RUSSIA IS BURNING:

Poems of the
Great Patriotic War

RUSSIA IS BURNING:

Poems of the
Great Patriotic War

Edited by
Maria Bloshteyn

Smokestack Books
1 Lake Terrace, Grewelthorpe, Ripon HG4 3BU
e-mail: info@smokestack-books.co.uk
www.smokestack-books.co.uk

Copyright of
the Russian texts
remains with the authors
and their estates.

English translations
copyright the translators.

Introduction copyright 2020,
Maria Bloshteyn.

The publication was effected under the auspices
of the Mikhail Prokhorov Foundation
TRANSCRIPT Programme to Support
Translations of Russian Literature.

 transcript

ISBN 9781916012110

Smokestack Books
is represented
by Inpress Ltd

Dedicated with love and gratitude

to my father,
Roman Isaakovich Bloshteyn (1925–1998)
who fought on the Kalinin Front;

to my maternal grandfather,
Yeremei Aronovich Rubinraut (1897–1977)
who fought on the Leningrad Front;

and to my paternal grandfather,
Isaak Moiseevich Bloshteyn (1901–1962)
who fought on the Baltic Front.

Содержание

Contents

Вспоминая Войну

The War Remembered

Introduction

It is February, 1943 on the Kalinin Front, near Moscow. A 17-year-old Soviet soldier is crouching beside a BM13 multiple rocket launcher, consisting of eight 13-cm diameter barrels, mounted on a truck. When a battery of BM13s fires, the ground shakes and the impact on the Germans is devastating. The Soviet troops gave it the appreciative tongue-in-cheek nickname 'Katyusha,' after the lyrics of a song written by one of the most popular songwriters of the war, Mikhail Isakovsky. Young Katyusha stands on a riverbank and sings a song of love, which she hopes her beloved, who is fighting at the front, will hear. The distinctive song of a battery of BM13s – a horrifying high-pitched howl – is heard by anything living for miles around. The terrified German troops, who don't have anything like this in their military repertoire, call it '*Stalinorgel,*' or 'Stalin's Organ.'

The young soldier beside one of the Katyushas is tall, athletic, blue-eyed, dark-haired and proud to be a part of the six-man BM13 crew. He started trying to enlist when the war broke out – which is when his father enlisted – but he was too young. Instead, he dug anti-tank trenches around Leningrad, where he lived with his mother and younger sister. Then the three were evacuated to the Urals. He was finally allowed to join the army in December of 1942, ending up in the artillery, with the Katyushas. Stalin called artillery 'the God of War,' and the Katyushas are as divine as it gets, especially when the Soviet army finally begins to push the Germans back. The battle for Stalingrad had been won only two weeks earlier, on 2 February and troop morale is high.

The soldier is relieved to finally be at the front – he was afraid the Nazis might be finished off without him. He is proud of the formidable Katyushas. He thinks victory is around the corner and that life will be all roses once the war is won. At seventeen, he also likes poetry. When he was younger, he wrote poems. Now he doesn't, but he still enjoys reading poetry – which is lucky, because poetry is all around him. The army newspapers, including the Kalinin Front's own paper, *Vpered na vraga!* along with the most popular military newspaper, *Krasnaia Zvezda* and the nation's leading newspapers like *Pravda* and *Izvestiia,* all publish poems about the war written by special war correspondents, by regular soldiers fighting on the frontlines, and by poets on the home front. Poetry is on posters, on leaflets of all kinds, on instruction sheets, and it is also read to soldiers during the mandatory political instruction sessions. Poetry is on the radio and, put to music, it is played on portable record players and sung by the soldiers.

The young soldier has no inkling of the future. He doesn't know that only two weeks later he'll be wounded by shrapnel, that sepsis will set in, and that he'll have to have surgery and treatment in one of Moscow's military hospitals. The woman surgeon, feeling sorry for the young good-looking lad, will bring him homemade soup to help him heal, but even she won't have much hope for his complete recovery. He doesn't know that he'll survive against all odds, but with a damaged heart, and that, for the rest of his life, he'll be considered an invalid. He doesn't know that victory, when it does come in May of 1945, will be followed by a severe government clampdown on freedoms, and by vicious campaigns against the intelligentsia, against nationally respected poets and writers, and against the 'rootless cosmopolitans' (largely a euphemism for Jews, like the young soldier), culminating in the Night of the Murdered Poets and the infamous Doctors' Plot, which terminated only with Stalin's own demise in March of 1953. He doesn't know that after the war, when his father, a dyed-in-the-wool Communist and member of the Party since 1924, will ask him, a member of the Komsomol, why he doesn't want to join the Party, he'll retort: 'Would *you* have joined now?' and his father will pause and then slowly say, 'No, I don't think I would have.' He also doesn't know that in a different century and in a very different country, many years after his death at the age of 73, his younger daughter will try to gain a fuller sense of the Russian poetry of the War, by asking questions about the poetry he had access to during the war years and by thinking back to how he remembered the war in his later years.

Over the years of working on this anthology, I thought of my father a great deal. Both of my grandfathers also fought in the War (my maternal grandfather on the Leningrad Front; my paternal grandfather on the Baltic Front), but I hardly knew them: the first died when I was six, the second, a decade before my birth. My father never spoke about the war, only very occasionally dropping a phrase or two, but he didn't have to: he lived his life with the damage the war had wreaked on his body. All first visits to the many health specialists he needed to see over the years would begin with my mother's introductory phrase: 'My husband was wounded in the Second World War.'

I began my work on the anthology with a series of simple questions that ultimately determined the structure of this book. I wanted to know what Russian poems and songs about the war were available to a young Soviet soldier during the Second World War; what Russian poems about the war were off-limits to him or her; and what Russian poems and songs helped them to work through their experiences and memories of the war and its aftermath.

The first question was fairly easy to answer – the most popular Russian wartime poets had been celebrated and anthologized back in the Soviet era, and there have also been many compilations of Soviet war songs. Less easy to find were examples of the unofficial songs composed anonymously and sung by Soviet soldiers, but some songs of this type were included in various post-Soviet articles on military folklore. These popular poems and songs from the years 1941 to 1945 make up the section 'Voices Heard.' Many appear here in new translations, and some have been translated for the first time.

Then came the more difficult question, which opened up a host of thorny issues. I wanted to know what Russian wartime poetry *wasn't* available to a young soldier fighting in the Soviet army. Obviously enough, this category included all the poets writing in Russian whose work couldn't be published in the Soviet Union. When unpacked, this consisted of: (1) Soviet poets who wrote all or some of their poems 'for the desk drawer'; (2) poets interned in the Gulag; (3) poets who switched sides and either supported the German invaders or ended up aligned with them through various circumstances; and (4) émigré poets. Many poems in each grouping were readily available to the researcher – some in post-Soviet publications of poems by individual poets; others in post-Soviet anthologies of Gulag poets; still others in émigré journals and poetry chapbooks.

These poems – these poets and their life stories – did not mingle easily with each other or with the poems of the 'Voices Heard' section. It felt awkward and potentially offensive to have them share the same space, particularly when it came to the work of those few poets in Occupied Russia who aligned themselves with the Nazi regime – just how offensive was brought home to me when a friendly Russian editor of a poetry anthology cut off correspondence with me when he learned *whose* poems I was including in this anthology. I understood only too well why these feelings ran so strongly. I recalled an exchange I witnessed many years ago in Southern Ontario cottage country between two old men, both Soviet vets, whose lives took very different paths. One of them, who became a Nazi collaborator and ended up in Germany early in the war, reminisced about how beautiful life had been when he was sitting with Fräulein N. in a cozy little café in Berlin: 'You really couldn't believe that somewhere out there the war was raging,' he concluded cheerily. The other, who spent the entire war at the front, including Stalingrad, frowned and clenched his fists. 'You and I,' he finally managed, 'were on different sides of the barricades.'

It is precisely because these poetic perspectives on the war come from such uncomfortably different and mutually hostile places, however, that they are so valuable. To borrow an insight from Boris Pasternak, poetry is the one thing that moves easily above barriers and barricades, and the mosaic of voices and experiences in these Russian poems adds up to a panoramic, multiangle picture of the War that has never been seen before – even by Russian readers. The émigré poems included in this section also serve as a reminder of a seemingly obvious but constantly overlooked fact: if, for Soviet poetry, the war started on 22 June 1941, with Germany's attack on the Soviet Union, then for Russian poetry the war started several years before Operation Barbarossa. Russian émigré poets living in the West (such as Georgy Ivanov, Irina Knorring, Lev Gomolitsky, and countless others) experienced the first onslaught of the War when most of Europe did – in 1939 – and wrote about it in poems full of anguish, horror, and foreboding of worse things to come. All in all, this section, which I called 'Muted Voices,' stretches from 1939 to several years after the end of the War, includes many poems that have never been anthologized or translated before, and is many ways the most challenging and thought-provoking part of the anthology.

I have adopted a similarly inclusive approach to the final section of the anthology, 'Remembering the War,' which addresses how the memory of the war continued to inform the lives of those who took part in it (or who experienced it either as children; or through the stories of their parents) and how poems helped them to deal with these memories and their experiences. Throughout, I remembered my father, in 1980s Toronto, grimly listening to Alexander Galich's searing poem-songs about the War, quietly repeating the words. The section opens with poems written about a decade after the war, when Khrushchev's Thaw made it seem as if things could finally be said openly, and a number of Soviet frontline poets who survived the war began to speak on behalf of their generation. Even so, this limited and fragile freedom (soon restricted in a new clampdown) did not mean that everything could be said: on the contrary, many poems had to be written for the desk drawer – and some of these are also included in this section. Once again, I've attempted to incorporate a broad selection of poets and perspectives (including both Soviet-era and post-Soviet émigré poets). Of particular interest are poetic attempts to come to terms with the respective postwar fates of Germany and the Soviet Union and to rethink the meaning of the war after the collapse of the USSR.

Some poets are represented across several sections of the anthology. For example, the poems of Olga Berggolts, known as 'the voice of blockaded Leningrad,' are found in each of the three sections. In the first section, she is represented by her celebrated poems about the siege; in the second, by a poem she wrote for the desk drawer about the injustices she saw immediately after the end of the war; in the third, by a poignant and in certain ways subversive poem she wrote many years after the war, remembering Anna Akhmatova watching for German incendiary bombs in Leningrad in 1941. Some poets included are represented by several poems in the same section, either because they were particularly significant for their times or because they said things that no one else had managed to say.

Taken together, the poems in this anthology push out the narrow boundaries that are usually drawn to define Russian verse from the War and easily overturn the assumptions frequently made about this body of work both in the West and in Russia itself. At the same time, the poets and poems included in this book are just a tiny sample of the extraordinary treasure hoard of Russian poetry from the Second World War. It is my deep regret that so many first-rate poets were left out of the anthology and so many unforgettable poems were not included. This inevitable failure, however, only proves the truth of what has been maintained by those who examined the subject, like the poet, writer, and scholar Dmitry Bykov, who said that no other country produced so much good poetry during the War as the Soviet Union.

I have included an essay at the back of the book that provides a historical, political, and cultural context for the poems, brief notes about the individual poets (on the Russian side of the text) and the poems they wrote (on the translated side of the text). I hope these notes will help readers contextualize the verse without interfering with their enjoyment, because despite the often harrowing subject matter, the work gathered in this anthology includes some of the finest poetry written in Russian in the past eight decades.

In the process of preparing the anthology, I gained a deeper understanding of the terrible blow struck by the War to Russian poetry. An entire generation of poets was annihilated on the frontlines and in concentration camps. Among these were the young poets associated with the Moscow IFLI (the so-called 'Red Lyceum' – the Moscow Institute of Philosophy, Literature, and History), the rising stars of the Russian poetic world, whose poetry showed so much energy, ambition, and promise, most of whom enlisted immediately after Germany attacked and many of whom were promptly killed. Just as tragic were the fates of émigré poets who lived in France and were killed in concentration camps in the first years of the war. As a tribute to the fallen, the anthology opens with seven poems for each of the seven years 1939–45, each written by a Russian poet killed in the war.

Maria Bloshteyn, Toronto, 2020

Семь убитых поэтов

Seven Poets Killed

1939
1940
1941
1942
1943
1944
1945

МИХАИЛ ВАЛЕНТИНОВИЧ КУЛЬЧИЦКИЙ

Kulchitsky, barely published at the time of his death and known only to a small but influential group connected with Moscow's IFLI, was one of the great hopes of Russian poetry. Lilya Brik considered him Mayakovsky's poetic successor.

'Мечтатель, фантазер, лентяй-завистник...'

Мечтатель, фантазер, лентяй-завистник!
Что? Пули в каску безопасней капель?
И всадники проносятся со свистом
вертящихся пропеллерами сабель.
Я раньше думал: «лейтенант»
звучит вот так: «Налейте нам!»
И, зная топографию,
он топает по гравию.
Война – совсем не фейерверк,
а просто – трудная работа,
когда, черна от пота,
вверх
скользит по пахоте пехота.
Марш!
И глина в чавкающем топоте
до мозга костей промерзших ног
наворачивается на чеботы
весом хлеба в месячный паек.
На бойцах и пуговицы вроде
чешуи тяжелых орденов.
Не до ордена.
Была бы Родина
с ежедневными Бородино.

24 декабря 1942

MIKHAIL KULCHITSKY (1919–1943)

Kulchitsky gave this poem to Lilya Brik when he visited her in December of 1942. They were planning to celebrate New Year's together, but Kulchitsky was sent to fight in Stalingrad, where he was killed in action in January 1943. This is his last known and most famous poem.

'Dreamer, Stargazer, Envious Slacker...'

Dreamer, stargazer, envious slacker!
Still think helmets halt bullets righter than rain?
And cavalry whips by, their whirling sabres
putting propellers to shame.
I used to think 'lieutenant'
sounds like 'lets have a round!'
And, guided by topographical notes,
he stomps on top of gravel roads.
War is nothing like fireworks
it's just hard work,
when black with sweat
soldiers skid up
tilled fields.
Forward march!
And feet frozen to the marrow
stomp in the squelching mud
that clings to boots
heavy like a month's bread ration.
Even soldiers' buttons
hang like heavy medals.
No one's trying for a medal.
Just let the Motherland be well,
even if it takes a daily Borodino battle.

24 December 1942

ВСЕВОЛОД ЭДУАРДОВИЧ БАГРИЦКИЙ

The son of the poet Eduard Bagritsky, Vsevolod showed great promise as a young poet and playwright, publishing his work from a precociously young age. He was rejected for military service because of poor eyesight, but enlisted in the frontline press corps. He was killed by shrapnel on assignment, in the middle of an interview.

'Я приехал сюда...'

Я приехал сюда
И, не скрою, плюю
На твои холода,
На старинную Каму твою.

Есть глухая тоска
В белоснежных полях
До озноба в виске,
До тумана в глазах.

Как я быстро привык
О друзьях забывать,–
Спросят нас, кто погиб,
И начнешь бормотать.

Удилами исхлестаны губы,
Опрокинуты дни на дыбы.
Тех, кого мы любили, – на убыль!
Тех, кого схоронили,– забыть!

Самовар, словно маленький карлик,
Задыхался, мычал и укачивал.
Мы с тобой этот вечер украли
У голодных степей азиатчины.

1 Ноябрь 1941

VSEVOLOD BAGRITSKY (1922–1942)

Bagritsky wrote this poem in his diary after he was evacuated from Moscow, arriving to the provincial and isolated town of Chistopol' (Tatarstan) on the shores of the Kama river. His father had died years earlier, his mother was in the Gulag – he was alone and desperately lonely, despite meeting some friends from his Moscow theatre studio.

'I've Come Here for Now...'

I've come here for now
but I don't give two bits
for your famed Kama river
and your iced-over streets.

There's a sadness past telling
in these fields gleaming white
which sends chills to the temples,
and a mist to the eyes.

See how fast I got used
to forgetting old friends –
If you ask me who perished,
I just mumble their names.

The bridle had whipped our lips bloody,
our racing days reared up in shock.
Forget your dead and your loved ones –
there's no bringing anyone back!

Our fairy-tale dwarf of a samovar
wheezed, cooed, and lulled us to sleep.
You and I stole this evening away
from the starved Asian steppe.

1 November 1941

ПАВЕЛ ДАВИДОВИЧ КОГАН

Unpublished and unknown outside his circle, Kogan was the acknowledged leader of young poets associated with IFLI and Ilya Selvinsky's seminars. Rejected for military service, he went to the front as a military interpreter to a mountain rifle regiment. He was killed leading a reconnaissance mission near Novorossiysk.

Письмо

Жоре Лепскому

Вот и мы дожили,
Вот и мы получаем весточки
В изжеванных конвертах с треугольными
                                штемпелями,
Где сквозь запах армейской кожи,
Сквозь бестолочь
Слышно самое то,
То самое, –
Как гудок за полями.
Вот и ты,
        товарищ красноармеец
                        музвзвода,
Воду пьешь по утрам из заболоченных
                                речек.
А поля между нами,
А леса между нами и воды.
Человек ты мой,
Человек ты мой,
Дорогой ты мой человече!

А поля между нами,
А леса между нами.
(Россия!
Разметалась, раскинулась

PAVEL KOGAN (1918–1942)

*Georgy (Zhora) Lepskiy was Kogan's childhood friend and cowriter.
By 1940, Lepskiy was already conscripted (Kogan was still a civilian)
and Germany had invaded a number of countries—a major war
seemed inevitable. The mention of Western Ukraine obliquely refers
to its occupation by Soviet troops, after the Soviet-Nazi pact of 1939.*

A Letter

to Zhora Lepskiy

So we're finally there –
it's finally our turn
to get letters in crumpled envelopes with triangular
                                        postmarks,
and through the smell of army leather,
through all the blather
you can hear it,
the real thing –
like a horn blast across the fields.
Finally,
you too,
          Comrade Red-Army-
                         Military-Band man,
get to drink muddy river water
                    in the mornings.
Now vast fields divide us,
vast forests, rivers, and fens.
My old friend,
my old friend,
my cherished old friend!

Vast fields divide us,
vast forests divide us.
(Russia!
She sprawls and spreads

По лежбищам, по урочищам.
Что мне звать тебя?
Разве голосом ее осилишь.
Если в ней, словно в памяти,
	словно в юности:
Попадешь – не воротишься.)
А зима между нами.
(Зима ты моя,
Словно матовая,
Словно ро́сшитая,
На большак, большая, хрома ты,
На проселочную горбата,
А снега по тебе, громада,
Сине-синие, запорошенные.)
Я и писем тебе писать не научен.
А твои читаю,
Особенно те, что для женщины.
Есть такое в них самое,
Что ни выдумать, ни намучить,
Словно что-то поверено,
Потом потеряно,
Потом обещано.
(...А вы все трагической героиней,
А снитесь – девочкой-неспокойкой.
А трубач «та́ри-та́ри-та́» трубит:
					«по койкам!»
А ветра сухие на Западной Украине.)
Я вот тоже любил одну, сероглазницу,
Слишком взрослую, может быть,
	слишком строгую.
А уеду и вспомню такой проказницей,
Непутевой такой, такой недотрогою.
Мы пройдем через это.
Мы затопчем это, как окурки,
Мы, лобастые мальчики невиданной
					революции.
В десять лет мечтатели,
В четырнадцать – поэты и урки.

over lairs, over tracts.
No use calling out!
You can't shout her down.
She's like memory,
    or like youth itself:
once you're in, you won't find your way back.)
And winter divides us.
(O winter, snow colossus,
with your dull glow,
and your lacy throws!
Your highways are horrid,
your byways are lurid,
your snow mounds are storied –
tinted brightest-blue, dusted with fresh snow.)
I've never learned to write proper letters,
so I'm reading yours.
Especially those you wrote to a woman.
There's something so real about them –
can't make it up, can't force it out –
as if something is being confided,
then derided,
at last requited.
(...You keep acting the tragic heroine;
but I remember you as a young worrywart.
The bugler is now playing *ta-ti-ta, ta-ti-ta*
                              for *Lights out!*
And dry winds blow across Western Ukraine.)
I too loved a grey-eyed girl once,
too grown-up perhaps, a bit too stern,
but once we'd part, I'd think her
a tease, an ice maiden,
all about her – an act she put on.
We'll leave all that behind us.
We'll stomp it out like cigarette butts.
We, the brainy boys of the ultimate
                              revolution;
at ten years of age – we're dreamers,
at fourteen – poets and criminals.

В двадцать пять – внесенные в смертные реляции.
Мое поколение –
                это зубы сожми и работай,
Мое поколение –
                это пулю прими и рухни.
Если соли не хватит –
                хлеб намочи пóтом,
Если марли не хватит –
                портянкой замотай тухлой.
Ты же сам понимаешь, я не умею бить
                в литавры,
Мы же вместе мечтали, что пыль, что
                ковыль, что криница.
Мы с тобою вместе мечтали пошляться
                        по Таврии
(Ну, по Крыму по-русски),
А шляемся по заграницам.
И когда мне скомандует пуля
                        «не торопиться»
И последний выдох на снегу воронку
                        выжжет
(Ты должен выжить, я хочу, чтобы ты
                        выжил),
Ты прости мне тогда, что я не писал
                        тебе писем.
А за нами женщины наши,
И годы наши босые,
И стихи наши,
И юность,
И январские рассветы.
А леса за нами,
А поля за нами –
Россия!
И, наверно, земшарная Республика
                        Советов!

At twenty-five – entries on the casualty list.
My generation is –
        clench your teeth and work hard,
My generation is –
        take the bullet, drop dead.
Not enough salt?
        Salt your bread with your sweat.
Not enough bandages?
        Use fetid footcloths instead.
You know me, I'm not one
        to grandstand,
hadn't the two of us dreamed – never mind the dust,
        needle grass, and seepage springs –
hadn't we dreamed of tramping
        across Tavria
(that's to say, our native Crimea,)
but instead we're marching on foreign lands.
And when a bullet meant for me orders,
        'At ease,'
and I fall in the snow, my last breath melting
        a crater
(I want you to come back alive and you'd
        better),
forgive me then that I hadn't written you
        any letters.
So we're leaving behind
our women,
our barefooted years,
our poems,
and youth,
and January sunrises.
We're leaving behind vast forests,
and vast fields –
the whole of Russia!
And, probably, the coming pan-global
        Soviet Republic!

Вот не вышло письма.
Не вышло письма,
Какое там!
Но я напишу,
Повинен.
Ведь я понимаю,
Трубач «та́ри-та́ри-та́» трубит:
  «по койкам!»
И ветра сухие на Западной Украине.

Декабрь, 1940

Well, this is no letter.
No, this is no letter.
I blew it!
But I'll write you yet,
I'll try again.
Because I get it:
the bugler is blowing *ta-ti-ta, ta-ti-ta,*
    for *Lights out!*
and dry winds blow across Western Ukraine.

December 1940

ВАДИМ КОНСТАНТИНОВИЧ СТРЕЛЬЧЕНКО

Strelchenko was a metal worker and wrote many poems celebrating the joy of labour. Alexey Surkov wrote in 1965, 'all the poets of those days had no doubts that Vadim would turn into the most powerful and interesting of all poet-workers. He grew from poem to poem.'

Промельк

Есть, порой, на московской площади
Тихий промельк, секунда одна:
Ни троллейбуса вдруг, ни лошади –
Непонятная тишина.

Словно время на размышление
Всем идущим на миг дано,
Словно сбудется во мгновение
Все, чем сердце порой полно.

Словно всех незнакомых ранее
В этот полдень сошлись пути,
Узнаванье пойдет, братание
Всех,
С кем вместе жить и идти.

Вот уж кажется: начинается!
(...Дальний оклик, веселый вскрик...)
...Но вот тут-то и появляется
Неожиданный грузовик.
Вновь машин легковых мелькание,
Ветра легкая полоса.

Но не ветер, людей дыхание
Овевает мои волоса.

1940

VADIM STRELCHENKO (1912–1942)

After the Terror the late 1930s, for some the war against an external enemy seemed almost a relief. Strelchenko's poem, patriotic but never jingoistic, speaks to the sense of genuine unity and comradeship felt by so many at that time. He joined the volunteer corps and was killed near Vyazma in 1942.

A Flash

At times there are, on Moscow squares,
flashes of quiet, fleeting islands:
no horses and no trolley-cars –
only unfathomable silence.

As if a moment's thought were granted
to every person passing through;
as if what every heart had wanted
would, in a moment, all come true;

as if these people – perfect strangers –
were meant to meet that afternoon,
were meant to recognize each other,
to walk together,
and commune.

Yes, yes: it's happening, it's starting!
(... A distant hail, a cheerful cry ...)
... But suddenly, without a warning,
a lorry thunders by.
Again, the sound of engines revving –
ribbons of wind float through the air.

But what's that blowing through my hair?
Not wind – but people, breathing.

1940

ЕЛЕНА МИХАИЛОВНА ШИРМАН

Shirman was the only woman at Ilya Selvinsky's famed poetry seminar to enlist. She edited an army newspaper Direct Fire *which was published in Rostov-on-Don. In 1942, she was captured by the Germans with issues of the paper, and was tortured and executed.*

Приезд

Состав, задыхаясь, под арку влетит,
Навстречу рванутся и окна, и гомон,
И холод, и хохот. И кто-то навзрыд
Заплачет. И все это будет знакомо,
Как в детстве, в горячке.
Ведь так на роду
Написано мне по старинной примете -
И то, что тебя я опять не найду,
И то, что меня ты опять не встретишь.
И лица. И спины. И яркий перрон.
И кто-то толкает меня. Громогласен
Гудок паровозный. И это не сон,
Что нету тебя. И приезд мой напрасен.
Клубясь и вращаясь, прокатит вокзал,
Сверкание залов и темь коридоров.
И площадь пуста. И фонарь, как запал,
Мигнет, поджигая покинутый город.
И площадь взлетит, как граната, гремя,
И хлынут осколки разорванных улиц.
...Кто-то с панели поднимет меня
И спросит заботливо:
                        'Вы не споткнулись?'

Февраль 1940, Москва

ELENA SHIRMAN (1908–1942)

This poem is addressed to Shirman's great unrequited love, Valery Marchikhin, a poet turned soldier, killed in the early days of the war. Shirman never learned of his death. The poem describes their non-meeting during her visit to Rostov-on-Don. The image of the exploding train station eerily prefigures its destruction by the Germans in 1941.

The Visit

My panting train shoots through the archway,
met by a rush of cold, windows galore,
loud laughter, a real ruckus. Someone
bursts into tears. I felt like this before –
back in my childhood, struck with fever.
This was my fate from birth
foretold by age-old omens –
that yet again I would not find you;
that you would fail to meet me yet again;
that there'd be all these faces, people's backs,
this bright platform.
That I'd be shoved. A whistle
blast. You aren't there –
this is no dream. I've come in vain.
The station passes by, churning and swirling,
with its glittering halls and its dark corridors.
The plaza's empty. A streetlight turned fuse
flashes, and the abandoned town's ablaze.
The plaza hurls up like a grenade. A boom –
and shards of broken streets come tumbling.
...Someone will raise me from the pavement
and kindly say,
'You must have stumbled.'

February 1940, Moscow

ЮРИЙ ВЛАДИМИРОВИЧ МАНДЕЛЬШТАМ

Mandelshtam, who left Moscow as a child with his family in 1920, lived in Paris, where he graduated from the Sorbonne. He was active in émigré literary circles as a poet aligned with the poetics of the 'Paris Note' and a sensitive literary critic who published in a number of journals and newspapers.

'Нет, не воем полночной сирены...'

Нет, не воем полночной сирены,
Не огнем, не мечом, не свинцом,
Не пальбой, сотрясающей стены,
Не угрозой, не близким концом –

Ты меня побеждаешь иначе,
Беспросветное время войны:
Содроганьем в безропотном плаче
Одинокой сутулой спины,

Отворотом солдатской шинели,
Заколоченным наспех окном,
Редким звуком шагов на панели
В наступившем молчаньи ночном.

194?

YURI MANDELSHTAM (1908–1943)

Mandelshtam's life was tragic: his young wife for whom he converted into Orthodox Christianity (she was Stravinsky's daughter) died of TB, his beloved young daughter was raised by relatives. He thought his conversion was a safeguard and didn't leave Paris, but he was arrested as a Jew and sent to Auschwitz concentration camp, where he perished.

'No, it isn't the Midnight Sirens...'

No, it isn't the midnight sirens,
raging fires, sharp steel, howling lead,
the wall-shaking force of the bullets,
the danger, the imminent end –

that's not how war overtakes me,
how its darkness gets under my skin:
it's the sight of a lonely man weeping –
resigned but convulsing within,

it's the flap of a soldier's greatcoat,
boarded windows that keep out the light,
it's the echo of steps on the pavement,
in the hush that descends in the night.

194?

ЕЛИЗАВЕТА ЮРЬЕВНА КУЗМИНА-КАРАВАЕВА (МАТЬ МАРИЯ)

Poet, writer, and memoirist, who was part of Nikolai Gumilyov's first Guild of Poets, Kuzmina-Karavaeva debuted with a book of poems in 1912. She emigrated in 1920, settling in Paris. When the Germans invaded France, she helped Jews and others who were persecuted. She was arrested by the Gestapo and died in Ravensbrück in 1945.

'Прощайте берега. Нагружен мой корабль...'

Прощайте берега. Нагружен мой корабль
Плодами грешными оставленной земли.
Без груза этого отплыть я не могла бы
Туда, где в вечности блуждают корабли.
Всем, всем ветрам морским открыты ныне снасти.
Все бури соберу в тугие паруса.
Путь корабля таков: от берега где страсти,
В бесстрастные Господни небеса.
А если не доплыть? А если сил не хватит?
О, груз достаточен... неприхотливо дно.
Тогда холодных, разрушительных объятий
Наверно миновать не суждено.

Париж, 1941

ELIZAVETA KUZMINA-KARAVAEVA (MOTHER MARIA) (1891–1945)

Mother Maria was a legendary figure – first, for her early poetic fame and her memorable encounter with the poet Alexander Blok; then, for her altruism and self-sacrifice. She took monastic vows in 1931, writing memoirs, prose and lyrical poems with a mystical import.

'Farewell, Old Shores. My Ship Embarks...'

Farewell, old shores. My ship embarks
bearing the sinful fruits of my forsaken home.
Without this freight I couldn't set off sailing
to that eternity where all ships roam.
Now the sea winds tug at my riggings,
my sails swell up with the storms,
as I journey from shores of passion
to the peaceful skies of the Lord.
But what if my load is too heavy?
What if I run out of strength?
Then there won't be escaping the seabed,
with its cold and destructive embrace.

Paris, 1941

Услышанные
голоса

Voices
Heard

КОНСТАНТИН МИХАЙЛОВИЧ СИМОНОВ

Simonov was the best-known and best-loved Russian poet during the War – his poems were published in the main newspapers, carried into battle, recited like prayer, sent home from the frontlines and turned into songs. His name and his poems have become synonymous with the war.

Жди меня

Валентине Серовой

Жди меня, и я вернусь.
Только очень жди,
Жди, когда наводят грусть
Желтые дожди,
Жди, когда снега метут,
Жди, когда жара,
Жди, когда других не ждут,
Позабыв вчера.
Жди, когда из дальних мест
Писем не придет,
Жди, когда уж надоест
Всем, кто вместе ждет.

Жди меня, и я вернусь,
Не желай добра
Всем, кто знает наизусть,
Что забыть пора.
Пусть поверят сын и мать
В то, что нет меня,
Пусть друзья устанут ждать,
Сядут у огня,
Выпьют горькое вино
На помин души...
Жди. И с ними заодно
Выпить не спеши.

KONSTANTIN SIMONOV (1915–1979)

Simonov dedicated this poem to the actress Valentina Serova. At first, Simonov thought it too intimate for publication, but the poem made its way to the front in hand-written copies and became instantly famous. Military newspapers rejected the poem as insufficiently upbeat and heroic.

Wait for Me

To Valentina Serova

Wait for me and I'll come back!
Wait with all your might!
Wait when dreary yellow rains
Tell you nothing's right;
Wait when snow is falling fast;
Wait when summer's hot;
When no one waits for other men
And all the past's forgot!
Wait when those that wait with you
Are bored and tired and glum,
And when it seems, from far away,
No letters ever come!

Wait for me and I'll come back!
Wait in patience yet
When they tell you off by heart
That you should forget;
And when my mother and my son
Give up on me at last
And friends sit sadly round the fire
And talk about the past
And drink a bitter glass of wine
In memory of me –
Wait! No rush to drink with them!
Tell them to wait and see!

Жди меня, и я вернусь,
Всем смертям назло.
Кто не ждал меня, тот пусть
Скажет: Повезло. –
Не понять не ждавшим им,
Как среди огня
Ожиданием своим
Ты спасла меня.
Как я выжил, будем знать
Только мы с тобой,—

Просто ты умела ждать,
Как никто другой.

1941

Wait for me and I'll come back,
Escaping every fate!
'Just a lot of luck!' they'll say,
Those that didn't wait.
They will never understand
How, amidst the strife,
By your waiting for me, dear,
You had saved my life!
Only you and I will know
How you got me through!

Simply – you knew how to wait!
No one else but you!

1941

With You and Without You, *Simonov's 'lyrical diary,' spoke movingly of the complexities of wartime love. Prudish Stalin quipped that it should have been published in two copies only ('for him and for her') but approved it nonetheless.*

'Я, перебрав весь год, не вижу...'

Я, перебрав весь год, не вижу
Того счастливого числа,
Когда всего верней и ближе
Со мной ты связана была.

Я помню зал для репетиций
И свет, зажженный, как на грех,
И шепот твой, что не годится
Так делать на виду у всех.

Твой звездный плащ из старой драмы
И хлыст наездницы в руках,
И твой побег со сцены прямо
Ко мне на легких каблуках.

Нет, не тогда. Так, может, летом,
Когда, на сутки отпуск взяв,
Я был у ног твоих с рассветом,
Машину за ночь доконав.

Какой была ты сонной-сонной,
Вскочив с кровати босиком,
К моей шинели пропыленной
Как прижималась ты лицом!

Как бились жилки голубые
На шее под моей рукой!
В то утро, может быть, впервые
Ты показалась мне женой.

Although this poem was criticized for demoralizing soldiers and demeaning women, it became an instant classic and a readers' favourite.

'As I Recall the Year That's Ending...'

As I recall the year that's ending
I can't decide the happy time
When, more than any other moment,
I truly felt that you were mine.

Was it that night at your rehearsal?
The light that came on suddenly –
And your admonitory whisper
'You mustn't – everyone can see!'

Your starry robe for the old drama,
The riding whip held in your palms,
And how you ran to me so swiftly,
Straight from the stage into my arms...

Oh no, not then... Perhaps last summer,
I had a 24-hour pass
And reached you just as it was dawning
By all night driving on the gas.

And half awake and half still sleeping,
You jumped up barefoot from the bed
And tight against my dusty greatcoat
You pressed your sleepy little head.

Upon your neck, your veins were beating;
My hand could feel the pulse of life!
That morning, more than any other,
It seemed to me you were my wife....

И все же не тогда, я знаю,
Ты самой близкой мне была.
Теперь я вспомнил: ночь глухая,
Обледенелая скала...

Майор, проверив по карманам,
В тыл приказал бумаг не брать;
Когда придется, безымянным
Разведчик должен умирать.

Мы к полночи дошли и ждали,
По грудь зарытые в снегу.
Огни далекие бежали
На том, на русском, берегу...

Теперь я сознаюсь в обмане:
Готовясь умереть в бою,
Я все-таки с собой в кармане
Нес фотографию твою.

Она под северным сияньем
В ту ночь казалась голубой,
Казалось, вот сейчас мы встанем
И об руку пойдем с тобой.

Казалось, в том же платье белом,
Как в летний день снята была,
Ты по камням оледенелым
Со мной невидимо прошла.

За смелость не прося прощенья,
Клянусь, что, если доживу,
Ту ночь я ночью обрученья
С тобою вместе назову.

1941

And yet I felt you once still closer.
One night you gave me strength to fight -
Now I remember – it was winter,
That icy cliff at dead of night.

The major, checking through our pockets,
Had said no documents must go.
The scout must have no name or number
If he should perish in the snow.

We reached the other side at midnight,
Deep in the snow prepared for war,
The lights were twinkling in the distance
In Russia, on the other shore.

I now admit to a deception:
As I prepared (perhaps) to die,
I kept the picture in my pocket
You gave me when we said goodbye.

Seen by the northern light, your portrait
Seemed, in the darkness, almost blue.
I felt that when I must go forward,
Your hand in mine, you would go too.

Just as you were when it was taken,
Dressed in the same white summer frock,
Silent, unseen, you climbed beside me,
High on that cliff of icy rock.

I ask no pardon for deciding
That (if I live) I swear we'll say
That was the night of our betrothal.
That we shall call our wedding day.

1941

Simonov wrote this on the Bryansk Front. He later wrote, 'this feeling... that either you'll kill the enemy, or he'll kill you, pushed me to the desk and literally forced me to write this poem.' It was published on the second day of the Battle for Stalingrad.

Убей его!

Если дорог тебе твой дом,
Где ты русским выкормлен был,
Под бревенчатым потолком,
Где ты в люльке качаясь плыл,
Если дороги в доме том
Тебе стены, печь и углы,
Дедом, прадедом и отцом
В нем исхоженные полы,
Если мил тебе бедный сад
С майским цветом, с жужжанием пчел,
И под липой, сто лет назад,
В землю вкопанный дедом стол,
Если ты не хочешь, чтоб пол
В твоем доме немец топтал,
Чтоб он сел за дедовский стол
И деревья в саду сломал...

Если мать тебе дорога.
Тебя выкормившая грудь,
Где давно уж нет молока.
Только можно щекой прильнуть,
Если вынести нету сил.
Чтобы немец, ее застав,
По щекам морщинистым бил,
Косы на руку намотав,
Чтобы те же руки ее,
Что несли тебя в колыбель,
Немцу мыли его белье
И стелили ему постель...

The poem was reprinted, broadcast, and dropped from planes during the war. Mikhail Alekseev, who fought in the Battle for Stalingrad, said, 'All I had to do [as a political instructor] was to read the soldiers Simonov's poem 'Kill Him!' that appeared just around that time... it shook us to the core.'

Kill Him

If your house means a thing to you
Where you first dreamed your Russian dreams
In your swinging cradle, afloat
Beneath the log ceiling beams.
If your house means a thing to you
With its stove, corners, walls and floors
Worn smooth by the footsteps of three
Generations of ancestors,
If your small garden means a thing:
With its May blooms and bees humming low,
With its table your grandfather built
Neath the linden – a century ago.
If you don't want a German to tread
The floor in your house and chance
To sit in your ancestors' place
And destroy your yard's trees and plants...

If your mother is dear to you
And the breast that gave you suck
Which hasn't had milk for years
But is now where you put your cheek;
If you cannot stand the thought
Of a German doing her harm,
Beating her furrowed face
With her braids wound round his arm.
And those hands which carried you
To your cradle – washing instead
A German's dirty clothes
Or making him his bed...

Если ты отца не забыл.
Что качал тебя на руках.
Что хорошим солдатом был
И пропал в карпатских снегах,
Что погиб за Волгу, за Дон,
За отчизны твоей судьбу,
Если ты не хочешь, чтоб он
Перевертывался в гробу,
Чтоб солдатский портрет в крестах
Немец взял и на пол сорвал,
И у матери на глазах
На лицо ему наступал...

Если ты не хочешь отдать
Ту, с которой вдвоем ходил,
Ту, что долго поцеловать
Ты не смел, так ее любил.
Чтобы немцы ее живьем
Взяли силой, зажав в углу,
И распяли ее втроем
Обнаженную на полу.
Чтоб досталось трем этим псам,
В стонах, в ненависти, в крови,
Все, что свято берег ты сам.
Всею силой мужской любви...

Если ты не хочешь отдать
Немцу, с черным его ружьем,
Дом, где жил ты, жену и мать,
Все, что Родиной мы зовем,
Знай – никто ее не спасет,
Если ты ее не спасешь.
Знай – никто его не убьет,
Если ты его не убьешь.
И пока его не убил.
То молчи о своей любви –
Край, где рос ты, и дом, где жил,
Своей Родиной не зови.

If you haven't forgotten your father
Who tossed you and teased your toes,
Who was a good soldier, who vanished
In the high Carpathian snows,
Who died for your Motherland's fate,
For each Don and each Volga wave,
If you don't want him in his sleeping
To turn over in his grave,
When a German tears his soldier picture
With crosses from its place
And before your own mother's eyes
Stamps hobnailed boots on his face.

If you don't want to give away
Her you walked with and didn't touch,
Her you didn't dare even to kiss
For a long time – you loved her so much,
And the Germans cornering her
And taking her alive by force,
Crucifying her – three of them
Naked on the floor; with coarse
Moans, hate, and blood,
Those dogs taking advantage of
All you sacredly preserved
With your strong, male love...

If you don't want to give away
To a German with his black gun
Your house, your mother, your wife –
All that's yours as a native son –
No: No one will save your land
If you don't save it from the worst.
No: No one will kill this foe,
If you don't kill him first.
And until you have killed him, don't
Talk about your love – and
Call the house where you lived your home,
Or the land where you grew up your land.

Если немца убил твой брат,
Если немца убил сосед –
Это брат и сосед твой мстят,
А тебе оправданья нет.

За чужой спиной не сидят,
Из чужой винтовки не мстят,
Если немца убил твой брат –
Это он, а не ты, солдат.
Так убей же немца, чтоб он,
А не ты на земле лежал,
Не в твоем дому чтобы стон –
А в его – по мертвом стоял.
Так хотел он, его вина –
Пусть горит его дом, а не твой,
И пускай не твоя жена,
А его – пусть будет вдовой.
Пусть исплачется не твоя,
А его родившая мать.
Не твоя, а его семья
Понапрасну пусть будет ждать.

Так убей же хоть одного!
Так убей же его скорей!
Сколько раз увидишь его,
Столько раз его и убей!

18 июля 1942

If your brother killed a German,
If your neighbour killed one too,
It's your brother's and neighbour's vengeance,
And it's no revenge for you.

You can't sit behind another
Letting him fire your shot.
If your brother kills a German,
He's a soldier; you are not.
So kill that German so he
Will lie on the ground's backbone,
So the funeral wailing will be
In *his* house, not in your own.
He wanted it so – It's his guilt –
Let *his* house burn up, and his life.
Let *his* woman become a widow;
Don't let it be *your* wife.
Don't let *your* mother tire from tears;
Let the one bore him bear the pain,
Don't let it be yours, but his
Family who will wait in vain.

So kill at least one of them
And as soon as you can. Still
Each one you chance to see!
Kill him! Kill him! Kill!

18 July 1942

This poem marks the emergence in Soviet war poetry of the previously censored values of Russian Orthodoxy, Russian folk traditions and national roots, a shift in Stalin's policy that culminated in the State's consent to the election of the Moscow Patriarch in 1943. Russian émigrés were particularly moved by this poem and viewed Simonov as a hero.

'Ты помнишь, Алеша, дороги Смоленщины'

А. Суркову

Ты помнишь, Алеша, дороги Смоленщины,
Как шли бесконечные, злые дожди,
Как кринки несли нам усталые женщины,
Прижав, как детей, от дождя их к груди,

Как слезы они вытирали украдкою,
Как вслед нам шептали: – Господь вас спаси! –
И снова себя называли солдатками,
Как встарь повелось на великой Руси.

Слезами измеренный чаще, чем верстами,
Шел тракт, на пригорках скрываясь из глаз:
Деревни, деревни, деревни с погостами,
Как будто на них вся Россия сошлась,

Как будто за каждою русской околицей,
Крестом своих рук ограждая живых,
Всем миром сойдясь, наши прадеды молятся
За в бога не верящих внуков своих.

Ты знаешь, наверное, все-таки Родина –
Не дом городской, где я празднично жил,
А эти проселки, что дедами пройдены,
С простыми крестами их русских могил.

Dedicated to Simonov's friend, the poet Alexey Surkov, the poem describes the retreat and losses of the Soviet army in the First Battle of Smolensk during the advance on Moscow. Both men broke through the encirclement near Mogilyov, the site of a devastating battle that Simonov never forgot (he asked that his ashes be scattered there).

Smolenshchina

to A. Surkov

Remember, Alyosha, the roads of Smolenshchina,
Remember the rain and the mud and the pain,
The women, exhausted, who brought milk in pitchers,
And clasped them like babies at breast, from the rain.

The whispering words as we passed them – 'God bless you!'
The eyes where they secretly wiped away tears!
And how they all promised they would be 'soldatki',
The words of old Russia from earlier years.

The road disappearing past hills in the distance,
Its length that we measured with tears on the run.
And villages, villages, churches and churchyards,
As if all of Russia were gathered in one.

It seemed that in each Russian village we passed through,
The hands of our ancestors under the sod
Were making the sign of the cross and protecting
Their children, no longer believers in God.

You know, I believe that the Russia we fight for
Is not the dull town where I lived at a loss
But those country tracks that our ancestors followed,
The graves where they lie, with the old Russian cross

Не знаю, как ты, а меня с деревенскою
Дорожной тоской от села до села,
Со вдовьей слезою и с песнею женскою
Впервые война на проселках свела.

Ты помнишь, Алеша: изба под Борисовом,
По мертвому плачущий девичий крик,
Седая старуха в салопчике плисовом,
Весь в белом, как на смерть одетый, старик.

Ну что им сказать, чем утешить могли мы их?
Но, горе поняв своим бабьим чутьем,
Ты помнишь, старуха сказала: Родимые,
Покуда идите, мы вас подождем.

«Мы вас подождем!» – говорили нам пажити.
«Мы вас подождем!» – говорили леса.
Ты знаешь, Алеша, ночами мне кажется,
Что следом за мной их идут голоса.

По русским обычаям, только пожарища
На русской земле раскидав позади,
На наших глазах умирали товарищи,
По-русски рубаху рванув на груди.

Нас пули с тобою пока еще милуют.
Но, трижды поверив, что жизнь уже вся,
Я все-таки горд был за самую милую,
За горькую землю, где я родился,

За то, что на ней умереть мне завещано,
Что русская мать нас на свет родила,
Что, в бой провожая нас, русская женщина
По-русски три раза меня обняла.

1941

I feel that for me, it was countryside Russia
That first made me feel I must truly belong
To the tedious miles between village and village,
The tears of the widow, the women's sad song.

Remember, Alyosha, the hut at Borisov,
The girl and her passionate, desperate cry,
The grey-haired old woman, her velveteen jacket,
The old man, in white as if ready to die!

What could we say? With what words could we comfort them?
Yet seeming to gather the sense of our lack,
The old woman said, 'we shall wait for you, darlings!
Wherever you get to, we know you'll come back!'

'We know you'll come back!' said the fields and the pastures,
'We know you'll come back!' said the woods and the hill.
Alyosha, at nights I can hear them behind me.
Their voices are following after me still.

Because we are Russian, just fire and destruction
Are all we abandon behind as we go.
And fighting beside us, our comrades are dying
And Russians die only the face to the foe.

Alyosha, till now we've been spared by the bullets.
But when (for the third time) my life seemed to end,
I yet still felt proud of the dearest of countries,
The great bitter land I was born to defend.

I'm proud that the mother who bore us was Russian;
That Russian I'll fall as my ancestors fell;
That going to battle, the woman was Russian,
Who kissed me three times in a Russian farewell!

1941

АЛЕКСЕЙ АЛЕКСАНДРОВИЧ СУРКОВ

Surkov, poet and war correspondent, wrote this love poem for his wife after breaking through an encirclement in 1941. In 1942, the composer Konstantin Listov put it to music. It was published, picked up by the soldiers, and became one of the most popular songs of the War.

В землянке

Софье Кревс

Бьется в тесной печурке огонь,
На поленьях смола, как слеза.
И поет мне в землянке гармонь
Про улыбку твою и глаза.

Про тебя мне шептали кусты
В белоснежных полях под Москвой.
Я хочу, чтобы слышала ты,
Как тоскует мой голос живой.

Ты сейчас далеко, далеко,
Между нами снега и снега...
До тебя мне дойти нелегко,
А до смерти – четыре шага.

Пой, гармоника, вьюге назло,
Заплутавшее счастье зови.
Мне в холодной землянке тепло
От моей негасимой любви.

1941

ALEXEY SURKOV (1899–1983)

The ever-vigilant Soviet war censors took issue with the words 'just four steps divide me from death,' as being too defeatist, and destroyed the entire 1942 run of the song's recording. They subsequently tried to change the offending line, but everyone knew the words and sang it as it was written.

In the Dugout

to Sofia Krevs

Restless flames twist and toss in the stove,
Resin shines on the wood like a tear,
And accordion sings about love,
And your eyes and your smile reappear.

Bushes whispered about you to me
In the snowfields near Moscow, near home.
Ah, my love, if it only could be,
If you heard me here singing alone!

You are far, far away at this hour –
Snows between us and winter's hard breath,
To rejoin you is not in my power,
Though just four steps divide me from death.

Sing, accordion, scorning the storm,
Call back joy, drive off sorrow and doubt.
In the cold of the dugout I'm warm,
For the fire of our love won't go out.

1941

АЛЕКСАНДР ТРИФОНОВИЧ ТВАРДОВСКИЙ

Tvardovsky, one of the most remarkable and celebrated poets of the War, wholeheartedly believed in the Soviet project, but was troubled by the gap between ideals and reality, and by the cost of this in human lives. He wrote that the central questions facing his generation were those of 'personal conscience and the meaning of life.'

Две строчки

Из записной потертой книжки
Две строчки о бойце-парнишке,
Что был в сороковом году
Убит в Финляндии на льду.

Лежало как-то неумело
По-детски маленькое тело.
Шинель ко льду мороз прижал,
Далеко шапка отлетела.
Казалось, мальчик не лежал,
А все еще бегом бежал
Да лед за полу придержал...

Среди большой войны жестокой,
С чего – ума не приложу,
Мне жалко той судьбы далекой,
Как будто мертвый, одинокий,
Как будто это я лежу,
Примерзший, маленький, убитый
На той войне незнаменитой,
Забытый, маленький, лежу.

1943

ALEXANDER TVARDOVSKY (1910–1971)

Tvardovsky served as a war correspondent during the Winter War with Finland. This so-called 'minor' war, the ethics of which were privately questioned by many, resulted in more than 120,000 Soviet dead, young IFLI poets among them. In his diaries, Tvardovsky reflected with shock about how quickly the individual dead are forgotten in a war.

Two Lines

Found in my tattered notepad:
two lines about a soldier-lad,
killed back in Finland, whom I saw
in nineteen-forty, in the snow.

He looked so awkward as he lay,
small as a child on that cold day.
His overcoat was frozen stiff,
his cap had rolled so far away.
It seemed as if he wasn't done,
it looked like he was running on,
only the ice had held him down...

Amid this big and ruthless war,
I cannot say exactly why,
I feel such pity for this lad,
as if he's showing me my fate,
as if I am the one who lies
small, frozen-solid, downed
during that war of no renown,
forgotten on the ice.

1943

The first Tyorkin poem was published on September 4, 1942. The poems were instantly popular, but their folksy idiom and down-to-earth charm obscures their artfulness. When Boris Pasternak was asked to name the best text written about the war, he answered, 'Tyorkin!' The usually reserved Ivan Bunin enthused, 'what freedom, what wonderful bravado... what exactitude, what precision!'

Смерть и воин

За далекие пригорки
Уходил сраженья жар.
На снегу Василий Теркин
Неподобранный лежал.

Снег под ним, набрякши кровью,
Взялся грудой ледяной.
Смерть склонилась к изголовью:
– Ну, солдат, пойдем со мной.

Я теперь твоя подруга,
Недалеко провожу,
Белой вьюгой, белой вьюгой,
Вьюгой след запорошу.

Дрогнул Теркин, замерзая
На постели снеговой.
– Я не звал тебя, Косая,
Я солдат еще живой.

Смерть, смеясь, нагнулась ниже:
– Полно, полно, молодец,
Я-то знаю, я-то вижу:
Ты живой, да не – жилец.

Мимоходом тенью смертной
Я твоих коснулась щек,
А тебе и незаметно,
Что на них сухой снежок.

Tyorkin, a Russian Everyman, is quick-witted, cheerful, practical, and strikingly apolitical (Stalin and the Party are never once mentioned in the entire verse-novel). This story of Tyorkin's fight to stay alive after being wounded, takes its roots in a Russian folk tale, 'Death and the Soldier,' where a Russian soldier tricks Death itself into retreating.

Death and the Soldier

Beyond the distant hills and valleys
the sound of shooting died away.
And our friend, Tyorkin (Vasili)
in the snow unheeded lay.

The snow beneath him, mixed with blood,
had chilled his failing body.
Death bent over him and said:
'Now soldier, come with me.

We do not have that far to walk,
and I will be your lover now:
the wind will blow and fill your tracks
with powdered shifting snow.'

Tyorkin shivered, cold and lonely,
on his frozen bed.
'I'm no lover of yours, you bony
wench... and I'm not dead.'

Death, with a chuckle, bent still lower:
'Yes, that's right, there-there, my love,
I know all about you, soldier:
you're living, you've not long to live.

I laid down my deathly shadow
on your cheeks as I slid past,
and you don't even feel the snow
that falls on them so fast.

Моего не бойся мрака,
Ночь, поверь, не хуже дня...
– А чего тебе, однако,
Нужно лично от меня?

Смерть как будто бы замялась,
Отклонилась от него.
– Нужно мне... такую малость,
Ну почти что ничего.
Нужен знак один согласья,
Что устал беречь ты жизнь,
Что о смертном молишь часе...

– Сам, выходит, подпишись? –
Смерть подумала.
– Ну что же, –
Подпишись, и на покой.
– Нет, уволь. Себе дороже.
– Не торгуйся, дорогой.

Все равно идешь на убыль. -
Смерть подвинулась к плечу. -
Все равно стянулись губы,
Стынут зубы...
– Не хочу.

– А смотри-ка, дело к ночи,
На мороз горит заря.
Я к тому, чтоб мне короче
И тебе не мерзнуть зря...

– Потерплю.
– Ну, что ты, глупый!
Ведь лежишь, всего свело.
Я б тебя тотчас тулупом,
Чтоб уже навек тепло.

Don't be afraid of the coming darkness,
night is nothing worse than day...
'Hey, come on, you're not my mistress:
what is it you want from me?'

Death was taken a little aback,
and withdrew a step or two.
'What do I want? What do I lack?
Nothing, really... nothing new.
All I need's a sign that you agree
that you're tired of pushing on,
that you yearn for Death to set you free...'

'You mean, you'll give me something to sign?'
Death thought a little.
'Yes, why not?
Sign and you'll have peace and ease.'
'No, I'm worth much more than that.'
'Oh, come on, don't bargain, please.

You're done for, that's the short of it.'
Death bent down and said, 'Let's go.
'Your lips are freezing shut,
your teeth are chattering...'
'I said no.'

'Oh, come on. Look, night is falling,
red sky at night means a heavy frost.
I'm on the clock, there's no point stalling:
all is lost, and you are lost...'

'I will survive.'
'Come off it, idiot!
You're lying there and starting to freeze.
I could give you a lambskin coat
to keep you warm and at your ease.

Вижу, веришь. Вот и слезы,
Вот уж я тебе милей.
– Врешь, я плачу от мороза,
Не от жалости твоей.

– Что от счастья, что от боли –
Все равно. А холод лют.
Завилась поземка в поле.
Нет, тебя уж не найдут...

И зачем тебе, подумай,
Если кто и подберет.
Пожалеешь, что не умер
Здесь, на месте, без хлопот...

– Шутишь, Смерть, плетешь тенета.
Отвернул с трудом плечо. –
Мне как раз пожить охота,
Я и не жил-то еще...
– А и встанешь, толку мало, –
Продолжала Смерть, смеясь. –
А и встанешь - все сначала:
Холод, страх, усталость, грязь...
Ну-ка, сладко ли, дружище,
Рассуди-ка в простоте.

– Что судить! С войны не взыщешь
Ни в каком уже суде.

– А тоска, солдат, в придачу;
Как там дома, что с семьей?
– Вот уж выполню задачу –
Кончу немца – и домой.
– Так. Допустим. Но тебе-то
И домой к чему прийти?
Догола земля раздета
И разграблена, учти.
Все в забросе.

You see, you get it. Now you're crying,
and see that I am in the right.'
'No, that's not it at all. You're lying:
it's the cold that makes me cry.'

'Cry from happiness, cry from pain,
it doesn't matter. Cold is king.
The snowstorm whirls across the plain.
They'll not find you, nor anything...

And just think what's going to happen
even if they do find you.
You didn't die, but you'll be sad you didn't,
out here calmly, in the snow...'

'You're just prick-teasing, Death,' he grunted,
and sighed as he turned his back.
I'm here to live, like I've always wanted,
and aim to make my mark...'
'Get on up, then, you'll be sorry,'
Death said with a grin.
'If you get up, it's all before you –
cold and pain, begin again...
Just tell me if that's what you ask,
straight out, is that OK?'

'What do you mean? This is my task,
to fight till the war's out of the way.'

'What about your sad life, soldier;
your home and family?'
'I need to set this world in order:
smash the Nazis, then I'll be on my way.'
'Right. Let's say you do that, then.
Will you have a home remaining?
The land is stripped down to a ruin,
plundered till its strength is fading.
All's in pieces.'

– Я работник,
Я бы дома в дело вник,
– Дом разрушен.
– Я и плотник...
– Печки нету.
– И печник...

Я от скуки – на все руки,
Буду жив – мое со мной.
– Дай еще сказать старухе:
Вдруг придешь с одной рукой?
Иль еще каким калекой, –
Сам себе и то постыл...

И со Смертью Человеку
Спорить стало свыше сил.
Истекал уже он кровью,
Коченел. Спускалась ночь...

– При одном моем условье,
Смерть, послушай... я не прочь...

И, томим тоской жестокой,
Одинок, и слаб, и мал,
Он с мольбой, не то с упреком
Уговариваться стал:
– Я не худший и не лучший,
Что погибну на войне.
Но в конце ее, послушай,
Дашь ты на день отпуск мне?
Дашь ты мне в тот день последний,
В праздник славы мировой,
Услыхать салют победный,
Что раздастся над Москвой?
Дашь ты мне в тот день немножко
Погулять среди живых?
Дашь ты мне в одно окошко
Постучать в краях родных?

'I'm a worker,
I'll sort my house out right away.'
'Your house is destroyed.'
'I'm a carpenter...'
'Your stove's been smashed.'
'I can work with clay...

Look, I'm pretty good with my hands,
and I think I more or less know how to deal...'
'Oh, let me speak, a poor old woman:
what about if you're left a cripple?
Lose an arm or lose an eye,
that'll stop you being so cheery...'

This arguing with Death that night
had tired the Man, he was so weary.
He was bleeding free and fast,
and night was falling. He was cold...

'Look, I'll sign up with you at last,
but please, there's one more thing I'm owed...'

And now, overwhelmed with sadness,
lonely, weary, weak as sin,
begging now, in his great tiredness,
Tyorkin tried to bargain:
'I'm not the best and I'm not the worst
to die in this or any battle.
When it's over, can I rejoice
and celebrate with all the people?
Will you grant me one last day,
when the confetti and rice is thrown,
to hear the people shout 'Hooray!'
and parties rage in Moscow?
Will you let me take that day
to walk among the living?
Will you let me tap like Cathy
on a window... I mean like Heathcliff?

И как выйдут на крылечко, –
Смерть, а Смерть, еще мне там
Дашь сказать одно словечко?
Полсловечка?
– Нет. Не дам...

Дрогнул Теркин, замерзая
На постели снеговой.

– Так пошла ты прочь, Косая,
Я солдат еще живой.

Буду плакать, выть от боли,
Гибнуть в поле без следа,
Но тебе по доброй воле
Я не сдамся никогда.

– Погоди. Резон почище
Я найду, – подашь мне знак...

– Стой! Идут за мною. Ищут.
Из санбата.
– Где, чудак?
– Вон, по стежке занесенной...
Смерть хохочет во весь рот:
– Из команды похоронной.
– Все равно: живой народ.

Снег шуршит, подходят двое.
Об лопату звякнул лом.

– Вот еще остался воин.
К ночи всех не уберем.

– А и то устали за день,
Доставай кисет, земляк.
На покойничке присядем
Да покурим натощак.

When my family comes outside,
oh Death, will you permit me to
say just one word, a sweet goodbye?'
'No, dear,
the answer's no...'

Tyorkin shivered, cold and lonely,
on his frozen bed.

'Then be on your way, you bony
wench... I'm not yet dead.

I shall weep and howl in pain,
and die without trace on this field,
but I'll never once give in
to you: I'll never yield.'

'Fair enough. I'll find a better
reason for you to sign...'

'Wait, they're coming for me. Here!'
'What's that,
oh lover mine?'
'Here, they're coming down the trail...'
Death laughs and shows her teeth.
'That's the corpse-gatherers on patrol.'
'I don't care: they're alive.'

Crunch of snow, two people come over.
Crowbar banging on a spade.

'Here's another fallen soldier.
We'll never clear all the dead.'

'And the day's been pretty hard,
so why not roll me a gasper?
Let's sit down on this dead comrade
and get our shit together.'

– Кабы, знаешь, до затяжки –
Щей горячих котелок.
– Кабы капельку из фляжки.
– Кабы так – один глоток.

– Или два...
И тут, хоть слабо,
Подал Теркин голос свой:
– Прогоните эту бабу,
Я солдат еще живой.

Смотрят люди: вот так штука!
Видят: верно, – жив солдат,

– Что ты думаешь!
– А ну-ка,
Понесем его в санбат.

– Ну и редкостное дело, –
Рассуждают не спеша. –
Одно дело – просто тело,
А тут – тело и душа.
– Еле-еле душа в теле...
– Шутки, что ль, зазяб совсем.
А уж мы тебя хотели,
Понимаешь, в наркомзем...

– Не толкуй. Заждался малый.
Вырубай шинель во льду.
Поднимай.

А Смерть сказала:
– Я, однако, вслед пойду.

Земляки – они к работе
Приспособлены к иной.
Врете, мыслит, растрясете
И еще он будет мой.

'Maybe we should eat our chow first –
my mess-tin's full of cabbage soup.'
'Maybe we should hit my flask.'
'That's quite some plan, give me a shot.'
'Or maybe two...'

And here, though weakly,
Tyorkin let his voice be heard:
'Get rid of this bony lady,
I'm still live and kicking, lads.'

They look around: what's going on?
But yes, it's true, the man's not dead.

'What d'you reckon?'
'What do I reckon?
Let's get him to a hospital bed.'

'It's a rare thing, out of the ordinary,
but we can deal with it as well.
Sometimes a body's just a body,
but this is a body with a soul.'
'Well, my soul's just about in place...'
'You speak the truth, you're pretty lucky.
We might have had to find you space
on the Devil's Central Committee...'

'Don't push so much. Let's get a move on.
Cut his coat from out the ice.
One, two, three... heave!'

Death, sotto voce:
'I'll stick with him, he'll pay the price.

They're peasants, and they're pretty used
to work of other sorts.
They'll shake him and shiver him, cook his goose
and I'll still get my corpse.'

Два ремня да две лопаты,
Две шинели поперек.
– Береги, солдат, солдата.
– Понесли. Терпи, дружок.

Норовят, чтоб меньше тряски,
Чтоб ровнее как-нибудь,
Берегут, несут с опаской:
Смерть сторонкой держит путь.
А дорога – не дорога, –
Целина, по пояс снег.
– Отдохнули б вы немного, Хлопцы...
– Милый человек, –
Говорит земляк толково, –
Не тревожься, не жалей.
Потому несем живого,
Мертвый вдвое тяжелей.
А другой:
– Оно известно.
А еще и то учесть,
Что живой спешит до места, –
Мертвый дома – где ни есть.

– Дело, стало быть, в привычке, –
Заключают земляки. –
Что ж ты, друг, без рукавички?
На-ко теплую, с руки...

И подумала впервые
Смерть, следя со стороны:
'До чего они, живые,
Меж собой свои – дружны.
Потому и с одиночкой
Сладить надобно суметь,
Нехотя даешь отсрочку'.

И, вздохнув, отстала Смерть.

1944

Two leather belts and two metal shovels,
two army greatcoats bound across tight.
'Soldier, careful with the soldier.'
'I've got him. Hey, you'll be alright.'

They try their best to keep him comfy,
make sure he's level as he rides,
they carry him most carefully:
and Death walks slowly at their side.
The road here is no road at all:
it's untilled soil, waist-deep in snow.
'Hey, if you want to make a pause, lads...'
'No, that's alright, you know,'
one of the peasants says quite chattily,
'don't worry about us, kid.
You're alive, so we'll move you happily;
you'd weigh much more if you were dead.'
His friend chimes in:
'That's the truth, yes,
and I'll tell you the reason why.
A live man's trying to find his place,
and a dead man's home already.'

That's one way of seeing it,
the two of them conclude.
'What's up, mate, have you lost your glove?'
'Take mine, you've got more need...'

And as she still paced on beside them,
Death thought of her failed lover:
'That's what they've got, this love inside them
that binds them to one another.
It's only when they're on their own
that I can win the day,
and so I guess I'll leave this one.'

With a sigh, Death walked away.

1944

ВАСИЛИЙ ИВАНОВИЧ ЛЕБЕДЕВ-КУМАЧ

Lebedev-Kumach was one of the founders of Soviet popular song – he proudly called himself 'the Bard of the Stalin era' (he composed the 'Anthem of the NKVD'). Many of his lyrics, put to music by the best Soviet composers, were enormously popular and are still performed today.

Священная война

Вставай, страна огромная,
Вставай на смертный бой
С фашистской силой темною,
С проклятою ордой!

Пусть ярость благородная
Вскипает, как волна, –
Идет война народная,
Священная война!

Как два различных полюса,
Во всем враждебны мы:
За свет и мир мы боремся,
Они – за царство тьмы.

Дадим отпор душителям
Всех пламенных идей,
Насильникам, грабителям,
Мучителям людей!

Не смеют крылья черные
Над Родиной летать,
Поля ее просторные
Не смеет враг топтать!

VASILY LEBEDEV-KUMACH (1898–1949)

The poem, put to music by Alexander Aleksandrov, became the unofficial Soviet war anthem. It was first performed four days after the war began, but wasn't broadcasted because it spoke of 'mortal war' – officially, Soviet victory would come easily. After 15 October 1941, when major Soviet cities fell, it was played every morning on the All-Union Radio.

Sacred War

Arise, my giant country,
arise for mortal war,
against dark fascist forces
against their cursed hordes!

Let righteous wrath mount higher,
let it soar and soar,
the people's war is coming –
a sacred, holy war!

We're enemies in every sense –
we're two opposing poles:
we fight for light and peace,
and they – for evil's rule!

We'll stand up to those stranglers
of truths they cannot ban,
those raiders and aggressors,
vile torturers of men!

The enemy must never dare
to darken our fair skies,
or trample our verdant fields
that stretch for endless miles!

Гнилой фашистской нечисти
Загоним пулю в лоб,
Отребью человечества
Сколотим крепкий гроб!

Пойдём ломить всей силою,
Всем сердцем, всей душой
За землю нашу милую,
За наш Союз большой!

Встает страна огромная,
Встает на смертный бой
С фашистской силой темною,
С проклятою ордой.

Пусть ярость благородная
Вскипает, как волна,
Идет война народная,
Священная война!

24 Июня 1941

For putrid fascist scum
a bullet to the head!
Deleted, cancelled, coffined
nailed down and dead!

Rip into them with all we've got,
our hearts, our souls, our might!
It's for the Soviet Union,
It's for our land we fight!

A giant country rises,
prepared for mortal war,
Against dark fascist forces,
against their cursed hordes!

Let righteous wrath mount higher,
Let it soar and soar,
The people's war is being fought –
A sacred, holy war!

24 June 1941

СЕРГЕЙ СЕРГЕЕВИЧ НАРОВЧАТОВ

A member of the poetic brotherhood at Moscow's IFLI, Narovchatov emerged as a poet during the War, when he served as a war correspondent. Together with the poet Mikhail Lukonin, he was encircled near Bryansk. When they broke through, they were arrested and interrogated (they were eventually released). Narovchatov wrote about the horrors they saw on enemy-occupied territory.

В те годы

Я проходил, скрипя зубами, мимо
Сожженных сел, казненных городов,
По горестной, по русской, по родимой,
Завещанной от дедов и отцов.

Запоминал над деревнями пламя,
И ветер, разносивший жаркий прах,
И девушек, библейскими гвоздями
Распятых на райкомовских дверях.

И воронье кружилось без боязни,
И коршун рвал добычу на глазах,
И метил все бесчинства и все казни
Паучий извивающийся знак.

В своей печали древним песням равный,
Я сёла, словно летопись, листал
И в каждой бабе видел Ярославну,
Во всех ручьях Непрядву узнавал.

Крови своей, своим святыням верный,
Слова старинные я повторял, скорбя:
– Россия, мати! Свете мой безмерный,
Которой местью мстить мне за тебя?

1941

SERGEI NAROVCHATOV (1919–1981)

Narovchatov sent an early version of this poem into blockaded Leningrad, to the poet Olga Berggolts, with whom he was in love, telling her that it was written after his encirclement experience, commenting, 'There is not a line here that I didn't actually see and live through... In Khatun, the Germans slaughtered everyone... and crucified the teacher.'

Those Years

Grating my teeth in pain, I passed
Burned-down village and tortured town;
Through war-torn Russia, my very own,
The heritage of a cherished past.

They sank in my heart, the tossing flames,
The smouldering windswept ashes,
Girls crucified in the streets and lanes,
On doors and window sashes.

The ravens gorged without shame or fear,
The buzzards clawed corpses bare and stark,
And all the horrors both far and near
Were marked with the crawling spider's mark.

Watching the widows bent with their woes
I re-felt the sorrow of ancient songs,
At one with the trees in their mournful rows,
With the streams running tears and the country's wrongs.

I passed by ruins to find still more,
Through my country scathed by the flames of war,
'Russia, mother, light of my eyes,
Can any revenge suffice?'

1941

ИЛЬЯ ЛЬВОВИЧ СЕЛЬВИНСКИЙ

By 1941, Selvinsky was famous as an experimental poet who had once feuded with Mayakovsky and as a mentor to young Moscow poets. He volunteered to go to the front as a war correspondent but ended up fighting (as a commissar), rising to the rank of lieutenant-colonel. Many of his poems became popular wartime songs.

Тамань

Когда в кавказском кавполку я вижу казака
На белоногом скакуне гнедого косяка,
В черкеске с красною душой и в каске набекрень,
Который хату до сих пор еще зовет «курень», –
Меня не надо просвещать, его окликну я:
«Здорово, конный человек, таманская земля!»

От Крымской от станицы до Чушки до косы
Я обошел твои, Тамань, усатые овсы,
Я знаю плавней боевых кровавое гнильцо,
Я хату каждую твою могу узнать в лицо.
Бывало, с фронта привезешь от казака письмо –
Усадят гостя на топчан под саблею с тесьмой,
И небольшой крестьянский зал в обоях из газет
Портретами станичников начнет на вас глазеть.
Три самовара закипят, три лампы зажужжат,
Три девушки наперебой вам голову вскружат,
Покуда мать не закричит и, взяв турецкий таз,
Как золотистого коня, не выкупает вас.

Тамань моя, Тамань моя, форпост моей страны!
Я полюбил в тебе уклад батальной старины,
Я полюбил твой ветерок военно-полевой,
Твои гортанные ручьи и гордый говор твой.

ILYA SELVINSKY (1899–1968)

Taman was captured as part of the German attempt to control the Caucasus' oil fields and only liberated following fierce fighting and heavy losses on both sides. Selvinsky, from the Crimea himself, fought there as part of a Cossack cavalry regiment. War correspondents, many of whom were also poets, knew this poem by heart.

Taman

When I see a Cossack ride a white-legged cavalry horse
In the mounted regiment of a Caucasian force,
Wearing a broad-shouldered cloak, his helmet set askew,
A Bolshevik who uses Cossack terms his fathers knew,
Not one question need I ask, I hail the cavalry man:
'Hey there, rider, I can plainly see you're from Taman!'

I have roamed your fields of whiskered oats, Taman, you see,
All the way from Krymskaya to Chushka by the sea.
Well I know your bloody swamps that took so many lives
And there's not a cottage door I do not recognise...
When I'd bring a letter from a soldier at the front
They'd insist that I be seated on a wooden bunk
With a sword hung on the wall, newspapers everywhere
Pasted up from which the local villagers would stare.
Then three samovars would simmer and three lamps sing
And three pretty girls would set a man's heart fluttering
Till their mother reprimanded them and taking hold
Of a Turkish basin bathe me like a horse of gold.

My Taman, Taman, brave outpost of this land of mine!
I adore your martial ways that date from olden time,
I adore the breeze that breathes of armies on the go
Your gurgling streams, the way your phrases proudly flow.

Кавалерийская земля! Тебя не полонить,
Хоть и бомбежкой распахать, пехотой
    боронить.
Чужое знамя над тобой, чужая речь в дому,
Но знает враг:
      никогда
         не сдашься ты ему.
Тамань моя, Тамань моя! Весенней кутерьмой
Не рвется стриж с такой тоской издалека домой,
С какую тянутся к тебе через огонь и сны
Твои казацкие полки, кубанские сыны.

Мы отстоим тебя, Тамань, за то, что ты века
Стояла грудью боевой у русского древка;
За то, что где бы ни дралось, развеяв чубовье,
Всегда мечтает о тебе казачество твое;
За этот дом, за этот сад, за море во дворе,
За красный парус на заре, за чаек в серебре,
За смех казачек молодых, за эти песни их,
За то, что Лермонтов бродил на берегах твоих.

1943

Cavalry land! You never shall be held by enemy troops
Though you're ploughed by bombs and harrowed by their
     heavy boots.
Alien flags fly over you and alien speech is here.
But the foe knows:
    your surrender
       he shall never hear.
My Taman, Taman! When bustling spring brings merry days
No migrating birds come racing home from faraway
With such love through thick and thin the land of home to scan
As your Cossack sons do, racing home to the Kuban.

We shall fight for you, Taman, because you many a time
Stood with martial courage in the Russian battle line;
And no matter where they fought with forelock in the breeze
Your bold Cossack sons would ever see you in their dreams;
For your homes we'll fight, your orchards and doorstep waves,
For your silver gulls, your boats with glowing sunset sails,
For the laughter of your Cossacks and the songs they sing
And for Lermontov along your coastline wandering.

1943

ИЛЬЯ ГРИГОРЬЕВИЧ ЭРЕНБУРГ

Ehrenburg, already an internationally famous writer, poet, essayist, became one of the most important Soviet war correspondents, the author of much-anticipated and much-loved articles that raised troop morale, both for the military newspapers and civilian press. Hitler promised to have Ehrenburg hanged, declaring him Germany's worst enemy.

Возмездие

Она лежала у моста. Хотели немцы
Ее унизить. Но была та нагота,
Как древней статуи простое совершенство,
Как целомудренной природы красота.
Ее прикрыли, понесли. И мостик шаткий
Как будто трепетал под ношей дорогой.
Бойцы остановились, молча сняли шапки,
И каждый понимал, что он теперь – другой.
На Запад шел судья. Была зима как милость,
Снега в огне и ненависти немота.
Судьба Германии в тот мутный день решилась
Над мертвой девушкой, у шаткого моста.

1942

ILYA EHRENBURG (1891–1967)

In 1942, Soviet forces began to retake some of the territories previously occupied by the German army. According to those who witnessed it, the devastation they found fueled their hatred of the enemy and their resolve more than any military orders or any exhortations of the army's political officers.

Retribution

She lay beside the bridge. The German troops had reckoned
To cheapen her by this. Instead, her nakedness
Was like an ancient statue's unadorned perfection,
Was like unspotted Nature's loveliness and grace.
We covered her and carried her. The bridge, unsteady,
Appeared to palpitate beneath our precious load.
Our soldiers halted there, in silence stood bare-headed,
Each transformed, acknowledging the debt he owed.
Then Justice headed westward. Winter was a blessing,
With hatred huddled mute, and snows a fiery ridge.
The fate of Germany that murky day was settled
Because of one dead girl, beside a shaky bridge.

1942

The battle for Rzhev (1942–43) was so horrific and casualties were so catastrophic, that veterans called it the Rzhev meatgrinder. There were forests and valleys of death, where corpses lay three or four deep. The shelling permanently changed the landscape in and around Rzhev. The corpses attracted birds of prey and changed the fauna of the area.

'Слов мы боимся, и все же прощай....'

Слов мы боимся, и всё же прощай.
Если судьба нас сведет невзначай,
Может, не сразу узнаю я, кто
Серый прохожий в дорожном пальто,
Сердце подскажет, что ты – это тот,
Сорок второй и единственный год.
Ржев догорал. Мы стояли с тобой,
Смерть примеряли. И начался бой...
Странно устроен любой человек:
Страстно клянется, что любит навек,
И забывает, когда и кому...
Но не изменит и он одному:
Слову скупому, горячей руке,
Ржевскому лесу и ржевской тоске.

1944

The theme of betrayal became especially relevant, when the State limited wartime freedoms. Ehrenburg later wrote euphemistically, 'In 1943, the clouds began to gather that five years later would cover the entire sky'. He had hoped the shared horror of Rzhev would become a touchstone, ensuring integrity when the war ended.

'We Distrust Words, But I Will Say Farewell.'

We distrust words, but I will say, 'Farewell.'
If our paths cross again, I might not tell
at once who is that passerby I see,
in a grey coat, brushing past me.
But then my heart will whisper that it's you,
with whom in one-and-only forty-two
I sized-up death and watched Rzhev burn,
while all around the battle had raged on...
Some of us men are strangely put together:
we swear our love will last forever,
but then forget to whom we swore and why...
But even such a man would not betray
those spare words, and that searing handshake,
Rzhev's forests, and Rzhev's heartache.

1944

ЯРОСЛАВ ВАСИЛЬЕВИЧ СМЕЛЯКОВ

Smelyakov became famous in the 1930s for his unique poetic voice and notorious for his fall from grace when Gorky denounced him as a Bohemian hooligan (followed by three years in the Gulag). He fought in the War, was taken prisoner in 1941, then exchanged in 1944, only to be interred in a Soviet filtration camp.

Судья

Упал на пашне у высотки
суровый мальчик из Москвы;
и тихо сдвинулась пилотка
с пробитой пулей головы.

Не глядя на беззвездный купол
и чуя веянье конца,
он пашню бережно ощупал
руками быстрыми слепца.

И, уходя в страну иную
от мест родных невдалеке,
он землю теплую, сырую
зажал в костнеющей руке.

Горсть отвоеванной России
он захотел на память взять,
и не сумели мы, живые,
те пальцы мертвые разжать.

Мы так его похоронили –
в его военной красоте –
в большой торжественной могиле
на взятой утром высоте,

YAROSLAV SMELYAKOV (1913–1972)

Smelyakov wrote this poem in a Soviet filtration camp, working in the coal mines. His poet friends in Moscow did everything they could to secure his release (he returned in 1947) and published his poems – including this frequently anthologized one – in the important literary journal Znamia. *Smelyakov was rearrested and sent to the Gulag in 1951.*

The Judge

Under a hillock, in a field,
a stern young boy from Moscow fell,
and, quietly, his cap slid off
his bullet-riddled head.

Not looking at the starless dome,
and sensing that his end was imminent,
he felt the field – carefully,
with the quick touch of the blind.

Departing for another world,
not very far from that in which he grew,
he clutched his warm, native earth
in his already stiffening hand.

Clutching at the keepsake he desired –
a handful of the Russia won in war;
we, the living, were unable
to unclasp his dead hand.

We buried him thus –
in his warrior beauty –
in a large solemn grave
on the hill we took this morning.

И если, правда, будет время,
когда людей на Страшный суд
из всех земель, с грехами всеми,
трехкратно трубы призовут, –

предстанет за столом судейским
не бог с туманной бородой,
а паренек красноармейский
пред потрясенною толпой,

держа в своей ладони правой,
помятой немцами в бою,
не символы небесной славы,
а землю русскую свою.

Он все увидит, этот мальчик,
и ни йоты не простит,
но лесть – от правды, боль – от фальши
и гнев – от злобы отличит.

Он все узнает оком зорким,
с пятном кровавым на груди –
судья в истлевшей гимнастерке,
сидящий молча впереди.

И будет самой высшей мерой,
какою мерить нас могли,
в ладони юношеской серой
та горсть тяжелая земли.

1945

And if there really comes a time
when trumpets thrice shall summon all the people
from all the lands, with all their sins,
to greet the Day of Judgment –

Then before the shaken crowd will stand
not God with misty beard,
but a young Red Army lad
presiding in the judgment,

Holding, in the palm of his right hand,
which the Germans crushed in battle,
not symbols of celestial majesty,
but the earth of Russia, which was his.

And he will see everything, this boy,
and not one detail be forgiven;
but he will distinguish truth from flattery,
pain from falsehood, wrath from spite.

He will sit there silently before us all,
his penetrating gaze detecting everything,
this judge – a decayed field shirt on his back,
and bloodstains on his breast.

The highest criterion
by which we can possibly be judged
will be that heavy handful of earth
clutched in that young grey palm.

1945

МАРГАРИТА ИОСИФОВНА АЛИГЕР

Aliger debuted as a poet in the 1930s, as a passionate believer in the Soviet project, celebrating the heroic romanticism and optimism of her contemporaries, and receiving a State Prize at the behest of Stalin himself. During the War, her husband, a composer, was killed in combat. She was a war correspondent in blockaded Leningrad.

Отрывок из поэмы 'Зоя'

Навсегда сохрани фотографию Зои.
Я, наверно, вовеки ее позабыть не смогу.
Это девичье тело,
не мертвое
и не живое.

Это Зоя из мрамора
тихо лежит на снегу.
Беспощадной петлей перерезана тонкая шея.
Незнакомая власть в запрокинутом лике твоем.
Так любимого ждут,
сокровенной красой хорошея,
изнутри озаряясь таинственным женским огнем.
Только ты не дождалась его, снеговая невеста.
Он – в солдатской шинели,
на запад лежит его путь,
может быть, недалеко от этого страшного места,
где ложились снежинки на строгую девичью грудь.
Вечной силы и слабости неповторимо единство.
Ты совсем холодна, а меня прожигает тоска.
Не ворвалось в тебя, не вскипело в тебе материнство,
теплый ротик ребенка не тронул сухого соска.
Ты лежишь на снегу.
О, как много за нас отдала ты,
чтобы гордо откинуться чистым, прекрасным лицом!

MARGARITA ALIGER (1915–1992)

Aliger wrote the long poem 'Zoya' shortly after an 18-year-old Soviet partisan Zoya Kosmodemyanskaya was tortured then hanged by Nazi troops. The poem became instantly famous as a poetic monument to Zoya's heroism; sections of it were memorized and recited by generations of schoolchildren.

from 'Zoya'

You must keep Zoya's photograph forever.
As for me, I couldn't forget if I tried
that photo – a young woman's body,
neither dead
nor alive.

Zoya, you seem made of marble,
as you quietly lie on the snow,
a pitiless noose round your slender neck.
There's a strange power in your upturned face –
that's how a girl awaits her beloved,
glowing with that inward grace,
that mysterious womanly flame.
But you've waited in vain, snowy bride –
he's in a soldier's overcoat,
marching west,
not far, maybe, from that terrible place
where snowflakes fell on your young breast,
where your eternal strength and weakness fused into one.
You are cold through and through but sorrow scalds me –
motherhood never surged within you,
a baby's warm lips never brushed your dry nipple.
You lie on the snow.
O how much you've given up for us,
to proudly raise up your pure, beautiful face!

За доспехи героя,
за тяжелые ржавые латы,
за святое блаженство быть храбрым бойцом.
Стань же нашей любимицей,
символом правды и силы,
чтоб была наша верность, как гибель твоя, высока.
Мимо твоей занесенной снегами могилы –
на запад, на запад! –

                  идут,
                  присягая,
                  войска.

1942

Yours are the hero's armour,
the heavy rusty breastplates,
the sacred ecstasy of a fearless fighter.
Now you'll be our beloved,
a symbol of truth and strength.
Our loyalty will be as great as your death.
Troops pass the grave where you rest,
                              make a vow,
                              and press on—
                              to the West, to the West!

1942

МИХАИЛ АРКАДЬЕВИЧ СВЕТЛОВ

Svetlov began as a poet of the Revolution. His most famous poem of the 1920s was the wildly popular 'Grenada,' about a young Ukrainian revolutionary who dreams about 'giving the land back to the peasants of Spain.' In the 1930s, horrified by Soviet political developments, he concentrated on playwriting but returned to poetry as a war correspondent in the War.

Итальянец

Черный крест на груди итальянца,
Ни резьбы, ни узора, ни глянца, –
Небогатым семейством хранимый
И единственным сыном носимый...

Молодой уроженец Неаполя!
Что оставил в России ты на поле?
Почему ты не мог быть счастливым
Над родным знаменитым заливом?

Я, убивший тебя под Моздоком,
Так мечтал о вулкане далеком!
Как я грезил на волжском приволье
Хоть разок прокатиться в гондоле!

Но ведь я не пришел с пистолетом
Отнимать итальянское лето,
Но ведь пули мои не свистели
Над священной землей Рафаэля!

Здесь я выстрелил! Здесь, где родился,
Где собой и друзьями гордился,
Где былины о наших народах
Никогда не звучат в переводах.

MIKHAIL SVETLOV (1903–1964)

Many Italian soldiers were killed on the Eastern Front (the entire Eighth Italian Army was destroyed in Stalingrad). The Italians were not demonized to the same extent as the Germans, a fact that allowed Svetlov to movingly reflect on the ethics of killing another human being in a war.

The Italian

The Italian had a cross round his neck –
it was simple – unvarnished and black.
A humble family's modest bequest,
that their only son wore on his chest...

Let me ask you, young native of Naples,
what brought you to our Russian fields?
Why couldn't you cheerfully stay
back home by your famous bay?

I, who killed you near Mozdok, can say now
how I dreamt of your distant volcano!
How I longed, on Volga's vast tide,
to go – just once! – for a gondola ride!

But then I was never the one
to come wreck your world with my gun,
and I never let my bullets hail
over the blessed land of Raphael!

I shot my gun where I was born,
where I learned to take pride in my own,
where the epics of our nation
are never read out in translation.

Разве среднего Дона излучина
Иностранным ученым изучена?
Нашу землю – Россию, Расею –
Разве ты распахал и засеял?

Нет! Тебя привезли в эшелоне
Для захвата далеких колоний,
Чтобы крест из ларца из фамильного
Вырастал до размеров могильного...

Я не дам свою родину вывезти
За простор чужеземных морей!
Я стреляю –и нет справедливости
Справедливее пули моей!

Никогда ты здесь не жил и не был!..
Но разбросано в снежных полях
Итальянское синее небо,
Застекленное в мертвых глазах...

1943

Was it a foreign explorer
who first traced the course of Don River?
Was the farming of our land –
of our Russia – done by your hand?

No! You were brought here by train,
to claim colonies for your Empire's gain,
so the cross that your family saved
would swell to the size of your grave...

I shall not stand to see my homeland
plundered, shipped overseas, undone!
I shoot, and there's no justice greater
than the bullet blasting out of my gun!

This isn't your home, you're a stranger!
But now the Italian blue skies
are fused with our snow-covered fields
in your dead and glazed-over eyes...

1943

ОЛЬГА ФЕДОРОВНА БЕРГГОЛЬЦ

Berggolts was born in Leningrad and refused to leave her city during the siege. She continued to write poems, work on the radio, and broadcast her poems in the blockaded city. She starved, developed dystrophy.

Разговор с соседкой

Пятое декабря 1941 года. Идет четвертый месяц блокады. До пятого декабря воздушные тревоги длились по десять – двенадцать часов. Ленинградцы получали от 125 до 250 граммов хлеба.

Дарья Власьевна, соседка по квартире,
сядем, побеседуем вдвоем.
Знаешь, будем говорить о мире,
о желанном мире, о своем.

Вот мы прожили почти полгода,
полтораста суток длится бой.
Тяжелы страдания народа –
наши, Дарья Власьевна, с тобой.

О, ночное воющее небо,
дрожь земли, обвал невдалеке,
бедный ленинградский ломтик хлеба –
он почти не весит на руке...

Для того чтоб жить в кольце блокады,
ежедневно смертный слышать свист –
сколько силы нам, соседка, надо,
сколько ненависти и любви...

Столько, что минутами в смятенье
ты сама себя не узнаешь:
– Вынесу ли? Хватит ли терпенья?
– Вынесешь. Дотерпишь. Доживешь.

OLGA BERGGOLTS (1910–1975)

Between September 1941 and January 1944, over 16,000 civilians died during the bombardment of Leningrad, and more than 600,000 died of hunger. The worst losses were sustained during the brutal winter of 1941–1942.

Conversation with a Neighbour

The fifth of December 1941. The fourth month of the blockade. Till the fifth of December air-raid alarms last until ten-twelve o'clock. The people of Leningrad receive from 125 to 250 grams of bread.

Darya Vlasyevna, my neighbour,
Let's sit down and have a talk together.
We'll have a talk about the world, you know,
the one we'd like, as well as what we've got.

We've survived now almost half a year,
One hundred and fifty days the battle's lasted.
The bitter hardships suffered by the people,
Darya Vlasyevna, are yours and mine.

O the howling of the night-time sky,
the trembling of the ground, the crash of masonry,
our Leningrad slice of bread, so thin
you can barely hold it in your hand...

To live in the ring of the blockade,
to hear the deadly whistle every day,
how much strength we need, neighbour,
how much hatred, how much love...

So much that, at times, in your confusion,
you do not even recognize yourself:
'Can I stand it? Is there the endurance?'
– 'You will stand it. You'll endure. Survive.'

Дарья Власьевна, еще немного,
день придет – над нашей головой
пролетит последняя тревога
и последний прозвучит отбой.

И какой далекой, давней-давней
нам с тобой покажется война
в миг, когда толкнем рукою ставни,
сдернем шторы черные с окна.

Пусть жилище светится и дышит,
полнится покоем и весной...
Плачьте тише, смейтесь тише, тише,
будем наслаждаться тишиной.

Будем свежий хлеб ломать руками,
темно-золотистый и ржаной.
Медленными, крупными глотками
будем пить румяное вино.

А тебе – да ведь тебе ж поставят
памятник на площади большой.
Нержавеющей, бессмертной сталью
облик твой запечатлят простой.

Вот такой же: исхудавшей, смелой,
в наскоро повязанном платке,
вот такой, когда под артобстрелом
ты идешь с кошелкою в руке.

Дарья Власьевна, твоею силой
будет вся земля обновлена.
Этой силе имя есть – Россия.
Стой же и мужайся, как она!

5 Декабрь 1941

Darya Vlasyevna, one thing more:
a day will come – over our heads
the last alert will sound,
and the last all-clear ring out.

And how far, how long ago
will the war seem suddenly to you and me
that moment when we push the shutters open,
take the dark blinds down from the window.

Let our home be bright then, let it breathe,
let it fill with peace and springtime...
Weep more softly, laugh more softly then,
we shall enjoy the silence.

We shall break the fresh bread with our hands,
dark-golden, made of rye.
We shall drink slow and deep
of the rosy wine.

And they will put up a monument to you,
to you, yes, on the main square.
They'll engrave your simple image
in unfading, everlasting steel.

Just as you are now: emaciated, dauntless,
in a hastily tied kerchief,
holding a purse as you go out
under the bombardment.

Darya Vlasyevna, the whole land
will be renewed by your strength.
The name of this strength of yours is 'Russia.'
Like Russia, stand and take heart!'

5 December 1941

Berggolts experienced a number of personal tragedies before the war. She lost two young daughters to illness. She was arrested twice on charges of anti-Soviet activity, imprisoned, and tortured. On both occasions she was pregnant, and both times, she miscarried. The war allowed her to speak about pain and suffering of herself and others.

Дорога на фронт

...Мы шли на фронт по улицам знакомым,
припоминали каждую, как сон:
вот палисад отеческого дома,
здесь жил, шумя, огромный добрый клен.

Он в форточки тянулся к нам весною,
прохладный, глянцевитый поутру.
Но этой темной ледяной зимою
и ты погиб, зеленый шумный друг.

Зияют окна вымершего дома.
Гнездо мое, что сделали с тобой!
Разбиты стены старого райкома,
его крылечко с кимовской звездой.

Я шла на фронт сквозь детство – той дорогой,
которой в школу бегала давно.
Я шла сквозь юность,
                сквозь ее тревогу,
сквозь счастие свое – перед войной.

Я шла сквозь хмурое людское горе –
пожарища,
        развалины,
                гробы...
Сквозь новый,
        только возникавший город,
где здания прекрасны и грубы.

*In the south of Leningrad, the frontline was only several kilometers
from the city limits. You could see the German troops from the roofs
of the taller buildings. Busses travelled from the Kirov Factory to the
frontline and took the wounded back into the city. The enemy was at
the gates.*

The Road to the Battle Front

...We walked along towards the battle front,
familiar streets passed by us like a dream:
here stands our family home, our wooden fence,
here loomed a noisy, friendly maple tree.

He'd stretch his glossy branches through
our windows when the cool spring morning swelled.
But as this dark and coldest winter drew
like many men, green friend, you died as well.

The windows of the deadened house, my nest,
gape out like you and I were never there.
Old city hall, porch with the Kimovsk crest:
all down to ruins, desolate and bare.

I walked along across my childhood,
the road where I had run to school before.
I walked across my youth
            with its disquietude,
across my happiness – before the war.

I walked across the suffering of many
fires,
        wreckage,
                    graves...
Across a recent
        just created city,
Where stand its buildings, rough and great.

Я шла сквозь жизнь, сведя до боли пальцы.
Твердил мне путь давнишний и прямой:
– Иди. Не береги себя. Не сжалься,
не плачь, не умиляйся над собой.

И вот – река,
        лачуги,
                ветер жесткий,
челны рыбачьи, дымный горизонт,
землянка у газетного киоска –
наш
  ленинградский
              неприступный фронт.

Да. Знаю. Все, что с детства в нас горело,
все, что в душе болит, поет, живет, –
все шло к тебе,
            торжественная зрелость,
на этот фронт у городских ворот.

Ты нелегка – я это тоже знаю,
но все равно – пути другого нет.
Благодарю ж тебя, благословляю,
жестокий мой,
          короткий мой расцвет,

за то, что я сильнее, и спокойней,
и терпеливей стала во сто крат
и всею жизнью защищать достойна
великий город жизни – Ленинград.

Май 1942

I walked across it all, my fingers clenched,
And said to me the endless path of life:
'Go on. Don't ever try to save yourself.
Do not take pity on yourself and cry.'

And so – the river,
          shanties,
                    the bitter wind,
the fishermen's canoes, smoky horizon.
a simple earth lodge by a newsstand –
our own
    impregnable
              Leningrad front line

Yes. I know. All that we cried, survived, exulted,
all that burned within us as we came of age,
all lead to you
                    our march into adulthood
On these front lines at our city's gates.

You are not gentle – I know this too,
but all the same – there is no other way.
And so I thank and sanctify you
my cruel
          briefly blooming heyday

for all my strength and my composure steady
for giving me a patience unsurpassed
now that I am worthy of defending
the great city of life – my Leningrad.

May 1942

ВЕРА МИХАЙЛОВНА ИНБЕР

Vera Inber a wide-ranging poet who was endorsed by Stalin (despite being Trotsky's cousin), moved to Leningrad and lived there throughout the war. She kept a celebrated diary about life in the besieged city where she worked on the radio.

Заря в Блокадном Ленинграде

Зима роскошествует. Нет конца
Ее великолепьям и щедротам.
Паркетами зеркального торца
Сковала землю. В голубые гроты
Преобразила черные дворы.
Алмазы. Блеск... Недобрые дары!

Но чем закрыть? Без теплых испарений
Воздушный свод неизъяснимо чист.
Не тающий на ветках снег – сиренев,
Как дымчатый уральский аметист.
Закат сухумской розой розовеет...
Но лютой нежностью все это веет.

А в час, когда рассветная звезда
Над улиц перспективой несравненной
Сияет в бездне утренней, – тогда
Такою стужей тянет из вселенной,
Как будто бы сам космос, не дыша,
Глядит, как холодеет в нас душа.

1942

VERA INBER (1890–1972)

This segment is part of Inber's long poem about the siege (the poem and her siege diary Almost Three Years *won the Stalin Prize. The winter of 1941–1942 was extremely cold, with temperatures dipping below –30°.*

Dawn in Besieged Leningrad

Diamonds, Sparkling. Gifts that cannot ease
the agonies of a town where all the faces
are branded deep with hunger, death, disease.
What use then are these opalescent spaces,
this garden glint, this crystal light of trees?
They should be shrouded, like a shrouded mirror
in homes where death makes glittering things a horror.

How may we shroud them? There's no warming mists
curling to blur with clouds the aery dome.
Unmelting snow, like Ural amethysts,
has found on boughs its settled shining home.
No southern rose was like the sunset-rose.
All round a fiercely tender beauty glows.

And when, above the streets, the morning star
climbs up the sky to warn us of the dawn
and throbs and beams in lucid strength afar,
such a sharp iciness from earth is drawn
the universe seems gasping to behold
how souls themselves are frozen by the cold.

1942

ЕВГЕНИЙ АРОНОВИЧ ДОЛМАТОВСКИЙ

Dolmatovsky graduated from Moscow's Gorky Literary Institute. His father was executed as a people's enemy in 1939, the year that Dolmatovsky enlisted as a war correspondent. During the War he was best known as a songwriter, whose universally popular songs won multiple awards.

Бомбежка

Детей, завернутых в одеяла,
Несли на пристань.
Воронок язвой земля зияла,
Шел третий приступ.

На старой барже огонь косматый
С обшивкой грызся,
Сирена выла, и по канату
Бежала крыса.

По узким доскам, по переборкам,
По лужам масла,
Дыша безумьем, шла мать с ребенком
В пеленках красных.

Мы слишком много видали крови,
Чтоб ошибиться.
С тяжелой тучей почти что вровень
Парил убийца.

А вражьи роты уже в предместьях
Ползли, как змеи.
О чем, товарищ, коль не о мести,
Я думать смею?

19 Декабрь 1942

YEVGENY DOLMATOVSKY (1915–1994)

This poem was first published in the army newspaper Krasnaia Zvezda *in 1942, when Dolmatovsky was allowed to return to the army, after being encircled and then escaping. It is a well-written and hard-hitting propaganda piece that would later become a part of his cycle of poems* In a Besieged City.

Air Raid

The town was being bombed again –
streets gaped with craters.
Parents brought children to the wharf,
wrapped up in blankets.

On the old barge the fire raged
and gnawed the fittings,
the siren howled and down a rope
a rat came fleeing.

Across the planks, the bulkhead beams,
and spills of oil,
a distraught mother brought her child
in scarlet swaddling.

We've all seen too much blood by then,
to be mistaken.
His killer hovered near the clouds –
a storm was breaking.

The suburbs fell to enemy troops,
that slithering menace.
What do I dare to dream of now,
if not of vengeance?

19 December 1942

АЛЕКСАНДР ПЕТРОВИЧ МЕЖИРОВ

Mezhirov, who fought on the Leningrad front, published his first collection of poetry in 1947. He was an important member of the post-war poetic scene and influenced a number of young poets, including Yevtushenko.

Ладожский лед

Страшный путь!
    На тридцатой,
            последней версте
Ничего не сулит хорошего.
Под моими ногами
       устало
           хрустеть
Ледяное,
   ломкое
      крошево.
Страшный путь!
    Ты в блокаду меня ведешь,
Только небо с тобой,
       над тобой
           высоко.
И нет на тебе
     никаких одёж:
Гол как сокол
Страшный путь!
    Ты на пятой своей версте
Потерял
   для меня конец,
И ветер устал
     над тобой свистеть,
И устал
   грохотать
      свинец...
– Почему не проходит над Ладогой
          мост?! –

ALEXANDER MEZHIROV (1923–2009)

Mezhirov later said, 'I crossed into Leningrad across Lake Ladoga... I saw a dead city... frozen into the ice. Corpses were stacked one on top of the other... the defence line was metres away from the enemy.'

The Ice of Ladoga

Road of terror!
     The thirtieth,
         the final mile
Promises nothing good.
The icy,
   brittle
     chunks
Have tired
     of crunching
        under my feet.
Road of terror!
    You are taking me into the blockade,
Only the sky is with you,
      high
        above you.
And on you there is
     no clothing at all:
Poor
   and
      naked.
Road of terror!
    When I reached your fifth mile
I began to see
     no end to it,
And the wind tired
     of whistling above you,
And the shells
    grew tired
      of thundering...
– Why is there no bridge
        across Ladoga?!

Нам подошвы
        невмочь
              ото льда
                    оторвать.
Сумасшедшие мысли
            буравят
                  мозг:
Почему на льду не растет трава?!
Самый страшный путь
              из моих путей!
На двадцатой версте
            как я мог идти!
Шли навстречу из города
              сотни
                    детей...

Сотни детей!..
        Замерзали в пути...

Одинокие дети
        на взорванном льду –
Эту теплую смерть
              распознать не могли они сами
И смотрели на падающую звезду
Непонимающими глазами.

Мне в атаках не надобно слова «вперед»,
Под каким бы нам
            ни бывать огнем –
У меня в зрачках
            черный
                  ладожский
                        лед,
Ленинградские дети
        лежат
              на нем.

1944

We can't even
        tear
            our soles
                from the ice.
Insane thoughts
            pierce
                the brain:
Why doesn't grass grow on ice?!
The most terrible
            of all my roads!
At the twentieth mile
            how could I go on!
From the city come toward us
                hundreds
                    of children...

Hundreds of children!
            They froze to death on the way...

Lonely children
        on the bombed ice –
They themselves could not recognize
            this warm death
And in their innocent eyes, the bombs
Seemed to be falling stars.

In attacks I don't need the word 'forward,'
No matter what kind of fire
            we are under –
In my eyes is the
        black
            Ladoga
                ice,
and the children of Leningrad
            lying
                on it.

1944

АННА АНДРЕЕВНА АХМАТОВА

Akhmatova was in Leningrad for the first terrifying months of the siege, working on the fire brigade, digging anti-tank trenches, and broadcasting on the radio, until she was evacuated with other 'distinguished cultural workers,' on a list approved by Stalin himself. She ended up in Tashkent, where she continued to write about Leningrad and to mourn its dead.

Первый дальнобойный в Ленинграде

И в пестрой суете людской
Все изменилось вдруг.
Но это был не городской,
Да и не сельский звук.
На грома дальнего раскат
Он, правда, был похож, как брат,
Но в громе влажность есть
Высоких свежих облаков
И вожделение лугов –
Веселых ливней весть.
А этот был, как пекло, сух,
И не хотел смятенный слух
Поверить – по тому,
Как расширялся он и рос,
Как равнодушно гибель нес
Ребенку моему.

1941

ANNA AKHMATOVA (1889–1966)

The first explosions of German artillery shells in Leningrad came on September 4th, 1941. The artillery raids against the city took place during the day, usually from 10am to 7pm – casualties were high. This is one of the first poems Akhmatova wrote about the war while still in Leningrad, before she was evacuated.

The First Long-Range Artillery Shell in Leningrad

A rainbow of people rushing around,
And suddenly everything changed completely,
This wasn't a normal city sound,
It came from unfamiliar country.
True, it resembled, like a brother,
One peal of thunder or another,
But every natural thunder contains
The moisture of clouds, fresh and high,
And the thirst of fields with drought gone dry,
A harbinger of happy rains,
And this was an arid as hell ever got,
And my distracted hearing would not
Believe it, if only because of the wild
Way it started, grew, and caught,
And how indifferently it brought
Death to my child.

1941

This poem, part of a cycle Akhmatova started when she was evacuated to Tashkent, was published in Pravda *and marked her temporary return into the State's good graces as a national patriotic poet. Soviet readers hadn't seen her poems in official publications for nearly a decade. The poem was also immediately noticed by émigré readers.*

Мужество

Мы знаем, что ныне лежит на весах
И что совершается ныне.
Час мужества пробил на наших часах,
И мужество нас не покинет.
Не страшно под пулями мертвыми лечь,
Не горько остаться без крова,
И мы сохраним тебя, русская речь,
Великое русское слово.
Свободным и чистым тебя пронесем,
И внукам дадим, и от плена спасем
Навеки.

23 Февраля 1942 , Ташкент

While 'Courage' is a patriotic poem, Akhmatova's allegiance is not so much to the State or its leader, but to the continuity of Russian literary culture – the Russian language itself. This obvious point was ignored before Zhdanov's attack on Akhmatova in 1946, and then brought out as an accusation against the poet.

Courage

We know what's at stake and how great the foe's power,
And what now is coming to pass.
Every clock shows the same time – it's courage's hour,
And our courage will hold to the last.
The bullets can kill us, but cannot deter;
Though our houses fall, yet we will stand –
Through it all we will keep you alive, Russian word,
Mighty language of our Russian land.
Your sounds will remain pure and free on our tongues,
To be passed on unfettered through ages to come.
Forever!

23 February 1942, Tashkent

БОРИС ЛЕОНИДОВИЧ ПАСТЕРНАК

When war began, Pasternak dug trenches on the outskirts of Moscow, and took special courses for war correspondents. His war poems were published in the country's main newspapers, after a decade-long unofficial ban.

Одесса

Земля смотрела именинницей
И все ждала неделю эту,
Когда к ней избавитель кинется
Под сумерки или к рассвету.

Прибой рычал свою невнятицу
У каменистого отвеса,
Как вдруг все слышат, сверху катится:
'Одесса занята, Одесса.'

По улицам, давно не езженным,
Несется русский гул веселый.
Сапер занялся обезвреженьем
Подъездов и домов от тола.

Идет пехота, входит конница,
Гремят тачанки и телеги.
В беседах время к ночи клонится,
И нет конца им на ночлеге.

А рядом в яме череп скалится,
Раскинулся пустырь безмерный.
Здесь дикаря гуляла палица,
Прошелся человек пещерный.

Пустыми черепа глазницами
Глядят головки иммортелей
И населяют воздух лицами,
Расстрелянными в том апреле.

BORIS PASTERNAK (1890–1960)

This poem was first published in the newspaper Red Fleet *two days after the liberation of Odessa. It was originally published without the sixth stanza of the poem.*

Odessa

The waiting land was looking radiant,
she knew the day was coming soon,
when rescuers would finally reach her,
whether near dusk or breaking dawn.

The tide was growling angry nonsense
down by the rocky coastal cliff,
when suddenly we heard a thundering:
'They're here! Odessa has been freed!'

Streets long untravelled now resounded
with joyful sounds of Russian speech,
as sappers started on demining
the yards and buildings with their spades.

Here come the troops, and now the cavalry,
and rattling carts from left and right.
The days are filled with giddy banter,
which carries on into the night.

But skulls lie grinning in the ditches
and badlands stretch in endless blight,
where, brandishing his savage bludgeon,
a caveman ravaged all in sight.

The immortelles, just like the orbits
of skulls look up at us and stare –
the ghostly faces of those murdered
that April rise into the air.

Зло будет отмщено, наказано,
А родственникам жертв и вдовам
Мы горе облегчить обязаны
Еще каким-то новым словом.

Клянемся им всем русским гением,
Что мученикам и героям
Победы одухотворением
Мы вечный памятник построим.

1944

The evil done will be avenged,
but we must ease the awful grief
of widows and the victims' kin
with some new word that brings relief.

We pledge now by the Russian spirit,
to all the martyred heroes here:
we'll build a lasting monument
and elevate their victory.

1944

МИХАИЛ КУЗЬМИЧ ЛУКОНИН

Lukonin studied at the Gorky Literary Institute and became identified with the young generation of Moscow poets, together with Kogan, Kulchitsky and Narovchatov. He enlisted for the war, publishing poems in military newspapers.

Приду к тебе

Ты думаешь:
Принесу с собой
Усталое тело свое.
Сумею ли быть тогда с тобой
Целый день вдвоем?
Захочу рассказать о смертном дожде,
Как горела трава,
А ты –
            и ты жила в беде,
Тебе не нужны слова.
Про то, как чудом выжил, начну,
Как смерть меня обожгла,
А ты – ты в ночь роковую одну
Волгу переплыла.
Спеть попрошу,
            а ты сама
Забыла, как поют...
Потом
        меня
            сведет с ума
Непривычный уют.
Будешь к завтраку накрывать,
А я усядусь в углу,
Начнешь,
        как прежде,
                стелить кровать,
А я
    усну
        на полу.

MIKHAIL LUKONIN (1918–1976)

Lukonin began writing this poem in 1943, during the Battle for Prokhorovka. It was published in Znamia *in 1945, when the Soviet press was voicing concerns about soldiers' ability to adapt to the demands of peacetime.*

'I'll Come to You...'

You wonder:
Shall I bring home to you
This tired-out body of mine?
Shall we be able to live as two,
Together all the time?
I shall want to speak of death's leaden rain,
And how the grasses burned,
But you –
      you, too, lived in woe and pain,
And you do not need such words.
I shall start, how by miracles I survived,
How scorching near me death came.
But you –
      But you on one fatal night
Across the wide Volga swam.
I shall ask you to sing,
              but you will find
That you have forgotten how.
And then
      I shall go
           clean out of my mind
With comforts not used to now:
The breakfast tablecloth you will spread,
But I shall squat by the door.
You will start, as usual,
to make the bed,
But I
      shall sleep
          on the floor.

Потом покоя тебя лишу,
Вырою щель у ворот,
Ночью,
    вздрогнув,
        тебя спрошу:
– Стой! Кто идет?!
Нет, не думай, что так приду.
В этой большой войне
Мы научились ломать беду,
Работать и жить вдвойне.
Не так вернемся мы!
        Если так,
То лучше не приходить.
Придем работать, курить табак,
В комнате начадить.
Не за благодарностью я бегу –
Благодарить лечу.
Все, что хотел, я сказал врагу.
Теперь работать хочу.
Не за утешением –
        утешать
Переступлю порог.
То, что я сделал,
        к тебе спеша,
Не одолженье, а долг.
Друзей увидеть,
        в гостях побывать
И трудно
    и жадно
        жить.
Работать – в кузницу,
        спать – в кровать.
Слова про любовь сложить.
В этом зареве ветровом
Выбор был небольшой, –
Но лучше прийти с пустым рукавом,
Чем с пустой душой.

1944

I'll creep to the gate and dig a trench.
At night of you unaware,
I'll jump
        and shout,
                my fists tight-clenched,
'Halt! – Who goes there?'
No, do not think that so I shall come.
In this war's oppressive hell
We learned to conquer our woes as one.
To work and live twice as well.
Not so shall I come!
Were that it's like,
It were better never to come.
I shall come – I shall work,
             I shall light my pipe,
Make a proper fug in the room.
Not for gratitude do I hasten so,
But with gratitude back do I hark.
All that I wished to, I told the foe –
Now I just want to work.
Not for consolation –
           But to console,
Shall I cross the threshold I know
What I did as I hastened to you, was my goal,
Was my duty –
no debt you owe.
I shall meet my friends, be invited as guest,
Live hard
        And eagerly too.
I shall work – in the smithy,
             And sleep – in bed.
And write poems of love for you.
In that fiery glow fanned up by the breeze
The choice of me was small.

But better to come with an empty sleeve,
Than with an empty soul.

1944

СЕМЕН ПЕТРОВИЧ ГУДЗЕНКО

Gudzenko came into his own as a poet while fighting on the front and publishing in army newspapers. Ilya Ehrenburg made sure that Gudzenko's stark, hard-hitting poems reached a wide readership. Gudzenko died of wartime injuries nearly a decade after the war.

Перед атакой

Когда на смерть идут – поют,
а перед этим
       можно плакать.
Ведь самый страшный час в бою –
час ожидания атаки.
Снег минами изрыт вокруг
и почернел от пыли минной.
Разрыв –
       и умирает друг.
И значит – смерть проходит мимо.
Сейчас настанет мой черед,
За мной одним
       идет охота.
Будь проклят
       сорок первый год –
ты, вмерзшая в снега пехота.
Мне кажется, что я магнит,
что я притягиваю мины.
Разрыв –
       и лейтенант хрипит.
И смерть опять проходит мимо.
Но мы уже
       не в силах ждать.
И нас ведет через траншеи
окоченевшая вражда,
штыком дырявящая шеи.

SEMYON GUDZENKO (1922–1953)

Reviewing Gudzenko's first book of poetry in 1944, Ehrenburg observed: 'these words are truthful and courageous, there is nothing conventional about them, they breathe the grim air of battle.' The lines 'accursed nineteen forty-one/with infantry in snowdrifts frozen' were cut by the censors.

Before the Attack

When sent to certain death – we sing,
But faced with this
                we feel like wailing.
Before a battle soldiers shrink
From that last dreaded hour of waiting.
The snow is pockmarked, shelled, and mined,
And blackened by the mine dust drifting.
Explosion.
          And a comrade dies.
So death once more has left me living.
But soon enough my time will come.
The chase is on –
               now I am chosen.
Accursed
          nineteen forty-one,
With infantry in snowdrifts frozen.
I'm like a magnet in the smoke,
Attracting mines and every evil.
Explosion –
and a sergeant croaks.
And death again has left me living.
But now we can
no longer wait.
And we are led across the trenches
By numbed hostility and hate,
To bayonet the foe, unflinching.

Бой был короткий.
А потом
глушили водку ледяную,
и выковыривал ножом
из-под ногтей
          я кровь чужую.

Май 1942

The skirmish ended.
Then we drained
Some vodka from an icy bottle.
I scraped from underneath my nails
The blood
        from someone else's body.

May 1942

Gudzenko read this poem in various venues during and after 1945; many thought of it as an anthem of the wartime generation. It only published, however, ten years later, when Gudzenko was already dead, because its ultimate message was that it was the army, not Stalin, who won the war.

Мое поколение

Нас не нужно жалеть, ведь и мы никого б
    не жалели.
Мы пред нашим комбатом, как пред
    господом богом, чисты.
На живых порыжели от крови и глины
    шинели,
на могилах у мертвых расцвели голубые
    цветы.

Расцвели и опали... Проходит четвертая
    осень.
Наши матери плачут, и ровесницы молча
    грустят.
Мы не знали любви, не изведали счастья
    ремесел,
нам досталась на долю нелегкая участь
    солдат.

У погодков моих ни стихов, ни любви, ни
    покоя –
только сила и зависть. А когда мы
    вернемся с войны,
все долюбим сполна и напишем, ровесник,
    такое,
что отцами-солдатами будут гордится
    сыны.

As victory neared, the authorities began to reassert their control over the country. The press downplayed the role of veterans, with the State leadership taking all the credit. Concerns were also raised about the veterans' ability to reintegrate back into society. This was Gudzenko's answer.

My Generation

Don't feel pity for us, we wouldn't feel pity
  for others.
Before our CO we're as pure as
  before the Lord God.
Blood and earth leave red stains on the greatcoats worn
  by the living.
Blue flowers have sprung up and bloomed on the graves
  of the dead.

They flowered and faded... And now it is the fourth
  autumn.
Our mothers weep, sad and silent are the girls
  our own age.
We have not known love, or followed our chosen
  profession,
It is our lot to endure the soldier's difficult
  fate.

Men of my age have no love, no peace,
  and no poems –
Just envy and strength. And when we come back
  from the war,
We will more than make up for lost love, and get
  such things written,
That our sons will be proud of us, their fathers,
  who fought.

Ну, а кто не вернется? Кому долюбить не
    придется?
Ну, а кто в сорок первом первою пулей
    сражен?
Зарыдает ровесница, мать на пороге
    забьется, –
у погодков моих ни стихов, ни покоя, ни
    жен.

Кто вернется – долюбит? Нет! Сердца на
    это не хватит,
и не надо погибшим, чтоб живые любили
    за них.
Нет мужчины в семье – нет детей, нет
    хозяина в хате.
Разве горю такому помогут рыданья
    живых?

Нас не нужно жалеть, ведь и мы никого б
    не жалели.
Кто в атаку ходил, кто делился
    последним куском,
Тот поймет эту правду,- она к нам в
    окопы и щели
приходила поспорить ворчливым, охрипшим
    баском.

Пусть живые запомнят, и пусть поколения
    знают
эту взятую с боем суровую правду
    солдат.
И твои костыли, и смертельная рана
    сквозная,
и могилы над Волгой, где тысячи юных
    лежат, –
это наша судьба, это с ней мы ругались
    и пели,
подымались в атаку и рвали над Бугом
    мосты.

But how about those who'll have no chance to love, no
	homecoming?
Those who in forty-one, as the first bullets flew, lost their
	lives?
Girls will weep bitter tears, grieving mothers collapse on the
	doorstep, –
Men of my age have no poems, no peace, and no
	wives.

Will those who return love for them? No! We haven't
	the heart,
And the dead have no need of the living to love in
	their place.
With no man in the house there's no children, no head of
	the family.
Will help to lessen their grief if the living shed
	tears?

Don't feel pity for us, we wouldn't feel pity
	for others.
Those who went into attack, who shared out their food to
	the last,
Will know this is true, – it's a truth that we met in
	the trenches
When it argued its point in a deep voice, nagging and
	hoarse.

Let the living remember, and pass to the new
	generations
This truth that we captured in battle, a harsh soldier's
	truth.
Your crutches, and the deep gash of death-dealing
	wounds,
And the Volga, where thousands of young men lie in the
	earth, –
It is our fate, we cursed it and praised it
	in song,
As we mined the bridges over the Bug,
	and advanced.

...Нас не нужно жалеть, ведь и мы
    никого б не жалели,
Мы пред нашей Россией и в трудное время
    чисты.

А когда мы вернемся, – а мы возвратимся
    с победой,
все, как черти, упрямы, как люди,
    живучи и злы, –
пусть нам пива наварят и мяса нажарят к
    обеду,
чтоб на ножках дубовых повсюду ломились
    столы.

Мы поклонимся в ноги родным
    исстрадавшимся людям,
матерей расцелуем и подруг, что
    дождались, любя.
Вот когда мы вернемся и победу штыками
    добудем –
все долюбим, ровесник, и работу найдем
    для себя.

1945

Don't feel pity for us, we wouldn't feel pity
    for others.
Even when times are hard we are pure before Russia
    of ours.

But when we return, – and we'll be sure to come back
    as victors,
As stubborn as fiends, resilient and cussed
    as men,
Let beer be brewed and roast meat prepared for our
    dinner,
A feast that will make the legs of oak tables
    groan.

We'll bow to the ground before loved ones worn down
    with suffering,
Kiss our mothers and the women who waited for us,
    out of love.
And when we return and at bayonet-point win
    the victory –
Be sure we will love to the full, and find work
    for ourselves.

1945

ИОН ЛАЗАРЕВИЧ ДЕГЕН

A legendary Soviet tank commander who later became a pioneering surgeon, Degen wrote fierce, unblinking poems about the brutal reality of ground fighting. His poems were not published, but they travelled the fronts anonymously as part of the unofficial canon of wartime poems and songs.

'Мой товарищ, в смертельной агонии...'

Мой товарищ, в смертельной агонии
Не зови понапрасну друзей.
Дай-ка лучше согрею ладони я
Над дымящейся кровью твоей.
Ты не плачь, не стони, ты не маленький,
Ты не ранен, ты просто убит.
Дай на память сниму с тебя валенки.
Нам ещё наступать предстоит.

Декабрь 1944

ION DEGEN (1925–2017)

Although this poem was famous, no-one knew the identity of the author. Vasily Grossman referred to the poem in Life and Fate as being written by a lieutenant killed in the fighting. Later, the poem was condemned for its supposed depiction of marauding among Soviet troops.

'My Comrade, in Your Final Agony...'

My comrade, in your final agony,
don't bother calling to friends.
Better that your steaming blood
should warm my freezing hands.
Don't cry and moan, you're not a child,
you're not wounded, you're merely shot dead.
I'll take your boots to remember you by –
there's still lots of fighting ahead.

December 1944

Слова Народные

Although the official focus was on patriotic songs and humorous folk-songs (chastushki), there was also a lively and complex unofficial war-time folk-culture.

'На Базаре Бомбочка Рванула'

На базаре бомбочка рванула
Меня сразу к верху потянуло
Я лечу – верчу ногами
Бью по жопе кулаками
Началась великая война.

Граждане, воздушная тревога!
Граждане, спасайтесь ради бога!
Майки-трусики хватайте
И на кладбище тикайте –
Занимайте лучшие места.

Вызвали меня в военкомат,
и вручили ржавый автомат,
Дали мне бутылку водки
И кусок большой селедки,
Ты иди солдатик не скучай!

В первом же бою я отличился,
Вдоволь этой водочки напился,
Только вылез из окопа,
Получил три пули в жопу,
На тебе, солдатик, не скучай!

А очнулся я у вражеского дзота
Вижу офицера-бегемота...
Он смеется, он хохочет,
Он меня повесить хочет,
Словно сроду русских не видал!

ANONYMOUS

This satirical song was preserved in children's folklore and sung to the tune of the famous underworld song, 'Break-and-Entry'.

'When the First Bomb Fell on the Bazaar'

When the first bomb fell on the bazaar,
I was hurtled up into the stars,
I went flying, my legs thrashed,
my poor ass got quite a bash,
and that's how this great war begun.

Citizens, an air raid's on its way!
Citizens, get ready, come what may!
Grab whatever you can carry,
beeline for the cemetery –
get yourself a pick of their best graves!

Then the local draft board called me down,
handed me a rusty machine gun,
bottled vodka – not for sharing! –
with a piece of salted herring.
Go on soldier, have yourself a blast!

I downed that vodka right before the battle,
and brother, did I show them I had mettle:
left the trenches full of sass,
got three bullets in my ass.
Yes, we soldiers had ourselves a blast!

I came to behind the enemy lines,
right beside me stood a Nazi swine,
he was laughing fit to drop,
he just itched to string me up,
as if he'd never seen a Russian in his life!

Привели меня в большой сарай
Говорят, покажут фрицев рай
Били, били, колотили,
Морду в жопу превратили...
Говорят, лежи и не скучай!

А скучать я вовсе не собрался,
Только темной ноченьки дождался,
Часового хвать за глотку,
Сунул в рот ему обмотку...
Говорю – лежи и не скучай!

Так бежал из вражеского плена.
Целый полк убил одним поленом,
Сорок танков искалечил,
Двадцать пушек изувечил
И за это орден получил.

Fritz declared, 'Before you are a dead man,
we'll give you a taste of Nazi heaven!'
They beat me slow, they beat me fast,
until my face looked like an ass.
They told me, 'We hope you had a blast.'

Hanging out was not my plan at all,
I waited until night began to fall,
I jumped the guard, gave him a whack,
and stuffed my footcloth down his trap...
And I asked him, 'How is that for a blast?'

That's how I escaped the enemy that day,
I slew a whole brigade along the way,
turned forty tanks upside down,
smashed twenty canons to the ground,
and became a decorated hero!

This song was written in the beginning of the War and exists in many different versions, featuring pilots, partisans, sailors, etc. It is based on an old Russian miners' song, sung by a character in a 1939 Soviet film A Big Life, which was the national box office hit of 1940.

'На Поле Танки Грохотали'

На поле танки грохотали,
Солдаты шли в последний бой,
А молодого командира
Несли с пробитой головой.

В танк ударила болванка,
Прощай, родимый экипаж,
Четыре трупа возле танка
Дополнят утренний пейзаж.

Машина пламенем объята,
Вот-вот рванёт боекомплект.
А жить так хочется ребята,
Но вылезать уж мочи нет.

Нас извлекут из-под обломков,
Поднимут на руки каркас,
И залпы башенных орудий
В последний путь проводят нас.

И полетят тут телеграммы
Родных и близких известить,
Что сын ваш больше не вернётся.
И не приедет погостить.

В углу заплачет мать-старушка,
Смахнёт слезу старик-отец
И молодая не узнает,
Каков танкиста был конец.

This unofficial wartime song became famous again when it was sung by a tank crew in the 1968 Soviet film At the War, *based on a novel by Victor Kurochkin, a former tankman.*

'Down in the Fields the Tanks are Thundering'

Down in the fields the tanks are thundering,
our troops are making their last stand
but our young officer is downed –
he's badly wounded, it's the end.

An AP shell got us head on,
farewell, beloved crew,
four corpses lying by the tank
will frame this sunlit view.

Our tank is going up in flames,
the ammo's gonna blow,
we want to live, we're climbing out –
but this time we're too slow.

They'll find us lying in the wreckage,
lift us aloft and carry us away,
and salvos from a hundred tanks
will guide us to our resting place.

Swift telegrams will be sent flying,
and our families will learn
their sons won't come around to visit,
their sons will not return.

The tankman's mother will start weeping,
his father sob and turn aside,
and his young love will never learn
how her beloved died.

И будет карточка пылиться
На полке пожелтевших книг.
В военной форме, при погонах,
И ей он больше не жених.

The army photo he has sent her
will gather dust beside her bed,
he looks dashing in his uniform,
but now they'll never wed.

МИХАИЛ ЛЬВОВИЧ МАТУСОВСКИЙ

Matusovsky published his first books of poetry before the war, when he studied in Moscow's IFLI. He enlisted as a war correspondent in the War, writing articles in verse, poems, and songs. He is best-known for the international hit 'Moscow Nights.'

Счастье

Когда от неба и до земли
Летели клочья седого дыма,
И только люди сносить могли
Все, что для камней невыносимо,

Когда, одетый в огонь и дым,
Мир накренился, как в бурю судно,
И было трудно лежать живым,
А мертвым было уже нетрудно,

Когда под скрежет весенних льдин,
Прощаясь с миром последним взглядом,
Я оставался в снегу один,
А немцы были почти что рядом,

Когда, разбужен ночной стрельбой,
Весь лес был полон предсмертной дрожи,
Я не прельщался другой судьбой,
Я повторял лишь одно и то же:

Жить не украдкой, жить не ползком,
Подобно горной лететь лавине.
Мне нужно счастье все, целиком,
Мы не сойдемся на половине.

1945

MIKHAIL MATUSOVSKY (1915–1990)

The last stanza of the poem, with its call for a new fearless life and its rejection of compromise, shows why the State had such concerns about returning veterans, and had increased controls over post-war society in general.

Happiness

When tufts of smoke flew down
to earth all grey and tattered,
and only men could handle
what stones could never stand,

and when the blazing world
rolled like a storm-tossed ship,
and the living couldn't stay down
but dead men finally could,

and when I took my final glance –
the last man standing mid the snows
and crunching ice floes,
the Germans on my back,

and when the forest trembled,
roused by a vicious gun battle,
I envied no other fate nor fortune,
but kept repeating over and over:

I won't live stealthily, I won't crawl,
I'll thunder like an avalanche,
I demand happiness, I want it all,
I won't compromise on half!

1945

ЮЛИЯ ВЛАДИМИРОВНА ДРУНИНА

Drunina was one of the popular women poets to emerge from the War. She fought on several fronts, was wounded a number of times, earned the Medal for Valour, and was demobilized after a severe contusion in 1944. She began to publish her poetry during the war. Her first book of poems came out in 1948.

'Я только раз видала рукопашный...'

Я только раз видала рукопашный,
Раз наяву. И тысячу - во сне.
Кто говорит, что на войне не страшно,
Тот ничего не знает о войне.

1943

YULIA DRUNINA (1924–1991)

In 1941, Drunina's division was encircled. She broke out of the encirclement with 22 other fighters. In 1943, she was wounded and hospitalized; she spent the time writing a long poem about breaking through the encirclement, but was unhappy with the result, cutting out everything except for this quatrain. It became the most anthologized of her poems.

'Once I Saw Hand-to-Hand Combat...'

Once I saw hand-to-hand combat.
Then I dreamt it a myriad more.
Whoever says war is not frightening
knows nothing at all about war.

1943

It is estimated that almost a million Soviet women served in the war (women were first drafted into the army in 1941). Many were combat medics and doctors; many fought alongside men as snipers, tank personnel, pilots, partisans, and infantry. Drunina knew their lives first-hand.

Зинка

Памяти однополчанки – Героя Советского Союза Зины Самсоновой

Мы легли у разбитой ели,
Ждём, когда же начнёт светлеть.
Под шинелью вдвоём теплее
На продрогшей, сырой земле.

– Знаешь, Юлька, я против грусти,
Но сегодня она не в счёт.
Дома, в яблочном захолустье,
Мама, мамка моя живёт.

У тебя есть друзья, любимый.
У меня лишь она одна.
Пахнет в хате квашнёй и дымом,
За порогом бурлит весна.

Старой кажется: каждый кустик
Беспокойную дочку ждёт
Знаешь, Юлька, я против грусти,
Но сегодня она не в счёт.

Отогрелись мы еле-еле,
Вдруг приказ: 'Выступать вперёд!'
Снова рядом в сырой шинели
Светлокосый солдат идёт.

Drunina fought on the Belorussian Front alongside Zinaida Samsonova, a combat medic. The two teenagers were the only women in the regiment and became friends. Samsonova saved her battalion by leading the soldiers out of an encirclement near Orsha. She was later killed by a sniper's bullet while dragging a wounded soldier off the battlefield.

Zinka

To the memory of my fellow soldier Zinaida Samsonova, Hero of the Soviet Union.

We lay down by a blown-up pine tree
waiting for dawn to come,
huddling under one greatcoat
on the soggy and frigid ground.

'You know, Yulia, I'm not one for sadness,
but today that's of no account.
Back home, out in the backwoods
lives my mother, my elderly mom.

'You've got your friends, your beloved,
she's all I've ever had in my life.
Her hut smells of bread and the woodstove,
spring is brimming and teeming outside.

'And it seems to her every bush there
wants her restless child to come round.
You know, Yulia, I'm not one for sadness,
but today that's of no account.'

Just then orders came to get moving –
rest and warmth weren't our lot.
Once again, the blond-braided soldier
walked beside me in her damp overcoat.

С каждым днём становилось горше.
Шли без митингов и знамён.
В окруженье попал под Оршей
Наш потрепанный батальон.

Зинка нас повела в атаку.
Мы пробились по чёрной ржи,
По воронкам и буеракам,
Через смертные рубежи.

Мы не ждали посмертной славы,
Мы со славой хотели жить.
Почему же в бинтах кровавых
Светлокосый солдат лежит

Её тело своей шинелью
Укрывала я, зубы сжав.
Белорусские хаты пели
О рязанских глухих садах.

Знаешь, Зинка, я против грусти,
Но сегодня она не в счёт.
Дома, в яблочном захолустье
Мама, мамка твоя живёт.

У меня есть друзья, любимый
У неё ты была одна.
Пахнет в хате квашнёй и дымом,
За порогом бурлит весна.

И старушка в цветастом платье
У иконы свечу зажгла
Я не знаю, как написать ей,
Чтоб она тебя не ждала.

1944

Every day things grew darker and darker,
we marched without flags or salutes.
Near Orsha, our battered battalion
was encircled by enemy troops.

Zinka led us all into battle,
we broke through across fields of charred rye
crawling through gulleys and craters,
all those lines you cross only to die.

To go down in glory was never our plan –
we wanted to live with the glory.
So why does the blond-braided soldier
lie bloodied and lifeless before me?

I covered her with my greatcoat,
clenching my teeth not to cry.
Belorussian huts all around me
sang of Kazan, distant and wild.

You know, Zinka, I'm not one for sadness,
but today that's of no account.
Back home, out in the backwoods
Lives your mother, your elderly mom.

I've got my friends, my beloved,
you're all she had in her life.
Her hut smells of bread and the woodstove,
spring is brimming and teeming outside.

A brightly-robed old woman lights a candle –
before a family icon it will burn.
I don't know how to write to your mother
not to wait for you to return.

1944

СЕРГЕЙ СЕРГЕЕВИЧ ОРЛОВ

Orlov began writing poetry as a child in his native village; one of his childhood poems was praised by Kornei Chukovsky for its warmth and humour. He became a tankman in the war, and wrote poems about the harsh realities of battle combined with an optimistic vision of the future.

После марша

Броня от солнца горяча,
И пыль похода на одежде.
Стянуть комбинезон с плеча –
И в тень, в траву, но только прежде
Проверь мотор и люк открой:
Пускай машина остывает.
Мы все перенесем с тобой –

Мы люди, а она стальная...

1944

SERGEY ORLOV (1921–77)

The comparison of Soviet man's resolution and strength with steel was a cliché in wartime writing, but Orlov takes it one step further. Steel is not as strong as flesh, and a tank cannot be pushed beyond its limit (or easily replaced), while man can.

After the Campaign

The sun is blazing on the armour,
road dust is covering our clothes.
Oh, to pull off the coveralls and sink
into the shade, the grass, but first,
go check the motor, lift the hatch;
a tank must cool down – that's ideal.
We both can stand whatever comes –

we're men, a tank is only steel...

1944

Orlov published his first book of poetry in 1942. He fought his first battle as a tank commander in 1943 and his last battle as a commander of a tank platoon in 1944 (he managed to escape from his burning tank, but was severely burned). All the while, he wrote poems that were published in army newspapers.

'Его зарыли в шар земной...'

Его зарыли в шар земной,
А был он лишь солдат,
Всего, друзья, солдат простой,
Без званий и наград.

Ему как мавзолей земля –
На миллион веков,
И Млечные Пути пылят
Вокруг него с боков.

На рыжих скатах тучи спят,
Метелицы метут,
Грома тяжелые гремят,
Ветра разбег берут.

Давным-давно окончен бой...
Руками всех друзей
Положен парень в шар земной,
Как будто в мавзолей...

Июнь 1944

This poem, with its transcendent vision of a soldier's final resting place, is Orlov's most famous. Years after the war, when Orlov was talking poetry with friends in a bar, an ex-soldier sitting nearby declared that they would never write anything as fine as 'They Buried Him in Planet Earth.'

'They Buried Him in Planet Earth...'

They buried him in planet earth –
he was a soldier, nothing more.
No ranks, no decorations,
just a fighter in the corps.

The earth will be his mausoleum
for millenniums to come,
as countless milky galaxies
whip stardust all around.

Earth's storm clouds sleep on russet slopes,
its snows come drifting by,
its heavy thunders thunder past,
and winds get set to fly.

The battle ended long ago...
His friends took hold of him
and laid the lad in planet earth
as in a mausoleum.

June 1944

ВЕРОНИКА МИХАЙЛОВНА ТУШНОВА

Tushnova studied to be a doctor, but transferred to the Gorky Literary Institute on the advice of the poet Vera Inber. She began to publish during the war while working as a doctor. She was most famous for her intimate love lyrics, including 'The One Who Loves Does Not Forsake' (1944), which later became Alla Pugacheva's signature hit.

Кукла

Много нынче в памяти потухло,
а живет безделица, пустяк:
девочкой потерянная кукла
на железных скрещенных путях.

Над платформой пар от паровозов
низко плыл, в равнину уходя...
Теплый дождь шушукался в березах,
но никто не замечал дождя.

Эшелоны шли тогда к востоку,
молча шли, без света и воды,
полные внезапной и жестокой,
горькой человеческой беды.

Девочка кричала и просила
и рвалась из материнских рук, –
показалась ей такой красивой
и желанной эта кукла вдруг.

Но никто не подал ей игрушки,
и толпа, к посадке торопясь,
куклу затоптала у теплушки
в жидкую струящуюся грязь.

VERONICA TUSHNOVA (1911–1965)

Tushnova's poetic voice has been compared to a heartbeat. It is with that quietly persistent voice that Tushnova wrote about things that went unnoticed in the war. Her wartime poems about her little daughter attracted an enthusiastic reader response, but her 1945 book of poems was criticised for being 'excessively intimate,' like 'the salon dramas of Akhmatova.'

The Doll

I think of those days as a blur –
only odd little trifles remain:
a doll, loved by a small girl
but dropped on a railway line.

Engine steam shrouded the platform,
keeping low as it moved to the plain...
Warm raindrops fell on the birches,
and no one even noticed the rain.

Back then the trains rolled eastward,
silently, without water or light,
filled to the brim with that sudden
heartbreak, which can't be set right.

The girl was pleading and crying,
struggling in her mother's arms,
she so wanted her doll back,
entranced by its dollish charms.

But no one handed it to her,
and the crowd, in its rush to board,
stomped the doll by the train car
into the streaming dirt.

Маленькая смерти не поверит,
и разлуки не поймет она...
Так хоть этой крохотной потерей
дотянулась до нее война.

Некуда от странной мысли деться:
это не игрушка, не пустяк, –
это, может быть, обломок детства
на железных скрещенных путях.

1943

The child couldn't grasp parting,
or know what death is for,
but maybe this minuscule loss
taught her the meaning of war.

And I can't get away from the thought
that it was no toy, no trifle.
What I saw on the railway tracks
was the end of a small girl's childhood.

1943

АГНИЯ ЛЬВОВНА БАРТО

Barto was a children's poet and writer whose poems about childhood are still read and loved. She was ultra-loyal to the State, fiercely attacking anyone who fell short of her ideals. Her poems, however, remained lively, humorous, and full of love for their young subjects, a breath a fresh air during the war years, when they were widely published.

Наташа

Почтальон проходит мимо
И стучит не в нашу дверь.
Почтальон проходит мимо,
Мы не ждем его теперь.

Он обходит все квартиры,
Все соседние дома,
Только нам четвертый месяц
Ни открытки, ни письма.

Всем приходят письма с фронта...
У меня товарищ есть.
Он вчера перед уроком
Два письма мне дал прочесть.

Наш учитель от танкиста
Получил письмо вчера.
Только нам не пишет с фронта
Наша старшая сестра.

Но сегодня на рассвете
Вдруг соседи будят нас
И читают нам в газете
Напечатанный указ.

AGNIYA BARTO (1906–1981)

Barto travelled to the front to read her poems to soldiers. She felt that she was warmly received because her poems made the soldiers think of their own children. But her poems also spoke in a fresh and immediate way about everyday things that especially mattered in wartime: waiting for mail, for instance, from someone you loved and worried about.

Natasha

The postman walks right past us,
never stopping at our door.
The postman walks right past us,
we don't get mail anymore.

He goes to all the other flats
in buildings near and far,
but for months he's brought us nothing –
not a letter, not a card.

Everyone gets frontline letters...
In my school, I've got a friend –
yesterday, before the lesson,
he read me *two* that he was sent!

Just the other day, a tankman
wrote our teacher – so we heard.
While my sister on the frontlines
doesn't write a single word!

Then at dawn our neighbours woke us,
which we thought was pretty strange,
till they read us an announcement
on the newspaper's front page.

Там написано, в указе,
Кто получит ордена,
Там сестра моя Наташа.
Может, это не она?..

Говорят соседи маме:
– Ну конечно, ваша дочь.
Тут не может быть ошибки,
И фамилия точь-в-точь.'

Вслух сама читает мама:
–'В марте, первого числа,
Молодая санитарка
Двадцать раненых спасла'.

Мама плачет отчего-то,
Младший брат кричит: 'Ура!'
Молодец сестра Наташа,
Наша старшая сестра!

Вдруг я вижу почтальона.
Я кричу ему в окно:
– Вы не в пятую квартиру?
Писем не было давно!

На звонок выходит мама,
Отворяет дверь сама.
Почтальон дает ей сразу
От Наташи три письма.

1943

There it said who's getting medals
for their bravery in the war.
In the list was my big sister!
Wait... but maybe that's not her?

'It's your daughter, your Natasha,'
said the neighbours to my mom.
'There is no room for mistakes here,
Last name, first name – she's the one.'

Mother read aloud the entry:
'On March first,' (the words were terse)
'twenty of our wounded soldiers
were all saved by a young nurse.'

Mom starts crying for some reason,
my kid brother yells, 'Hurray!
My big sister is amazing!
Our Natasha saved the day!'

Then I saw the postman coming,
and I shouted down below:
'Any mail for number five now?
we've been waiting here, you know!'

The postman walked up to our flat,
my mom opened our door.
One letter from Natasha –
another – and one more!

1943

ВИКТОР МИХАЙЛОВИЧ ГОНЧАРОВ

Victor Goncharov, who started to publish his poems in the 1930s, fought in the infantry and was wounded several times. He gained fame not only as a poet and translator, but as an artist and sculptor.

Возвращение

А все случилось очень просто:
Открылась дверь, и мне навстречу –
Девчонка маленького роста,
Девчурка – остренькие плечи!

И котелок упал на камни!
Четыре с лишним дома не был.
А дочка, разведя руками,
Сказала: Дядя, нету хлеба.

А ее схватил и – к звездам!
И целовал кусочки неба...
Ведь это я такую создал!
Четыре с лишним дома не был....

1945

VICTOR GONCHAROV (1920–2001)

The theme of homecoming was, unsurprisingly, a central one in war-time poetry, before and after the actual return home. Goncharov's much-anthologised poem focuses on the reunification of families separated by the war.

The Homecoming

I knocked on the door and it opened
(in the end, that's how it turned out),
a little girl came, small and slight,
a skinny thing, a regular beansprout!

I dropped my mess kit in shock.
Four long years I hadn't been back.
And my daughter, with a helpless shrug
said, 'Sorry, we don't have any bread.'

I clasped her, tossed her up to the stars,
kissed this tiny bit of heaven – my own!
Would you look at what I've created!
Four long years I hadn't been home...

1945

МИХАИЛ ВАСИЛЬЕВИЧ ИСАКОВСКИЙ

Isakovsky became famous in the 1930s for his patriotic poems with strong ties to Russian folklore that were often turned into songs. During the War he achieved national fame, along with the composer Matvei Blanter, for hit songs like 'Farewell' and 'Katyusha' (the latter gave its name to the Katyusha multiple rocket launchers).

Враги сожгли родную хату

Враги сожгли родную хату,
Сгубили всю его семью.
Куда ж теперь идти солдату,
Кому нести печаль свою?

Пошел солдат в глубоком горе
На перекресток двух дорог,
Нашел солдат в широком поле
Травой заросший бугорок.

Стоит солдат – и словно комья
Застряли в горле у него.
Сказал солдат: «Встречай, Прасковья.
Героя-мужа своего.

Готовь для гостя угощенье,
Накрой в избе широкий стол.
Свой день, свой праздник возвращенья
К тебе я праздновать пришел...»

Никто солдату не ответил.
Никто его не повстречал,
И только теплый летний ветер
Траву могильную качал.

MIKHAIL ISAKOVSKY (1900–1973)

The poem-turned-song was written in 1945, published in Znamia *in 1946, but then banned because its tragic tone went against the Party's directive to stop dwelling on wartime losses. It was finally performed in 1960 by the singer Mark Bernes, after being championed by Marshal Vasily Chuikov.*

The Nazis Burnt his Home to Ashes

The Nazis burnt his home to ashes,
His family they murdered there,
Where shall the soldier home from battle
Go now, to whom his sorrow bear?

To where a lane the main road crosses,
Our soldier strode in grief profound
And saw all overgrown with mosses
A low and humble burial mound.

He stood with tears of sorrow welling
And scarcely able breath to draw
He said: 'Praskovya dear, come welcome
Your hero-husband back from war.

'Prepare a meal for merry making,
A cloth upon the table lay.
It's now we should be celebrating
My safe return, this holiday.'

But in reply there came no answer,
No welcome for the soldier brave.
Only a breeze that way came glancing
And stirred the grass upon the grave.

Вздохнул солдат, ремень поправил,
Раскрыл мешок походный свой,
Бутылку горькую поставил
На серый камень гробовой.

«Не осуждай меня, Прасковья,
Что я пришел к тебе такой:
Хотел я выпить за здоровье,
А должен пить за упокой.

Сойдутся вновь друзья, подружки.
Но не сойтись вовеки нам...»
И пил солдат из медной кружки
Вино и слезы пополам.

Он пил – солдат, слуга народа –
И с болью в сердце говорил:
«Я шел к тебе четыре года,
Я три державы покорил...»

Хмелел солдат, слеза катилась,
Слеза несбывшихся надежд,
И на груди его светилась
Медаль за город Будапешт.

1945

He paused awhile, his belt he straightened,
And, from the kitbag at his side
A flask of bitter vodka taking,
He placed it on her grave and sighed:

'Praskovya, please do not reproach me
That in this state I say my piece.
It was your health I'd have been toasting,
But now my toast is: 'Rest in peace!'

'Others shall meet the friends they treasure –
But we are parted for all time...'
And from his mug he drained a measure
Of sorrow half and half with wine.

This veteran to grief succumbing,
Had long and worthy service seen:
'It four long years I've been in coming,
A victor in three lands I've been...'

The soldier drank and wept for many
A broken dream, while on his chest
There shone a newly-minted medal
For liberating Budapest.

1945

САМУИЛ ЯКОВЛЕВИЧ МАРШАК

Marshak was a talented lyrical poet who debuted back in 1907, encouraged by Vladimir Stasov and Maxim Gorky. His national fame, however, rested in his children's poems, and later, his translations of Shakespeare. Marshak was one of the most published and respected poets during the war.

Берлинская Эпиграмма

'Год восемнадцатый не повторится ныне!'—
Кричат со стен слова фашистких лидеров.

А сверху надпись мелом: 'Я в Берлине'—
И надпись выразительная: 'Сидоров.'

1945

SAMUEL MARSHAK (1887–1964)

During the War, Marshak continued writing poetry and plays, but also became famous for his satirical poems. He wrote short poems and captions for war posters and caricatures, often working directly with the artists (he received the State Stalin Prize for this work in 1942). These were popular both at the front and the home front.

A Berlin Epigram

'We shan't relive the year nineteen-eighteen!'
Up on the walls the Nazi slogans scoff.

And over them, in chalk: 'I'm in Berlin!'
Signed simply and concisely, 'Sidorov.'

1945

Приглушенные
Голоса

Muted
Voices

ИРИНА НИКОЛАЕВНА КНОРРИНГ

Knorring's family emigrated after the Revolution and settled in France. She was active in émigré literary circles and brought out two well-reviewed books of poetry in the 1930s. Her husband was drafted into the French army and later joined the Resistance. Knorring died during the War of diabetes complications.

'Умеренный, твердый, железный...'

Под снегом холодной России,
Под знойным песком пирамид...
М.Ю. Лермонтов

Умеренный, твердый, железный,
Презревший лишенья и страх,
Взлетающий в звездные бездны,
Ныряющий в темных морях,
Еще – победитель-удачник –
(«Куда только мы ни зашли!»)
Немецкий мечтательный мальчик
Гуляет но карте земли.
Он так подкупающе молод,
Так бодро шагает вперед,
Неся разоренье и голод
Повсюду,
Куда ни придет.
Его на бульварах Парижа
Так радует каждый пустяк:
Он губы застенчиво лижет,
Косясь на французский коньяк.
У пестрых витрин магазинов
Часами стоит, не идет,
Совсем по-ребячьи разинув
Свой красный, смеющийся рот.

IRINA KNORRING (1906–1943)

Asked to review Knorring's poems in 1962, Akhmatova wrote that Knorring 'finds words that you must believe.' Her compassionate and compelling depiction of the enemy soldier about to die a senseless death in a harsh land could have no parallels in Soviet poetry due to the persistent dehumanization of the Germans in wartime Soviet press.

'He's Temperate, Dogged, Rock-Solid...'

Under the snows of cold Russia,
Under the scorching sands of the pyramids...
M. Lermontov

He's temperate, dogged, rock-solid,
he's scornful of both fear and ease,
he flies up to starry abysses
and dives into darkening seas.
Victorious destiny's darling,
('Wherever we've gone to, we won!')
see how this young German dreamer
traverses the globe up and down.
He's so endearingly youthful,
so briskly forges along,
bringing destruction and hunger
to every place
he has gone.
Here, in the city of Paris,
he takes joy in the least bric-a-brac,
shyly licking his lips
as he glances at local cognacs.
He can stand stock still for hours,
watching the stores' bright displays,
gaping his laughing red mouth
like a child intent on his play.

А завтра, послушный приказу,
С винтовкой на твердом плече
Пойдет... и не бросит ни разу
Простого вопроса: «Зачем?»
Зачем ему русские вьюги?
Разрушенные города?
На севере или на юге –
Везде – непременно – всегда?
Зачем ему гибнуть и драться
Среди разрушений и бед,
Когда за плечами лишь двадцать
Восторгом обманутых лет?
Неужто такая отрада –
Недолгих побед торжество?
Ведь запах смолы из Шварцвальда
Уже не коснется его.
И над безымянной могилой
Уже не поплачет никто.
Далекий, обманутый, милый...
За что?

18 Января 1942

But tomorrow, obedient to orders,
he'll march off, his rifle slung high...
Off he'll march, without ever asking
the one simple question: 'why?'
Why does he need Russian blizzards?
Why must cities be razed
in the South, in the North – wherever
he goes, till the end of his days?
Why must he fight and perish
amid destruction and woe,
when all he has lived are twenty
short years, deluded by awe?
Are short-lived victories that tempting
and promise him that much joy?
For the pine-scented breeze of Black Forest
won't ever again touch this boy.
And over his nameless grave
no one will ever cry.
So distant, so lied to, so sweet...
Why?

18 January 1942

МИХАИЛ НИКОЛАЕВИЧ ВОЛИН

Volin was born in China to a Russian family that included generals and diplomats. In Harbin he was a member of 'Young Churaevka' literary circle. He is best remembered for his poems of lost love, sung by Alexander Vertinsky.

Братья

Набежал солдат. Прикладом
Пехотинца сбил.
Сам винтовочным зарядом
Опрокинут был.
И в последнюю усталость
(Смерти тоже рад)
«Дейчланд, Дейчланд юбер аллес»,
Прохрипел солдат.
А другой сказал: «Россия,
Только ты одна...»
И закрыл глаза сухие
Для большого сна.
И, услышав хрип тревожный,
Нежностью томим,
Кто-то Ясный, Невозможный
Наклонился к ним.
Было видно – просветлели
Лица павших вдруг.
И уже не пули пели –
Сирины вокруг...
И тогда, от душной злобы
Страшно далеки,
Поднялись солдаты, оба,
Над землей легки.
И туда, где, погасая,
Пламенел закат,
Шли, земли едва касаясь,
Брат и рядом брат.

MIKHAIL VOLIN (1914–1997)

Volin who was born, lived, and died an émigré, was raised in a traditional Orthodox Russian family but became an adept of Eastern spirituality and taught Yoga and Eastern Mysticism as Swami Karmanand.

Brothers

One soldier downed another
with his rifle butt,
only to be killed himself
by a rifle shot.
Drifting off in his exhaustion
(he was glad to die)
'Deutschland, Deutschland über alles,'
the first hoarsely cried.
And the other whispered, 'Russia,'
there's you alone...'
And then shut his burning eyes,
too weary to go on.
There was One who heard their gasps –
filled with tender love,
Bright and Inconceivable,
He reached down from above.
And the faces of the fallen
brightened in response.
No more bullets whistled –
only mystic birds...
And released from anger
that had choked them both,
the two soldiers rose as one,
just above the earth.
And the two walked westward
to the dying light,
barely treading on the ground,
brothers, side by side.

НИКОЛАЙ НИКОЛАЕВИЧ ТУРОВЕРОВ

Born into a family of Don Cossacks, Turoverov fought in the Russian Army in WW1 and then in the White Army against the Bolsheviks. In 1920 he settled in France, where he eventually joined the Foreign Legion and fought against the Nazis. He published five well-reviewed books of poetry in France.

1942

Тебе не страшны голод и пожар.
Тебе всего уже пришлось отведать.
И новому ль нашествию татар
Торжествовать конечную победу?

О, сколько раз борьба была невмочь,
Когда врывались и насильники и воры!
Ты их вела в свою глухую ночь,
В свои широкие звериные просторы.

Ты их звала, доверчивых собак,
В свои трущобы, лютая волчица.
И было так, и снова будет так,
И никогда тебе не измениться.

1942

NIKOLAI TUROVEROV (1899–1972)

When Germany attacked Russia, many émigrés hoped that Communist Russia would be defeated. Turoverov, fooled neither by the false promises nor by Hitler's early successes, turned to Russian history, with its many enemy invasions, to predict what would happen to the invaders in the end.

1942

Hunger and fire don't scare you –
you've lived through it all before.
Do these new invading Tatars
think they will win this war?

O, how many raiders you've fought,
and each battle took its toll –
but you'd open your dark, wild expanses
and swallow the enemy whole!

You summoned them, vicious she-wolf,
and they came, like trusting dogs.
You're the same, you will never change –
it's the same as it always was.

1942

ИРИНА АЛЬФРЕДОВНА БЕМ

Bem was born in Petrograd in a Russified German family (her father was a well-known literary scholar and Dostoevsky specialist). In 1922 her family emigrated from Russia, ending up in Prague. In 1945 her father was arrested by Soviet secret service and disappeared without a trace.

Ныне Андромаха

I

Корютайолос Гектор, ты бился и умер героем...
Андромаха, жена твоя бедная, ткала и пела,
А потом увидала со стен многоветренной Трои,
Как влачил победитель когда-то прекрасное тело.
А потом она видела: сын твой, надежда и гордость,
Тот, что матери в старости будет опорою верной,
Тот, что Гектора будет отважней,
когда победители вторглись,
Был со стен многоветренной Трои
безжалостно свергнут.
А потом она видела, но уже тупо, без страха,
Как высокий приамовский дом разорили дотла.
Андромаха, сестра моя бедная,
белых локтей Андромаха,
Как могла пережить ты всё это – и пережила?

1941

IRINA BEM (1916–1981)

Although many Soviet poets wrote about the suffering of women in the War, this was usually within the specific parameters of propaganda. Bem contended that women always end up suffering most in wars.

Andromache Today

I

Bright-helmeted Hector, you fought and died like a hero.
Andromache, your poor wife, spun and sang,
then she watched from the walls of windy Troy,
how the victor dragged off your once beautiful body.
Then she watched your son, your hope and your pride,
who would be a support for his mother's old age,
who would be braver than Hector himself,
pitilessly cast off
the walls of windy Troy
when the victors burst in.
Then she watched, numb, without any fear now,
how of tall Priam's house stone was not left upon stone.
Andromache, my poor sister,
white-elbowed Andromache,
How could you live through it all – and go on?

1941

II

Сколько вас в наши страшные дни,
Андромах безызвестных!
Брат убит, муж убит, сын убит...
А от дома, от белого дома в зеленом предместьи
Только груда разрозненных плит.
И уже не отчаянье, только тупая усталость;
И уже нету слез, только пара потухших очей;
И уже за плечами стоит одинокая старость,
Смена дней без улыбок и страшных бессонных ночей.
Сколько вас, белокурых и темных, веселых и нежных,
Матерей и любовниц, утративших царство цариц...
Андромаха, сестра моя бедная, ныне как прежде,
И никто не закроет залитых слезами страниц.

1941–1942

II

There are so many of you these terrible days,
unknown Andromaches!
Your brother, husband, and son have been killed...
And your house, your white house in the green faubourg,
was reduced to a pile of fill.
And you feel no despair, just numb exhaustion;
you shed no tears, the light just went out of your eyes;
your lonely old age is just round the corner,
unsmiling days, followed by sleepless nights.
So many of you, blond and dark, joyful and tender,
mothers and mistresses, queens whose kingdoms are lost...
Andromache, my poor sister, today is as always,
and these tear-stained pages won't ever be closed.

1941–1942

ГЕОРГИЙ ВЛАДИМИРОВИЧ ИВАНОВ

Ivanov, one of the greatest poets of the emigration, intended to end his literary career with the publication in 1938 of the scandalous prose-poem Disintegration of the Atom. *But during the War he began writing poetry again.*

'Все на свете пропадает даром...'

Все на свете пропадает даром,
Что же Ты робеешь? Не робей!
Размозжи его одним ударом,
На осколки звездные разбей!

Отрави его горчичным газом
Или бомбами испепели –
Что угодно – только кончи разом
С мукою и музыкой земли!

GEORGY IVANOV (1894–1958)

Ivanov and his wife, the poet and memoirist Irina Odoevtseva, spent the war in Biarritz, where their villa was seized by the Germans and then bombed by the Allies. When the war ended the couple was left both homeless and destitute.

'All the World is Going to Wrack and Ruin...'

All the world is going to wrack and ruin.
What, You've lost your nerve? Oh, don't be shy!
Come and crush it all in one fell stroke,
Pulverize, make stardust in the sky!

Poison it with mustard gas or, better,
Bomb the whole damn thing to smithereens.
Do away at once with all this art and
Anguish of our planet – by all means!

Although Ivanov never took French citizenship, he didn't harbour nostalgic illusions about Russia's past, or develop sympathies for the regimes and leaders around him.

'Рассказать обо всех мировых дураках...'

Рассказать обо всех мировых дураках,
Что судьбу человечества держат в руках?

Рассказать обо всех мертвецах-подлецах,
Что уходят в историю в светлых венцах?

Для чего?
          Тишина под парижским мостом.
И какое мне дело, что будет потом.

1944

The war intensified Ivanov's visceral loathing of the world he saw and his own position of an individualistic bystander.

'Shall I Tell You of All of the World's Greatest Fools...'

Shall I tell you of all of the world's greatest fools,
With the fate of mankind in the palm of their hands?

Shall I tell you of all the dead crooks and the scum
Who have gone down in history, halo intact?

What's the use?
              All is calm under this Paris bridge.
And so what's it to me what tomorrow will bring?

1944

This poem was first published in New York. Although Ivanov's poetry was well-known to Russian émigrés all over the world, his poems were published in Russia only in 1989, after Perestroika and Glasnost.

'Лунатик В Пустоту Глядит...'

Лунатик в пустоту глядит,
Сиянье им руководит,
Чернеет гибель снизу.
И далее угадать нельзя,
Куда он движется, скользя,
По лунному карнизу.

Расстреливают палачи
Невинных в мировой ночи
Не обращай вниманья!
Гляди в холодное ничто,
В сияньи постигая то,
Что выше пониманья.

1948

In Ivanov's poetic universe, the words 'moon' and 'sleepwalker' are associated with the poet. The word 'shining' is laden with more complex associations – a symbol of poetic consciousness and, in later poems, of atomic destruction.

'Led by What is Shining...'

Led by what is shining,
the sleepwalker looks into a blank,
black is the death beneath him
and there's no knowing
where the moon's thin ledge
will slide him.

The innocent are executed
in a universal night –
look the other way.
Look into cold nothing
and let its moonshine take you
beyond all understanding.

1948

The émigré community was divided about Russia's victory over the Germans. Ivanov's own view was decidedly tragic: Russia was doomed, whether under the Tsars or under the Communists.

'Над Облаками И Веками...'

Над облаками и веками
Бессмертной музыки хвала –
Россия русскими руками
Себя спасла и мир спасла.

Сияет солнце, вьётся знамя,
И те же вещие слова:
«Ребята, не Москва ль за нами?»
Нет, много больше, чем Москва!

Теперь тебя не уничтожат,
Как тот безумный вождь мечтал.
Судьба поможет, Бог поможет,
Но – русский человек устал...

Устал страдать, устал гордиться,
Валя куда-то напролом.
Пора забвеньем насладиться,
А может быть – пора на слом...

...И ничему не возродиться
Ни под серпом, ни под орлом!..

1945/1949

Often published as two poems (the first two stanzas dated 1945 and titled 'On the Russian Taking of Berlin'), this poem is a despairing Spenglerian meditation on the fate of the Russian nation after winning the war.

'Immortal Music Tells the Story...'

Immortal music tells the story
through time and space extolled,
how Russia, standing on its own,
saved the entire world.

Now flags stream in the sunshine,
with the same stirring words as before:
'Lads, isn't Moscow *behind* us?'
Not only Moscow – so much more!

Now she won't be destroyed,
as that mad autocrat desired,
both destiny and God will aid her,
but the Russian man grew tired...

Tired of suffering, of taking pride,
of charging headlong all the while.
It's time to revel in forgetting,
or to head over to the junkyard pile...

...There's no rebirth for Russia's people
under the sickle or the eagle!..

1945/1949

ЮСТИНА ВЛАДИМИРОВНА КРУЗЕНШТЕРН-ПЕТЕРЕЦ

Kruzenshtern-Peterets grew up in Harbin (her family moved there as refugees, after her father, an officer, was killed in the First World War). She moved to Shanghai in the 1930s and was actively involved in a number of émigré literary circles. She spent the War in China and published her first book of poems there in 1946.

Россия

Проклинали... Плакали... Вопили...
Декламировали: 'Наша мать!'
В кабаках за возрождение пили,
Что опять наутро проклинать.
А потом вдруг поняли. Прозрели.
За голову взялись: 'Неужели?
Китеж! Воскресающий без нас!
Так-таки великая!
Подите ж!'
А она действительно, как Китеж,
Проплывает мимо глаз.

28 июля 1944

JUSTINA KRUZENSHTERN-PETERETS
(1903–1983)

The editors of the Shanghai émigré journal to which Kruzenshtern-Peterets contributed wrote in 1943: 'the great joy [we feel] at... the victories of the Red Army, combines... with the sadness from the knowledge that it's not our blood being spilled in those battles, that it's not our personal efforts that make those victories.'

Russia

We cursed her... we wailed and lamented...
'Mother Russia,' we called her, 'our own!'
Spent nights toasting her resurrection,
just to curse her again come dawn.
Then it struck us. We suddenly got it.
We clutched at our heads: 'Is it true?
She's Kitezh! She's rising without us!
Turns out, she's still great!
Well, who knew?!'
...And it's true – just like Kitezh of legend,
she sweeps past us, hidden from view.

28 July 1944

МАРИНА ИВАНОВНА ЦВЕТАЕВА

In 1939 Tsvetaeva was living in Paris. Earlier, she had lived in Prague and in Berlin, where she wrote some of her greatest poetry.

'О слезы на глазах...'

О слезы на глазах!
Плач гнева и любви!
О Чехия в слезах!
Испания в крови!

О черная гора,
Затмившая весь свет!
Пора – пора – пора
Творцу вернуть билет.

Отказываюсь – быть.
В Бедламе нелюдей
Отказываюсь – жить.
С волками площадей

Отказываюсь – выть.
С акулами равнин
Отказываюсь плыть
Вниз – по теченью спин.

Не надо мне ни дыр
Ушных, ни вещих глаз.
На твой безумный мир
Ответ один – отказ.

15 Марта–11 Мая 1939

MARINA TSVETAEVA (1892–1941)

In March of 1939, Tsvetaeva wrote to a friend: 'A new blow – my Czechia! When I see 'Prague' mentioned in the newspaper, I shake from head to toe... Czechia, for me, is not only a question of justice, but my love, and now – my open wound.'

O, I Refuse

These tears before my eyes!
Weeping with rage and love!
O, Czech-lands in tears!
Land of Spain in blood!

O, black mass, spread
Over all the world!
It's time – time – time I gave
Back our Creator's ticket.

I refuse – to be.
In inhuman Bedlam
I refuse – to live.
With the Roman wolves

I refuse – to do as they do.
With the sharks on land
I refuse to swim – down –
On the backs of their stream.

It's not as if I need ears to hear
Or eyes to prophesy.
To your senseless world my
One reply – I refuse.

15 March–11 May 1939

ЛЕВ НИКОЛАЕВИЧ ГОМОЛИЦКИЙ

Gomolitsky was born in St. Petersburg, to a Russified Polish family. The family emigrated to Poland after the Revolution, where Gomolitsky was active in Russian émigré circles as a poet, essayist, artist, and literary critic. He and his wife tried unsuccessfully to leave Warsaw in 1939.

Из 'Притч'

в дни истребления народа
они сидели в темноте
и спор вели: что зло на свете
– один сказал устало: жизнь
другой сказал с гримасой: чувства
гнездятся в чувствах страхи боль
а третий возразил им: память
не надо помнить лучших лет
там девочка была – в то время
ещо не отняли детей –
она сказала строго: роги
у зла острющие и хвост
– тут дверь пробитая прикладом
распалась и ворвалась та
кого они не помянули
ни разу между смертных зол
собравшись вскоре под землею
продолжить диспут мертвецы
они по-прежнему остались
при разных мнениях о зле.

Варшава 1942–1944

LEV GOMOLITSKY (1903–1988)

This excerpt is from Gomolitsky's second Book of Parables. Gomolitsky, who proudly wrote that his father always stood up for Jews when he saw them being oppressed, and whose wife Eva was Jewish, witnessed the destruction of Warsaw's ghetto.

from The Parables

while the nation was being destroyed
they sat in the dark
arguing about evil –
one said in a tired voice: it's life
the other said with a grimace: it's the senses
nestling in senses are fear and pain
the third countered: it's memory
you mustn't remember better times
a little girl was there –
they hadn't yet taken away the children –
she sternly said: evil has very
very sharp horns and a tail
– just then the door was shattered
by a rifle butt and in rushed
those never mentioned
among the mortal evils
the dead soon reconvened
to continue the dispute six feet under
but they still remained
divided on the nature of evil.

Warsaw 1942–1944

ОЛЬГА НИКОЛАЕВНА АНСТЕЙ

Anstei, a prominent poet of the second wave of emigration, was born in Kiev to a family of Russified Germans, Russians, Ukrainians, and Cossacks. She married the Russian-Jewish poet Ivan Elagin and managed to convince the occupying Nazi authorities that they were both volksdeutsch. After the War they emigrated to the USA.

Кирилловские Яры

I

Были дождинки в безветренный день.
Юностью терпкой колол терновник.
Сумерки и ковыляющий пень,
Сбитые памятники, часовни...
Влажной тропинкой – в вечерний лог!
Тоненькой девочкой, смуглой дриадой –
В тёплые заросли дикого сада,
Где нелюбимый и верный – у ног!..
В глушь, по откосам – до первых звёзд!
В привольное – из привольных мест!

II

Ближе к полудню. Он ясен был.
Юная терпкость в мерном разливе
Стала плавнее, стала счастливей.
Умной головкою стриж водил
На меловом горячем обрыве.
Вянула между ладоней полынь.
Чебрик дрожал на уступе горбатом.
Шмель был желанным крохотным братом!
Синяя в яр наплывала теплынь...
Пригоршнями стекала окрест
В душистое из душистых мест.

OLGA ANSTEI (1912–1985)

Kirillov Ravines is a series of ravines in Kiev that includes Babi Yar, where the city's Jews were massacred in September of 1941. Anstei witnessed it as it was happening. This was the first poetic response to the horror of Babi Yar.

Kirillov Ravines

I

Raindrops fell on that windless day.
Thorny sloes prickled with acerbic youth.
A limping tree stump in the twilight,
knocked-over tombstones, chapels...
A slip of a girl, a dusky Dryad –
down the damp path into the nocturnal ravine!
There, in the wild garden's balmy thicket,
unloved but faithful, he'll fall at my feet!...
Into the depths, down the slopes – until stars come out!
The most carefree of all carefree places!

II

Closer to noon. It was sunny and bright.
Youthful acerbity flows out gently,
growing more mellow, growing more joyful.
On the hot chalky bluffs the swift
turns his clever head.
Wormwood wilts, held between palms.
Thyme trembles on an angled ledge.
The bumblebee is a beloved tiny brother!
Blue warmth flows down into the Yar...
Handful by handful from all around
into the most fragrant of all fragrant places.

III

Дальше. Покорствуя зову глухому,
На перекрёсток меж давних могил
Прочь из притихшего милого дома,
Где у порога стоит Азраил –
Крест уношу, – слезами не сытый,
Смертные три возносивший свечи,
Заупокойным воском облитый,
Саван и венчик видавший в ночи...
Будет он врыт, подарок постылый,
Там, в головах безымянной могилы...
Страшное место из страшных мест!
Страшный коричневый скорченный крест!

IV

Чаша последняя. Те же места,
Где ликовала дремотно природа –
Странному и роковому народу
Стали Голгофой, подножьем креста.
Слушайте! Их поставили в строй,
В кучках пожитки сложили на плитах,
Полузадохшихся, полудобитых
Полузаваливали землёй...
Видите этих старух в платках,
Старцев, Как Авраам, Величавых,
И вифлеемских младенцев курчавых
У матерей на руках?
Я не найду для этого слов:
Видите – вот на дороге посуда,
Продранный талес, обрывки Талмуда,
Клочья размытых дождём паспортов!
Чёрный – лобный – запёкшийся крест!
Страшное место из страшных мест!

Декабрь 1941/1943

III

Onward. Obedient to some obscure call,
I go to the crossroad between older graves,
out of a hushed beloved house,
where Azrael stands at the threshold.
I carry a cross that still wants tears,
that raises three mortal candles
that is covered with wax drips
that saw a shroud and head-wreath in the night...
It will be dug into place there, a loathed gift,
at the head of a nameless grave...
The most frightening of all frightening places!
A frightening brown contorted cross!

IV

The last cup of all. The same place where
nature once drowsily luxuriated,
became Golgotha, the base of the cross
to a strange and fateful people.
Listen! They were lined up,
their belongings piled on the gravestones...
Half-smothered, half-killed,
then half-covered with soil...
Do you see those old women in kerchiefs,
elders, dignified like Biblical Abraham,
and curly-headed babes, like those in Bethlehem,
in their mothers' arms?
I can't find words for this.
Look: here on the road lie dishes,
a torn tallit, scraps of Talmud,
shreds of passports washed out by rain!
A black – murderous – blood-encrusted cross!
The most horrific of all horrific places.

December 1941/1943

БОРИС АНДРЕЕВИЧ ФИЛИППОВ

Filippov, a writer and literary scholar, was interned in the Gulag for being a member of a philosophical-religious circles in Leningrad. He thought the Germans would liberate Russia and welcomed the Occupation. He was part of Novgorod's collaborationist administration, wrote for and co-edited pro-Nazi newspapers.

'Города, города, города...'

Города, города, города,
Словно карточных домиков стадо,
Никому, никуда, никогда –
Ничего мне от жизни не надо.

По дорогам немецкой земли
Я влачу свою ветхую тачку,
И качаются кашки стебли,
Комары хороводят заплачку.

Никому, никуда, никогда –
Ничего мне от жизни не надо...
Деревень обозлившихся стадо...
Города, города, города...

1945

BORIS FILIPPOV (1905–1991)

Filippov wrote this poem while he was with the retreating German army. After the War he moved to the USA, where he was the driving force behind many important first editions of poets, including Mandelshtam, Gumilyov, and Akhmatova who weren't published in the Soviet Union.

'Town after Town after Town...'

Town after town after town,
just houses of cards bunched together.
There's nothing I want out of life...
No one... Nowhere... Never...

I'm pushing my rickety cart
on the roads across German land,
clover stems nod as I pass,
mosquitoes keen a lament.

There is nothing I want out of life –
Never... Nowhere... No one...
Angry villages bunched up together.
Town after town after town...

1945

НИКОЛАЙ ВАСИЛЬЕВИЧ ПАНЧЕНКО

Panchenko served as an airman in the War, until he was seriously wounded. Throughout the war he published poems in army newspapers. After the war, he edited the Komsomol newspaper in Kaluga, where he helped launch Bulat Okudzhava's career. Many of his war poems addressed tabooed subjects.

Баллада о расстрелянном сердце

Я сотни верст войной протопал.
С винтовкой пил.
С винтовкой спал.
Спущу курок – и пуля в штопор,
и кто-то замертво упал.
А я тряхну кудрявым чубом.
Иду, подковками звеня.
И так владею этим чудом,
что нет управы на меня.
Лежат фашисты в поле чистом,
торчат крестами на восток.
Иду на запад – по фашистам,
как танк – железен и жесток.
На них – кресты
и тень Христа,
на мне – ни Бога, ни креста:
– Убей его! –
и убиваю,
хожу, подковками звеня.
Я знаю: сердцем убываю.
Нет вовсе сердца у меня.
А пули дулом сердца ищут.
А пули-дуры свищут, свищут.
А сердца нет,
Приказ – во мне:
не надо сердца на войне.

NIKOLAI PANCHENKO (1924–2005)

Because of this poem's focus on the heartlessness and brutality expected of soldiers, and its dire predictions about what this would do to them post-war, Panchenko was unable to publish it until 1961, and in a literary almanac that he himself edited. The almanac was shut down after its very first issue.

A Ballad about a Heart Shot to Bits

I trekked hundreds of miles in the war.
I drank with my gun.
I slept with my gun.
I pulled the trigger, the bullet flew,
and someone hit the ground.
And I'd just nod my head and go,
my boots tapping clickety-clack,
I got so good at what I did
there was no holding me back.
The Nazis lay dead in open fields,
all facing East, like rigid Xs,
and I plowed West, right over them –
hard as a tank and just as callous.
The Nazis all wore crosses,
Christ's shadow fell on them,
I had no God, no scruples.
I was told, 'Kill him!' –
and so I did,
then tapped my boots and moved on.
But I knew my heart was fading,
and then my heart was gone.
The bullets looked and looked for my heart;
but couldn't find it to blow it apart.
I got the orders,
I knew the score –
no heart was needed in the war.

225

Ах, где найду его потом я,
исполнив воинский обет?
В моих подсумках и котомках
для сердца места даже нет.
Куплю плацкарт,
и скорым – к маме,
к какой-нибудь несчастной Мане,
к вдове, к обманутой жене:
– Подайте сердца!
Мне хоть малость! –
ударюсь лбом,
Но скажут мне;
– Ищи в полях, под Стрием, в Истре,
на польских шляхах рой песок:
не свист свинца – в свой каждый выстрел
ты сердца вкладывал кусок.
Ты растерял его, солдат.
Ты расстрелял его, солдат.
И так владел ты этим чудом,
что выжил там, где гибла рать.

Я долго-долго буду чуждым
Ходить и сердце собирать
– Подайте сердца инвалиду!
Я землю спас, отвел беду.
Я с просьбой этой, как с молитвой,
живым распятием иду.
– Подайте сердца! – стукну в сенцы.
– Подайте сердца! – крикну в дверь.
– Поймите, человек без сердца –
куда страшней, чем с сердцем зверь.

Меня «Мосторг» переодснст.
И где-то денег даст кассир.
Большой и загнанный, как демон,
Без дела и в избытке сил,
я буду кем-то успокоен:
– Какой уж есть, таким живи.

But where will I find a heart later,
when my soldier's job is done?
In all of my army bags
there is no space for one.
I'll buy a train ticket
and rush home to mama,
or else to some unhappy Manya,
a widow or a cheated wife:
'Spare me some heart!
A tiny bit will do!'
I'll beg and plead,
but they'll reply,
'Go search the fields by Stryi, or Istra,
sift through the sand of Poland's roads:
it wasn't just lead in those bullets –
your heart went into each shot.
It was lost bit by bit, soldier.
You had shot it to bits, soldier.
You got so good at what you did –
you lived while thousands were wiped out.'

I'll be a misfit for a long, long time,
begging for heart as a handout.
'Give to a war cripple, spare some heart!
I saved the land, I did my part.'
I'll wander like a living crucifix,
my plea turned to a prayer on my lips.
'Spare some heart!' I'll shout into doorways.
'Spare some heart!' I'll bang with my fist.
'Don't you see, a heartless man
is more fearsome than any beast.'

I'll get civilian clothes from 'Mostorg' shelves,
I'll get some money from a teller,
not knowing how to apply myself,
I'll loom about like a tormented demon,
till some advice brings me around:
'Live as you are – that is enough.'

И будет много шатких коек
скрипеть под шаткостью любви.
И где-нибудь, в чужой квартире,
мне скажут:
– Милый, нет чудес:
в скупом послевоенном мире
всем сердца выдано в обрез.

1944

And there'll be many shaky cots
creaking under a shaky kind of love.
And someone in a flat somewhere
will tell me,
'This postwar world is mean and hard;
don't look for miracles, my dear—
we all have a shortage of heart.'

1944

АННА АНДРЕЕВНА АХМАТОВА

Akhmatova considered this poem to be her life's work. She began it in Leningrad before the war and finished the first version in 1942, in Tashkent, where she had been evacuated. She then continuously revised it for the next two decades. Several excerpts were published in official press, but the full poem circulated only in Samizdat until the late 1980s.

Отрывок из 'Эпилога' (Поэма без героя)

Белая ночь 24 июня 1942 г. Город в развалинах. От Гавани до Смольного видно все как на ладони. Кое-где догорают застарелые пожары. И в Шереметьевском саду цветут липы и поет соловей. Одно окно третьего этажа (перед которым увечный клен) выбито, и за ним зияет черная пустота. В стороне Кронштадта ухают тяжелые орудия. Но в общем тихо. Голос автора, находящегося за семь тысяч километров, произносит:

Так под кровлей Фонтанного Дома,
Где вечерняя бродит истома
С фонарем и связкой ключей, –
Я аукалась с дальним эхом,
Неуместным смущая смехом
Непробудную сонь вещей,
Где, свидетель всего на свете,
На закате и на рассвете
Смотрит в комнату старый клен
И, предвидя нашу разлуку,
Мне иссохшую черную руку,
Как за помощью, тянет он.
Но земля под ногой гудела,
И такая звезда глядела
В мой еще не брошенный дом
И ждала условного звука...
Это где-то там – у Тобрука,
Это где-то здесь – за углом.

ANNA AKHMATOVA

The poem, in which Akhmatova meditates on the fate of her generation, is both a lament for blockaded Leningrad and an attempt to see the city and the horror of the war in the context of Russian history past and recent, including the horrors of the Gulag, where her own son was imprisoned at the time.

from 'Epilogue' (Poem Without A Hero)

The white night of June 24, 1942. The city in ruins. A panoramic view from the harbour to Smolny. Here and there old fires are burning themselves out. In the Sheremetev garden, lindens are blooming and a nightingale is singing. A third-floor window (with a crippled maple in front of it) is shattered, and behind it is a gaping black hole. The rumble of heavy artillery is coming from the Kronstadt area. But in general things are quiet. The voice of the author, seven thousand kilometers away, speaks:

Under the roof of the Fontanka House
Where the evening languor wanders round
Bearing a lamp and keys on a ring,
I hallooed and distant echoes answered,
And my inappropriate laughter
Troubled the unbroken sleep of things
In the place where each day, at dusk and dawn,
Witness to everything that goes on,
The old maple gazes into my room.
As it sees our parting in advance,
It extends to me a gnarled black hand
As if giving help, remaining true.
But the earth beneath me stirred and moaned,
And into my not-yet-abandoned home
Glared the star that heralds death and fear
Ready to march on the appointed day...
It's in Tobruk somewhere – still far away,
It's right around the block – it's almost here.

(Ты не первый и не последний
Темный слушатель светлых бредней,
Мне какую готовишь месть?
Ты не выпьешь, только пригубишь
Эту горечь из самой глуби –
Этой нашей разлуки весть.
Не клади мне руку на темя –
Пусть навек остановится время
На тобою данных часах.
Нас несчастие не минует,
И кукушка не закукует
В опаленных наших лесах...)

А за проволокой колючей,
В самом сердце тайги дремучей –
Я не знаю, который год –
Ставший горстью лагерной пыли,
Ставший сказкой из страшной были,
Мой двойник на допрос идет.
А потом он идет с допроса.
Двум посланцами Девки безносой
Суждено охранять его.
И я слышу даже отсюда –
Неужели это не чудо! –
Звуки голоса своего:

За тебя я заплатила
            Чистоганом,
Ровно десять лет ходила
            Под наганом,
Ни налево, ни направо
            Не глядела,
А за мной худая слава
            Шелестела

...А не ставший моей могилой,
Ты, крамольный, опальный, милый,
Побледнел, помертвел, затих.
Разлучение наше мнимо:

(You, not the first nor the last there'll be,
Dark listener to bright fantasy,
What revenge on me are you engaged in?
You're just sipping it, you won't drink up
This grief to the bottom of the cup –
The bitter news of our separation.
Don't lay your arm upon my shoulder,
Let the world never grow any older,
Let the hands of the watch you gave me freeze.
Ill fate and sorrow will not pass us by
And the cuckoo will no longer cry
Amid our leafless fire-blackened trees...)

Guard towers and barbed wire carve out a space
Deep within a measureless cold waste,
And there-but when, I don't know and won't guess –
Made an unperson, every trace wiped out,
Horrific facts changed to word of mouth,
My double's being taken to 'confess.'
Then, duly escorted by his keepers,
Two envoys of the noseless Reaper,
My double's being taken away.
And even as far distant as I am –
Truly an amazing happenstance! –
I hear what my own voice has to say:

No IOUs – I paid hard cash
*   For all you've done,*
A full ten years, no less, I've passed
*   Beneath the gun,*
I didn't dare look right or left
*   A single inch,*
And after me at every step
*   The slanders hissed.*

Where I faced doom but didn't perish,
You, city of granite, hellish, cherished,
Have fallen silent, turned deathly white.
My parting from you is only feigned.

Я с тобою неразлучима,
Тень моя на стенах твоих,
Отраженье мое в каналах,
Звук шагов в Эрмитажных залах,
Где со мною мой друг бродил,
И на старом Волковом Поле,
Где могу я рыдать на воле
Над безмолвием братских могил.
Все, что сказано в Первой части
О любви, измене и страсти,
Сбросил с крыльев свободный стих,
И стоит мой Город 'зашитый'...
Тяжелы надгробные плиты
На бессонных очах твоих.
Мне казалось, за мной ты гнался,
Ты, что там погибать остался
В блеске шпилей, в отблеске вод.
Не дождался желанных вестниц...
Над тобой – лишь твоих прелестниц,
Белых ноченек хоровод.
А веселое слово – дома –
Никому теперь не знакомо,
Все в чужое глядят окно.
Кто в Ташкенте, а кто в Нью-Йорке,
И изгнания воздух горький –
Как отравленное вино.
Все вы мной любоваться могли бы,
Когда в брюхе летучей рыбы
Я от злой погони спаслась
И над полным врагами лесом,
Словно та, одержимая бесом,
Как на Брокен ночной неслась...

И уже подо мною прямо
Леденела и стыла Кама,
И 'Quo vadis?' кто-то сказал,
Но не дал шевельнуть устами,
Как тоннелями и мостами
Загремел сумасшедший Урал.

Part of each other we still remain,
Upon your buildings my shadow lies,
Upon your waters my image falls,
My steps echo through the Hermitage halls,
Where my love and I once made our way,
And across old Volkovo Field,
Where my tears don't have to be concealed
Amid the quiet of common graves.
Everything written in the first part
About love, betrayal and the heart,
Free poetry has shaken off in flight,
And my city stands 'as good as new...'
A heavy burden lies upon you,
The gravestones placed on your sleepless eyes.
I fancied that you followed as I fled,
You who stayed behind to meet your death
With gleaming waters and spires of gold.
How you awaited bearers of good news –
They didn't come... Now all that's left to you
Is your white nights, still dancing as of old.
And the blest word – home – has become unknown,
All of us who have nowhere of our own
Peer through others' windows from outside.
Some are in New York, some in Tashkent,
And the bitter air of banishment
To the exile is like poisoned wine.
And all of you could marvel, if you wished,
When in the belly of a flying fish
I eluded the malice of foes,
And over war-ravaged forests I soared
Like she who, impelled by demonic force,
Into the air above Brocken rose.

Already I could see ahead
Where the icy Kama River stretched.
'Quo vadis?' I head someone ask,
But before I could have made a sound,
Across the mad Urals I was bound,
Their tunnels and bridges roaring past.

И открылась мне та дорога,
По которой ушло так много,
По которой сына везли,
И был долог путь погребальный
Средь торжественной и хрустальной
Тишины Сибирской Земли.
От того, что сделалась прахом,
....
Обуянная смертным страхом
И отмщения зная срок,
Опустивши глаза сухие
И ломая руки, Россия
Предо мною шла на восток.

Ташкент, 18 Августа 1942

And open before me lay the road
Along which so many were forced to go.
And my son, too, suffered that cruel command.
The track of the funeral column
Unfolded through the crystalline, solemn,
Silence of the Siberian land.
Seized by terror and overmastered

By dread of those who'd turned to ashes,
Knowing the length of retribution's reach
And acknowledging its hour had arrived,
Wringing her hands, with dry downcast eyes
Russia went before me to the east.

finished in Tashkent, 18 August1942

ПАВЕЛ ЯКОВЛЕВИЧ ЗАЛЬЦМАН

*Pavel Zaltsman was a half-German, half-Jewish artist and set designer,
and a student of Pavel Filonov. He also wrote poetry and prose. During
the siege of Leningrad, he painted over city landmarks in order to
protect them and disorient enemy pilots.*

Игра в карты

Первый признак – потный лоб,
Мы очень рады.
Когда едим горячий суп,
Свистят снаряды.

Второй – медали на груди
И бешеные строки.
Ах, мы не знаем, что впереди,
Какой там джокер...

Но мы прокладываем путь.
Там месят тесто.
Там у меня осталась мать,
Там ждет невеста.

Лети, лети, крылатый друг,
Спеши на праздник милый.
Ты не окончишь полукруг
Моей могилой.

Кто отстраняет их полет?
Не ты, конечно.
Но если, если Бога нет?
Нам безразлично.

PAVEL ZALTSMAN (1912–1985)

Zaltsman wrote a series of grotesque and heart-rending poems during the siege, capturing what it felt like to be bombed and to be dying of hunger in a besieged city – very different from the official, stoic depiction endorsed by the State.

A Game of Cards

First symptom is a sweaty brow –
we're having fun.
It's when we eat hot soup
that bombs come down.

The second – furious lines
and medals on the chest.
Who cares who holds the Joker,
when we don't know what's next!

But we still forge ahead
to where the dough is made,
to where my mother lives,
to where my bride awaits.

Rush to your festive do,
fly on, my winged friend.
I hope my grave won't mark
your semicircle's end.

Who makes these bombs fall past?
Not you, that's clear.
But what if there's no God?
We still don't care.

Бессмыслен праздник, если нет
Веселой встречи.
Мы оторвали свой обед,
Свисти короче.

Кто отстраняет их полет?
Мы очень рады,
Когда течет горячий жир с котлет,
И шоколаду.

Но если в небесах столбы
Родного дыма,
Мы воссылаем вам мольбы:
Валитесь мимо!

10 мая 1942 г., Ленинград, Николаевская, 73

What is a festive day
without a happy meeting?
We got our dinner anyhow,
so quit your bragging.

Who makes these bombs fly past?
We're very glad,
when there's chocolate
and burgers drip hot fat.

But when plumes of native smoke
rise high up in the sky,
we offer bombs our prayers:
Please pass us by!

10 May 1942, 73 Nikolaevskaia Street, Leningrad

Zaltsman's writings were influenced by the OBERIU avant-garde movement, which employed elements of the absurd, nonsense verse. They were declared to be class enemies. Daniil Kharms, the founder of OBERIU, died in the psychiatric ward of a Leningrad prison during the siege.

Псалом IV

Я еще плетусь за светозарным небом,
Но меня не выпускает ледяная тень.
Надо одеваться и идти за хлебом,
Мне сегодня что-то лень.

Я предлагаю кофе и открытки,
Я предлагаюсь весь,
Я сделался немой и кроткий,
И я с покорностью глотаю грязь.

Кускам подобранного с четверенек хлеба
Давно потерян счет.
Я, очевидно, никогда и не был
Ни весел, ни умен, ни сыт.

Еще висят холсты, еще рисунки в папках...
Но я теперь похож, –
Произошла досадная ошибка, –
На замерзающую вошь.

А впрочем, может, вши тебе дороже
Заеденных людей?
Если так, – выращивай их, Боже,
А меня – убей.

Но если что-нибудь над нами светит
И ты на небесах еси,
Я умоляю, хватит, хватит!
Вмешайся и спаси.

24 мая 1942 г., Ленинград, Николаевская, 73

Zaltsman knew that his poems were at odds with the times and never attempted to publish them. Polina Barskova has said that in this poem 'he explores the figure of a new Job: a Siege Job, the author of bitter psalms in which the contradictions of the siege ethos are fully expressed.'

Psalm IV

I'm still straggling under the luminous sky,
but an icy shadow holds me in thrall.
It's time to dress and line up for bread
but today I'm too lazy to go.

I'm offering coffee and postcards,
I'm offering up all of me.
I've become mute and meek
and gulp down muck obediently.

I've lost count of the pieces of bread
that I had picked up on all fours.
It seems that I was never
happy, intelligent, or full.

Canvasses hang, drawings fill folios...
But I resemble nothing as much as –
what a regrettable mistake! –
a slowly freezing louse.

But maybe you hold lice more precious
than people on which they feed?
If so – then multiply them, Lord,
but kill me dead.

But if hope glimmers above us
and you're truly up there in the skies,
I'm begging you, enough already!
Come down and save our lives.

24 May 1942, 73 Nikolaevskaia Street, Leningrad

НАТАЛЬЯ ВАСИЛЬЕВНА КРАНДИЕВСКАЯ

Born into a literary family, Krandievskaia began to write poetry precociously early. Her first book of poems was published in 1913 and favourably reviewed by some of the great poets of the age. She emigrated from Russia after the Revolution, returning in 1923. She lived in Leningrad with her two young sons during the siege.

'Шаркнул выстрел. И дрожь по коже...'

Шаркнул выстрел. И дрожь по коже,
Точно кнут обжёг.
И смеётся в лицо прохожий:
«Получай паек!»
За девицей с тугим портфелем
Старичок по панели
Еле-еле бредет.
«Мы на прошлой неделе
Мурку съели,
А теперь – этот вот...»
Шевелится в портфеле
И зловеще мяукает кот.
Под ногами хрустят
На снегу оконные стекла.
Бабы мрачно, в ряд
У пустого ларька стоят.
«Что дают?» – «Говорят,
Иждивенцам и детям – свекла».

Зима 1941–1942

NATALIA KRANDIEVSKAIA (1888–1963)

Krandievskaia wrote a poetic diary during the siege, describing the unprettified reality of life in the blockaded city – including the eating of cats and dogs – which contradicted the State-promoted story of the heroic and stoic Leningraders, who could never be brought as low as to eat their family pets.

'A Gunshot Cracks. I Shudder...'

A gunshot cracks. I shudder –
it feels like a whip slashing.
A passerby laughs at me,
'Just got your daily ration!'
A girl walks down the sidewalk
with a bulging briefcase,
an old man shuffles behind.
'Last week,
we ate Murka,
and now his time has come...'
The cat in the briefcase
stirs and darkly meows.
On the snow, windowpanes
crush under my feet.
Grim women line up
by an empty food stand.
'What's for sale?'
'For dependants and children – beets.'

Winter 1941–1942

Krandievskaia was planning to bring out a book of her siege poems in 1946, but this was abandoned after the political climate changed with Zhdanov's attack on Akhmatova, Zoshchenko, and the journals Zvezda *and* Leningrad. *Two books of her poetry were finally published in 1985.*

'В кухне крыса пляшет с голоду...'

В кухне крыса пляшет с голоду,
В темноте гремит кастрюлями.
Не спугнуть её ни холодом,
Ни холерою, ни пулями.

Что беснуешься ты, старая?
Здесь и корки не доищешься,
Здесь давно уж злою карою,
Сновиденьем стала пища вся.

Иль со мною подружилась ты
И в промёрзшем этом здании
Ждёшь спасения, как милости,
Там, где теплится дыхание?

Поздно, друг мой, догадалась я!
И верна и невиновна ты.
Только двое нас осталося –
Сторожить пустые комнаты.

1941

During the winter of 1941–42, when all the cats had been eaten, rats took over the blockaded city, frequently moving along the streets in large colonies. There were brigades for rat extermination, but nothing worked until the siege was broken in 1943 and trainloads of cats were brought into Leningrad.

'A Hungry Rat is Dancing in My Kitchen...'

A hungry rat is dancing in my kitchen,
in the dark, she clangs my pots.
Threaten her with cold, a gun or cholera,
but she still won't leave her spot.

Why are you rampaging, old girl?
You won't find a single crumb.
Hunger has become a scourge here
and all hope of food is gone.

Or is it that you befriended me
in this icy, frost-bound building,
and you're waiting for salvation,
help from anyone still breathing?

Ah, my friend, you're free of treachery!
Now I see as clear as ever!
Only two of us are left here –
guarding empty rooms together.

1941

АННА НИКОЛАЕВНА АЛЕКСЕЕВА

Alekseeva was born and lived in St. Petersburg/Petrograd/Leningrad her entire life. As a young woman interested in the arts, she attended the Institute of the Living Word, and was taught by Vsevolod Meyerhold and Anatoly Lunacharsky. She was a student at Nikolai Gumilyov's poetry seminar during the last year of his life.

Одиночество

После долгого небытия
Очнулась – кругом тишина,
Стараюсь припомнить, где же моя семья,
Вспоминаю – была война.
Какая? И нынче который год –
Семнадцатый иль сорок пятый?

Надо мной закопченный свод,
И в комнате воздух спёртый.
Подниматься с постели не хочется,
Знаю и там и здесь
Круглое одиночество
Мой дом заполняет весь.
Надо все начинать сначала,
И снова друзей искать,
И старое платье для бала
Заново перешивать.

5 Апреля 1945

ANNA ALEKSEEVA (1899–1945)

Alekseeva taught and worked during the siege. Her husband, the poet Vladimir Alekseev, died of hunger. Her father-in-law, the philosopher Sergey Alekseev, exiled in Novgorod, became a collaborationist and left with the retreating German troops. Alekseeva managed to send her son, Nikita, out of Leningrad, but he was killed in action. By 1945, she was totally alone.

Loneliness

After a long oblivion
I awaken – all around is quiet
I try to recall where my family have gone
I remember – there was a war.
Which one? And which year is it now –
'Seventeen or 'forty-five?
Above me a sooty vault
And the air in the room is foul.

I don't want to rise from my bed
I know what lies all about
Loneliness everywhere
It fills my house.
I have to begin everything afresh
Seek out new friends
There is my old dance dress
To patch up and mend.

5 April 1945

Alekseeva's first publication came many decades after her death, with the book This is Leningrad! Look and Listen! This is Leningrad under Siege, *including her letters and some of her wartime poems. Much of her poetic legacy remains unpublished to this day.*

'Мы плывем на нашем обстрелянном судне...'

Мы плывём на нашем обстрелянном судне,
Становясь с каждым днём всё спокойней и строже.
Величавая музыка ленинградских будней
Всех мелодий земли мне сейчас дороже.

Граждане, граждане ленинградцы!
Мне стыдно куда-то бежать и спасаться.
Ведь и предки мои костьми полегли,
Чтобы мы умереть здесь достойно могли –

От обстрела ли бешено-шалого
В жарких отблесках вечера алого
Иль на мягкой своей постели
Оттого, что три дня не ели.

29 Июля 1942

This poem was written after Alekseeva's husband starved to death during the worst winter of the siege, when corpses lay uncollected in frozen rooms. The winter passed, but the food shortages continued. This is the first publication of the poem, found among Alekseeva's recently discovered siege poems.

'Every Day We Grow Calmer and Sterner...'

Every day we grow calmer and sterner,
as our battered ship stays the course.
The grand chords of Leningrad's life
are more dear than all music on earth.

Fellow citizens, people of Leningrad!
I'd be ashamed to run off in dread.
My forebears laid down their lives
so that we could bravely face death –

whether in vicious bombardment,
one hot night, the sky glowing scarlet,
or lying in our soft beds,
after starving three days.

29 July 1942

ЗИНАИДА КОНСТАНТИНОВНА ШИШОВА

Shishova was a poet-turned-writer of the Odessan school. Her first husband, a poet, was shot by mistake. Her second husband was executed as an enemy of the people. She moved to Leningrad in 1940 and lived there until she was evacuated with severe dystrophy in 1942. She began to write poetry again during the siege.

Отрывок из поэмы 'Блокада'

Выходит на поверку, что тогда
Мы просто лгали близким и знакомым, –
Мы говорили: 'невская вода',
Мы говорили – 'в двух шага от дома'.
А эти два шага – четыре сотни.
Да плюс четырнадцать по подворотне.
Здесь не ступени – ледяные глыбы!
Ты просишь пить, а ноги отекли,
Их еле отрываешь от земли.
Дорогу эту поместить могли бы
В десятом круге в Дантовом аду...
Ты просишь пить – и я опять иду
И принесу – хотя бы полведра...
Не отступиться б только, как вчера!
Вода, которая совсем не рядом,
Вода, отравленная трупным ядом,
Ее необходимо кипятить,
А в доме даже щепки не найти...

1942

ZINAIDA SHISHOVA (1898–1977)

Shishova's The Siege *is a long poem about a mother trying to save her young son in blockaded Leningrad. A phone-call from the city's Party headquarters stopped Shishova's reading of the poem on Leningrad radio in July 1942: it was declared too dark and too unheroic. The poem was still published in 1943, but with many cuts.*

from The Siege

It turns out that we had lied
to family and friends,
when we said – 'the waters of the Neva,'
when we said – 'only two steps away.'
The two steps are actually four hundred
(plus the fourteen through the gateway).
Instead of stairs – ice slabs!
You're pleading for water, but my legs are swollen,
I can barely lift them as I walk.
This path to water would fit right into
the tenth circle of Dante's hell...
But you are pleading for water, so I'm going out again
to bring some, even if it's only a half-a-bucket...
I'm hoping I won't slip, like yesterday!
Water – that's not near at all.
Water – poisoned by cadaveric poison.
It must be boiled, but there's not a splinter of wood
with which to make a fire...

1942

КОНСТАНТИН ИЛЬИЧ ЛЕВИН

Levin was a commander of an anti-tank artillery unit, losing his leg in the fighting. His poetry wasn't published during his lifetime (he was accused of slandering Soviet reality in his poems), but several of his poems were well-known in postwar literary Moscow. Boris Slutsky considered him to be one of the most remarkable wartime poets.

Нас хоронила артиллерия

Нас хоронила артиллерия.
Она сначала нас убила
И, не гнушаясь лицемерием,
Клялась потом, что нас любила.

Она раскаивалась жерлами,
Но мы не верили ей дружно
Всеми искромсанными нервами
В руках полковников медслужбы.

Мы доверяли только морфию,
По самой крайней мере – брому,
А те из нас, что были мертвыми, –
Земле неверной, но знакомой.

А тех из нас, что были мертвыми,
Земля, кружась, не колебала,
Они чернели натюрмортами
Готического Калибана.

Нас поздравляли пэры Англии
И англичанки восковые,
Интервьюировали б ангелы,
Когда б здесь были таковые.

KONSTANTIN LEVIN (1924–1984)

This poem was prompted by Levin's arrival in Moscow as a disabled veteran in 1944. He was shocked by the apparent indifference of some civilians to the soldiers' sacrifices. This rift between the front and the home-front could not be officially acknowledged, in the same way that collateral damage was a prohibited topic.

Our Own Artillery Buried Us

Our own artillery buried us.
At first, it wiped us out,
then, stooping to hypocrisy,
it swore that we were loved.

Its canon muzzles mimed remorse
we thought false to the core,
with all our frazzled, shattered nerves
cared by the medical corps.

We trusted only morphine,
or bromide – at the worst,
but those of us already dead,
put their trust in the earth.

And those of us already dead,
unmoved as the earth spun,
lay strewn about like charred
remains of Gothic Calibans.

The British Peers applauded us,
as did their waxen misses,
the angels would've talked to us
had only they existed.

Но здесь одни лишь операторы
Из студии документальных фильмов
Накручивают аппаратами,
А их освистывают филины...

Один из нас, случайно выживший,
В Москву осеннюю приехал.
Он брел по улицам, как выпивший,
Он меж живыми шел, как эхо.

Кому-то помешал в троллейбусе
Ногой искусственной своею.
Сквозь эти мелкие нелепости
Он приближался к Мавзолею.

Там все еще ползут, минируют
И отражают контрудары,
А здесь уже иллюминируют,
Уже кропают мемуары.

И здесь, вдали от зоны гибельной,
Лиловым лоском льют паркеты,
Большой театр квадригой вздыбленной
Следит салютные ракеты.

И здесь, по мановенью Файера,
Взлетают стати Лепешинской,
И фары плавят плечи фрайера
И шубки женские в пушинках.

Солдаты спят. Им льет регалии
Монетный двор порой ночною.
А пулеметы обрыгали их
Блевотиною разрывною.

Но нас не испугает ненависть
Вечерних баров, тайных спален.
У нас защитник несравненный есть –
Главнокомандующий Сталин.

No angels here – just operators
from the documentary studios
who kept their cameras rolling
as eagle-owls hooted at them...

One of our own, a chance survivor,
made it to Moscow in the autumn.
He staggered round the city like drunk,
passing among the living like an echo.

His peg leg got in someone's way
when he rode on the tram.
As these inanities went on
he neared the Mausoleum.

Back at the front they still laid mines
and fielded counter strikes,
but here they scribbled memoirs
and strung up festive lights.

And here, far from the killing zone,
floors gleamed with lilac glow
as the Bolshoi's reared-up horses
watched the salute rockets go.

And here, at Fayer's beckoning,
grand Lepeshinskaya took flight;
as the men's suits and women's furs
flowed in the cars' headlights.

The soldiers slept. At night
the mint struck medals for them,
but the machineguns struck them
with their projectile vomit.

Now we don't fear the hatred
of bars and rooms of assignation –
Supreme Commander Stalin
gave us his unmatched protection.

И отослав уже к полуночи
Секретарей и адъютантов,
Он видит: в дымных касках юноши
Свисают с обгорелых танков.

На них пилоты с неба рушатся,
Костями в тучах застревая.
Но не оскудевает мужество,
Как небо не устаревает.

Так пусть любовь и независимость
Нас отличат от проходимцев,
Как отличил Генералиссимус
Своих неназванных любимцев.

1945/1946

At midnight, after letting go
of secretaries and adjutants,
he sees young men in smoking helmets
slump out of burned-out tanks.

Pilots attack them from the skies,
right through the clouds, bones clashing,
but courage isn't growing scarce
just as the sky never goes out of fashion.

So may our independence and our love
set us apart from cheats and swindlers,
just as the great Generalissimo
has set apart his unnamed favourites.

1945/1946

In this semi-autobiographical poem, Levin reflected on the anti-Semitism in the Soviet army during the War. The poem, like the feat it describes, was an act of courage; writing about Jewish experience and addressing the issue of Soviet antisemitism was not tolerated.

'Мы непростительно стареем...'

Мы непростительно стареем
И приближаемся к золе...
Что вам сказать? Я был евреем
В такое время на земле.

Я не был славой избалован
И лишь посмертно признан был,
Я так и рвался из былого,
Которого я не любил.
Я был скупей, чем каждый третий,
Злопамятнее, чем шестой.
Я счастья так-таки не встретил,
Да, даже на одной шестой!
Я шёл, минуя женщин славных,
И шушеру лишь примечал,
И путал главное с неглавным,
И ересь с истиной мешал.

Но даже в тех кровавых далях,
Где вышла смерть на карнавал,
Тебя, народ, тебя, страдалец,
Я никогда не забывал.
Когда, стянувши боль в затылке
Кровавой тряпкой, в маяте,
С противотанковой бутылкой
Я полз под танк на животе –
Не столько честь на поле брани,
Не столько месть за кровь друзей –
Другое страстное желанье
Прожгло мне тело до костей.

Levin read this poem publicly when the State campaign against rootless cosmopolitans (mostly targeting Jews) was already gearing up. The poem was one of the reasons for Levin's expulsion from Moscow's Literary Institute, where he studied after the war.

'We're Aging Unforgivably...'

We're aging unforgivably,
all ashes and decline...
What can I say? I was a Jew
on earth at just that time.

Fame never came to spoil me:
death came, then recognition.
I longed to break free of the past
I viewed without affection.
I was more miserly than most
more grudge-bearing than many.
I never chanced on happiness,
not even here – not any!
I sidestepped lovely women,
and sidled up to broads,
and I confused what mattered
and muddled up the truth.

But in that gory yonder,
when death came to the fair,
my anguished, tortured nation –
I thought of you back there.
And when I tied a dirty rag
around my bleeding head,
and with a bottle firebomb
crawled underneath that tank –
it wasn't done for glory,
or just as an act of revenge,
another passionate yearning
burned deep within my chest.

Была то жажда роковая
Кого-то переубедить,
Пусть – в чистом поле умирая,
Под гусеницами сгорая,
Но – правоту свою купить.

Я был не лучше, не храбрее
Пяти живых моих солдат –
Остатка нашей батареи,
Бомблённой пять часов подряд.
Я был не лучше, не добрее,
Но, клевете в противовес,
Я полз под этот танк евреем
С горючей жидкостью КС.

1947

It was a dire longing
to make someone believe,
even if I'd end up dead –
crushed under that Panzer's tread,
but to prove my righteousness.

I was not better and not braver
than my five soldiers still alive –
the remnants of our squadron
bombed for full hours five.
I was not better and not kinder,
but as a counterweight to slander,
I crawled beneath a German Panzer –
a Jew clutching a bottle bomb.

1947

МАРК АНДРЕЕВИЧ СОБОЛЬ

Sobol was interred in the Gulag in the late 1930s, but was allowed to enlist in 1941. He was wounded and decorated (thus clearing his former record), and began to publish in army newspapers in 1943, becoming well-known for his patriotic poems. He also wrote some less upbeat poems, like this one, for the desk drawer.

Маршевая рота

Зябко поникла трава на лугах,
дождик безбожный...
Тысяча лет на моих сапогах
глиной дорожной.

В горле от этой пожухлой травы
горькая завязь.
Счастливы лица у тех, что мертвы, –
отвоевались.

Тяжкое званье советских бойцов
мы переносим
долгой дорогой среди мертвецов
и через осень.

Вот они, сполохи огненной мглы,
Дымного смрада!..
В серые спины нам смотрят стволы
заградотряда.

Что сторожите вы из-за бугра
взглядом-прицелом?
Не беспокойтесь: мы крикнем 'ура!'
перед расстрелом.

1943

MARK SOBOL (1918–1999)

Barrier troops were a part of Soviet war strategy from 1942, when Stalin issued the famous order, known as 'Not A Step Back!' creating penal troops, barrier troop, and forbidding retreat in any form. Barrier troops ensured that those who ran from the frontlines in fright or panic would be either returned to their positions or shot.

March Battalion

The meadow grass looks cold and wilted.
It's raining hard...
A thousand years encrust my boots
like roadside mud.

That wilted grass leaves a bitter taste
deep at the core.
The faces of the dead look joyful –
they're done with war.

The taxing title of 'Soviet soldiers,'
that heavy haul,
we carry on the roads amid the dead
and through the fall.

Here comes the stench of smoky gloom,
quick blazing bursts...
Our backs are targets for the guns
of barrier troops.

Why are you watching from behind,
cocking your guns?
Don't worry, we'll all shout 'Hurrah!'
as we're mowed down.

1943

ЮРИЙ ВАСИЛЬЕВИЧ ГРУНИН

Grunin was studying to be an artist when he was drafted into the army. In 1942, he was taken prisoner. He was active in an underground Komsomol organization in the POW camp, writing poetry as a survival strategy. In 1945, he returned to the Soviet Union and the army, but was arrested and sent to the Gulag.

Болотные солдаты

Загоняют нас в болото пленным строем.
Мы дорогу на болотах немцам строим.
От воды студёной ноги-руки сводит.
Нас приходит в лагерь меньше, чем уходит.
Коль конвой недосчитается кого-то,
значит, пленного покой – в глуби болота.

Ещё дома мне запала песня в душу –
песня доблестного немца Эрнста Буша.
До войны её в Германии сложили
те, что головы в концлагере сложили:

> *Болотные солдаты,*
> *несём свои лопаты...*

Я по радио ту песню дома слушал,
по-немецки пел ту песню вместе с Бушем:

> *Wir sind die Moorsoldaten*
> *und ziehen mit dem Spaten...*

Вот про эту распроклятую работу
пел тогда, как загоняют нас в болото.
Мы – те самые болотные солдаты,
безымянные голодные солдаты.

1942

YURI GRUNIN (1921–2014)

Some poems written in POW camps were published in Soviet press during the war, but Grunin's poetry was beyond the pale, because he was forced to build roads for the Germans and so was branded a collaborator. Attempts were made during the Thaw to publish his poems, but they only appeared during Glasnost.

Bog Soldiers

Into the bogs we're forced in captive rows,
down in the bogs we're building German roads.
The freezing water numbs our hands and feet,
and fewer make it back to camp than leave.
If the guards are short one after the slog –
a prisoner rests in the depths of the bog.

There was a song I loved to hear back home,
that brave man, Ernst Busch, sang the song.
It was a German song composed by those
who in the concentration camps were lost.

> *We are the peatbog soldiers,*
> *marching with our spades...*

Back home they broadcasted that song,
Busch sang it in German and I sang along.

> *Wir sind die Moorsoldaten*
> *und ziehen mit dem Spaten...*

I didn't know I sang about this accursed work,
about being forced to go into the bog.
We are those peatbog soldiers,
those nameless starving soldiers.

1942

ЯН САТУНОВСКИЙ

Satunovsky began the War as a platoon commander, was wounded in 1942, and served as a war correspondent for the rest of the war. He was a chemical engineer by profession, but his love was poetry. He was close to the constructivist circles in 1920s Moscow and became a notable figure in the avantgarde of the 1960s.

'Как я их всех люблю...'

Как я их всех люблю
(и их всех убьют).
Всех –
командиров рот:
«Ро-та, вперед, за Ро-о...»
(одеревенеет рот.)
Этих. В земле.
«Слышь, Ванька, живой?»
«Замлел».
«За мной, живей, е!»
Все мы смертники.
Всем
артподготовка в 6,
смерть в 7.

1942

YAN SATUNOVSKY (1913–1982)

Satunovsky called his poetry 'chopped-up prose' and 'poems made of inessential words.' His poetry's unconventional form and the bitter but clear-eyed depiction of wartime realities made them unsuitable for publication both during the war and after. Satunovsky published a number of children's books, but his poems were published only in the late 1980s.

'How I Love Them All...'

How I love them all
(they'll all be killed).
All of them –
the company commanders:
'Company chaaarge! For the Motherla-a..'
(their mouths go dry.)
These ones. Covered in soil.
'Hey, Vanya, you alive?'
'I passed out.'
'Follow me, on the double!'
We're all dead men.
For all of us,
preliminary bombing comes at 6,
death at 7.

1942

In the beginning of the War, more than 18 million people were evacuated from major Soviet urban centres to the east of the country. Many evacuees couldn't be properly accommodated (some were evacuated to the Stalingrad region and had to be evacuated a second time).

'У Нас Был Примус...'

У нас был примус.
Бывало, только вспомнишь – он шумит.
Там
мама возится с кастрюлями
и в спешке крышками гремит,
и разговаривает сама с собой
о дороговизне и о себе самой.

У нас был примус.
У нас был примус, чайник, кран.
У нас был свет.
Теперь у нас ничего нет.

Вы эвакуированные.

1941

Satunovsky was from Dnepropetrovsk. When he returned from the front, he found the city in shambles, after the German occupation from 1941 to 1943. His parents, wife, and two daughters were still in Samarkand, in evacuation.

'We Had a Primus Stove...'

We had a primus stove.
You just thought about it – it hissed into action.
Mom was busy with the pots
banging their lids as she rushed about,
talking to herself
about how expensive things were
and about herself.

We had a primus stove.
We had a primus stove, a kettle, a tap.
We had light.
Now we have nothing.

You're evacuees.

1941

МИХАИЛ ВИКТОРОВИЧ ПАНОВ

Panov was a linguist and a literary scholar, who graduated from Moscow's Pedagogical Institute in 1941 and immediately enlisted in the army. He wrote poetry throughout his life, including at the front, where he was wounded and decorated, but began publishing his poems only in 1998.

Из Памятки Солдата

Таблица расстояний видимости предметов:

Наименование предмета	*Расстояние (в км.)*
Большие башни, церкви, элеваторы	16-21
Ветряные мельницы	11
Фабричные трубы	6
Окна в домах	4

	(в м.)
Переплеты в окнах	530
Пуговицы	160
Лица людей	160

Но одно милое лицо –
сквозь муку
всех солдатских глухих переходов.
А подвиг?
Сквозь провалы в тысячи лет?
Да нет! И вплотную не виден.

1942

MIKHAIL PANOV (1920–2001)

Panov's poems written while he was fighting on the front are formally innovative, free of lofty sentiment, and striking in their immediacy.

From a Soldier's Reference List

A Table of Distances of Visible Objects:

Name of Object	*Distance (in km)*
Large towers, churches, grain elevators	16-21
Windmills	11
Factory smokestacks	6
Windows in buildings	4

	(in m)
Window sashes	530
Buttons	160
People's faces	160

But only one lovely face –
shows through
the agony of the unending footslogs.
And acts of heroism?
Through thousands of years?
Not one! Not even up close.

1942

АРСЕНИЙ АЛЕКСАНДРОВИЧ ТАРКОВСКИЙ

Tarkovsky was one the great Russian poets and literary translators of twentieth-century, who became a war correspondent. He wrote many popular patriotic poems that soldiers took into battle with them, as well as some much darker poems for the desk drawer.

'Немецкий автоматчик подстрелит на дороге...'

Немецкий автоматчик подстрелит на дороге,
Осколком ли фугаски перешибут мне ноги,

В живот ли пулю влепит эсесовец–мальчишка,
Но все равно мне будет на этом фронте крышка.

И буду я разутый, без имени и славы
Замерзшими глазами смотреть на снег кровавый.

1942

ARSENY TARKOVSKY (1907–1989)

Tarkovsky wrote this poem in 1942, when he joined the army. He began to work on a book of poems in 1944, but the editors took issue with the fact that there were no poems about Stalin, and the book never came out.

'Say a German Gunner Will Get Me in the Back...'

Say a German gunner will get me in the back,
or a piece of shrapnel will take out both my legs,

or a teenaged SS trooper will shoot me in the gut –
anyway, I'm done for, there is no way out.

I won't go down in glory – I'll lie unshod, unknown,
looking through my frozen eyes at the bloodied snow.

1942

ДАВИД САМУИЛОВИЧ САМОЙЛОВ

Samoilov once belonged to the close-knit IFLI brotherhood, decimated by war. He himself made it through the war, wounded and decorated. He frequently said that he wrote no poetry during the forties and fifties, but it turned out not to be true – he wrote some remarkable poems about his war experiences, that could only be published many decades later.

Бандитка

Я вел расстреливать бандитку.
Она пощады не просила.
Смотрела гордо и сердито.
Платок от боли закусила.

Потом сказала: «Слушай, хлопец,
Я все равно от пули сгину.
Дай перед тем, как будешь хлопать,
Дай поглядеть на Украину.

На Украине кони скачут
Под стягом с именем Бандеры.
На Украине ружья прячут,
На Украине ищут веры.

Кипит зеленая горилка
В белёных хатах под Березно,
И пьяным москалям с ухмылкой
В затылки тычутся обрезы.

Пора пограбить печенегам!
Пора поплакать русским бабам!
Довольно украинским хлебом
Кормиться москалям и швабам!

DAVID SAMOILOV (1920–1990)

In 1944, Samoilov took part in operations against the troops of Stepan Bandera, the nationalist Ukrainian leader. He later wrote that, at the time, he believed that whoever fought the Red Army was an enemy and a Nazi, although "Bandit Woman', written [just] after the war, testifies that my feelings were truer and more honest than my thoughts.'

The Bandit Woman

I led a bandit out, to shoot her.
She didn't beg, she didn't plead –
Just glared at me with pride and anger,
And bit her shawl in agony.

And then she said: 'Now listen, fella,
You're gonna shoot me anyway.
Before you lay me down forever,
Just let me look at my Ukraine.

Across Ukraine our horses gallop
Under the banner of Bandera.
Across Ukraine we're stashing weapons,
Searching for something we can honour.

Green moonshine boils in whitewashed huts
Around Berezne, in the woods –
We smirk and press our sawed-off guns
Against the Russkies' drunken heads.

Time for the Pechenegs to raid!
High time that Russian women sobbed!
There'll be no more Ukrainian bread
For all the Russkies and the Swabs!

Им не жиреть на нашем сале
И нашей водкой не обпиться!
Еще не начисто вписали
Хохлов в Россию летописцы!

Пускай уздечкой, как монистом,
Позвякает бульбаш по полю!
Нехай як хочут коммунисты
В своей Руси будуют волю...

Придуманы колхозы ими
Для ротозея и растяпы.
Нам все равно на Украине,
НКВД или гестапо».

И я сказал: «Пошли, гадюка,
Получишь то, что заслужила.
Не ты ль вчера ножом без звука
Дружка навеки уложила.

Таких, как ты, полно по свету,
Таких, как он, на свете мало.
Так помирать тебе в кювете,
Не ожидая трибунала».

Мы шли. А поле было дико.
В дубраве птица голосила.
Я вел расстреливать бандитку.
Она пощады не просила.

1946

Don't want them gorging on our lard,
Drinking our vodka, getting merry!
Your scribes – they haven't yet inscribed
Ukrainians into Russia's story!

Let the potato-eaters flee,
Their bridles jangling loud, like coins!
Let Commies realize their ideals
The way they want to back at home...

It's them that came up with the kolkhoz
Where all the bums can eat for free.
For us Ukrainians, what's the difference –
Gestapo or NKVD?'

And then I said: 'Come on, you fiend,
It's time you got what you deserved.
Wasn't it you who killed my friend,
Who knifed him dead without a word?

The world is full of scum like you.
There aren't enough good men around.
No sense in waiting for tribunals –
You'll soon be rotting in the ground.'

And on we went. The land was brutal.
A bird was crying in the trees.
I led a bandit out, to shoot her.
She didn't beg, she didn't plead.

1946

ВЛАДИМИР АНТОНОВИЧ БОБРОВ

Bobrov was born in Moscow, drafted in 1941 and ended the war in Eastern Prussia, wounded and decorated. He never published his poetry during his lifetime. His family discovered his earnest, powerful, and darkly compelling wartime poems after his death.

Победа

Был я там, где рвались мины,
слышал рядом визг свинца.
Долю фронтовой судьбины
честно вынес до конца.

Рад бы память не тревожить,
да забыть я не могу
вшей на заскорузлой коже,
кровь и трупы на снегу,

и карболовое счастье
лазаретов, где я гнил,
и оскаленные пасти
наспех вырытых могил,

и перед броском минуты...
Знаю, какова она –
отгремевшего салюта
настоящая цена.

И, мне думается, рано
подводить боям итог.
Нерубцующейся раной
мир лежит у наших ног.

1945

VLADIMIR BOBROV (1921–1977)

Bobrov's poem reads like a direct response to the official State policy of the time that everyone should work cheerfully on rebuilding of the Soviet State, and forget the horrors of the war.

Victory

I was there, where mines exploded,
sending howling shrapnel past.
I was fighting on the frontlines
honestly and to the last.

I'd be glad not to remember,
but I live with what I saw:
crusty skin crawling with lice,
blood and corpses in the snow,

the med units where I rotted
with their disinfected grace,
the open, snarling jaws
of the hastily dug graves,

and the minutes before battle...
So that you can take my word –
I know well how much it cost us,
the salute we all just heard.

And it still feels much too early
to draw up the final bill,
when the world spreads out before us
like a wound that will not heal.

1945

ГЕОРГИЙ НИКОЛАЕВИЧ ОБОЛДУЕВ

Connected to Moscow's avantgarde scene, Obolduev published only one poem in his lifetime (aside from children's poems and translations). In 1933, he was arrested for anti-Soviet propaganda and exiled internally. He was drafted in 1943 and served in front-line reconnaissance, where he was severely wounded.

Мы победили

Вот они мы, вернулись, чать,
А не сыграли в ящик!
Теперь уж, чур, не жульничать:
Слав ставьте настоящих.
Настроены умы
На радости и почести,
Мы победили, мы...
Подайте, сколько можете!

Пришли отцы и дедушки,
Мужья, браты–младенцы,
И валом валят девушки
Хлеб-соль на полотенца,
Вынают из сумы
Того-сего во множестве,
За что сражались мы.
Подайте, сколько можете...

Без слёз, без крестных знамений,
Храня любовь к отчизне,
За честь родного знамени
Шли, не жалея жизни.
Всесветной кутерьмы
Невиданные мощности
Мы своротили, мы...
Подайте, сколько можете.

GEORGY OBOLDUEV (1898–1954)

After the War Obolduev briefly hoped that some of his war poems might be published. To that end, he tried to make the harsh social criticism in this poem seem more innocuous by attributing it to British soldiers. It didn't work.

We Brought Back Victory

So here we are, we made it back,
we haven't bit the dust!
Now bring out first-rate glory,
not some cheap second-best.
There's plenty honour due to us,
we're set to get our share.
We brought back victory, we did...
Give us what you can spare!

Here come the dads, the husbands,
kid brothers and granddads,
and all the girls are pouring in
to roll out a big welcome mat.
They dig out of their sacks
huge heaps of sundry fare –
what we fought for, we did.
Give us what you can spare...

We didn't cross ourselves or cry
when we launched an attack:
with willingness we gave our lives
for fatherland and flag.
We took on great colossi
that bred chaotic fear,
and brought them crashing down, we did...
Give us what you can spare.

Крутые схватки выстояв
С достаточным упорством,
Полны желаньем истовым –
И обоюдоострым –
Уж, избежав чумы,
Забыть о всём ничтожестве
Того, чем были мы,
– (Подайте сколько можете)—

Терпели мы от голода,
Терпели от обжорства,
От сырости, от холода,
От мягко и от чёрство.
От лета и зимы
Спасаясь по возможности,
Без хворей мёрли мы...
Подайте, сколько можете.

Не ждали мы заранее
Ни славы, ни медали,
Когда за другом раненым
Под вихорь выползали,
Уздая ветер тьмы.
Припоминая вожжи те,
Мы отдыхаем, мы –
Подайте, сколько можете...

Мы не были ни пленными,
Ни даже в окруженьи:
За что ж от роду-племени
Терпеть нам возраженья?
Сонны мы; как сомы –
Малоподвижны... Что же, де:
Контуженые мы.
Подайте, сколько можете!

We stood our ground in battles,
we were obstinate and hard.
But once the plague had passed us,
one wish burned in our hearts:
to wipe out what we were back there,
the nullity we shared –
we tried to forget it all, we did.
(Give us what you can spare!)

We suffered from hunger,
we suffered from surfeit,
from dankness and cold,
from bitter and sweet.
We tried to shield ourselves
from snow and scorching glare –
stayed healthy till we croaked, we did...
Give us what you can spare.

We crawled to save our wounded friends
when battle raged and bullets hailed –
we weren't out for medals
when death itself we braved.
Remembering those moments
and what spurred us on out there,
we thought that we should rest, we did.
Give us what you can spare...

We weren't taken prisoner,
we weren't in encirclement.
So why should we put up with
complaints from our kith and kin?
They say we're somnolent like fish,
that we just sit and stare.
We told them we're contused, we did.
Give us what you can spare!

Возможно ль без мошенничеств,
Когда свистят стихии?
Пусть несколько средь женщин есть
Таких-сяких, какие
Поотдали внаймы
Своих сердец жилплощади:
Ан, вот – вернулись мы –
«Подайте, сколько можете».

Готовы наши ноженьки
Задрать, скакнув в постельку
Ленивицы иль неженки,
Медовую недельку.
Покрепче сулемы
Любовь дерет по кожице:
Мы здеся, тута мы,
Подайте, сколько можете!

Что – боя, что – тюрьмы
Мгновенья да не множатся:
Увоевались мы!!
И всё же – обезноживши,
Слепы, немы, хромы –
Мы счастливы в убожестве,
Мы победили, мы...
Подайте, сколько можете!

1947

There is no straight and narrow,
when chaos is unleashed.
Some trashy no-good floozies
had let their hearts on lease
to those who paid them cash for it,
which wasn't any fair.
But now we have returned, we did:
'Give us what you can spare!'

We're ready to hop into bed
and stretch our legs beside
a pretty little lazybones
who'll make us feel just right.
Love finds a way to all of us,
it tugs, corrodes, and tears –
and that's what we all missed, we did.
Give us what you can spare!

Let's hope that jails and battles
are done with and won't multiply,
because we're all fought out, you see...
But though we've lost our sight,
are lame, disfigured, mute now,
had more than we could bear,
we brought back Victory, we did...
Give us what you can spare!

1947

ОЛЬГА ФЕДОРОВНА БЕРГГОЛЬЦ

Berggolts, the voice of Blockaded Leningrad, who, like so many of her generation, had hoped for more freedoms after victory, was one of the many bitterly disappointed by the political clampdown that followed. She wrote a series of poems for the desk drawer, as part of a secret diary.

'На собранье целый день сидела'

На собранье целый день сидела –
    то голосовала, то лгала...
Как я от тоски не поседела?
    Как я от стыда не померла?..
Долго с улицы не уходила –
    только там сама собой была.
В подворотне – с дворником курила,
    водку в забегаловке пила...
В той шарашке двое инвалидов
    (в сорок третьем брали Красный Бор)
рассказали о своих обидах, –
    вот – был интересный разговор!
Мы припомнили между собою,
    старый пепел в сердце шевеля:
штрафники идут в разведку боем –
    прямо через минные поля!..
Кто-нибудь вернется награжденный,
    остальные лягут здесь – тихи,
искупая кровью забубённой
    все свои небывшие грехи!
И, соображая еле-еле,
    я сказала в гневе, во хмелю:
'Как мне наши праведники надоели,
    как я наших грешников люблю!'

1948–1949

OLGA BERGGOLTS

When Berggolts wrote this poem, war invalids were not receiving monthly payment for their military decorations (this ceased in 1948), and Victory Day was no longer celebrated. The press attacked Akhmatova (whom Berggolts defended at personal risk) and others, and there were sweeping arrests.

'I Spent All Day at the Meeting...'

I spent all day at the meeting,
    either lying or voting.
I'm surprised I didn't go grey
    or die of shame.
I wandered about the streets,
    where I could be myself again.
I had a smoke with a yardman –
    then a drink in a cheap kiosk
along with two amputees,
    who had fought at Krasny Bor.
Their complaints were something else –
    their conversation was real.
One memory led to another,
    as we stirred the ash in our hearts:
penal battalions sent on reconnaissance
    straight across minefields.
One man would return bemedaled;
    others would lie down for ever,
their trumped-up sins now redeemed
    with daredevil blood.
And I said in a drunken rage,
    barely able to string thoughts together,
'Oh how I hate our righteous ones,
    Oh how I love our sinners!'

1948–1949

АННА АЛЕКСАНДРОВНА БАРКОВА

In the 1920s Barkova moved to Moscow from the provinces, at the invitation of Lunacharsky himself, and became known as the 'proletarian Akhmatova.' Because of her unwillingness to lie and to compromise with the political and the literary establishments, she spent twenty years in prison.

Песня победителей

Чем торгуешь ты, дура набитая,
Голова твоя бесталанная?
Сапогами мужа убитого
И его гимнастёркой рваною.

А ведь был он, как я, герой.
Со святыми его упокой.

Ах ты, тётенька бестолковая,
Может, ты надо мною сжалишься,
Бросишь корку хлеба пайкового
В память мужа – его товарищу?

Все поля и дорооги залило
Кровью русскою, кровушкой алою.
Кровью нашею, кровью вражеской.
Рассказать бы всё, да не скажется!

Закоптелые и шершавые,
Шли мы Прагой, Берлином, Варшавою.
Проходили мы, победители.
Перед нами дрожали жители.

Воротились домой безглазые,
Воротились домой безрукие,
И с чужой, незнакомой заразою,
И с чужой, непонятною мукою.

ANNA BARKOVA (1901–1976)

Barkova was responding here to the State's shocking treatment of war veterans, especially amputees or disabled. The terrible poverty of these veterans, who were no longer paid out pension supplements for their medals and injuries, often made them turn to begging on the streets.

Victory Song

What's that you're selling, pathetic fool,
standing there in the dirt?
– My fallen husband's army boots
and his torn army shirt.

So he was a hero like me...
May he sleep with the saints, RIP.

Ah, poor daft woman, take pity:
spare a crust of your rationed bread
in your dead husband's memory,
for me – his former comrade!

The roads and the fields were aflood
with Russian blood, our bright red blood,
with our own blood and that of our foes.
The tale must be told, but how, no one knows!

We were filthy, grimy, the worst off –
but we took Prague, Berlin, and Warsaw.
We marched on for victory's sake,
and people quaked in our wake.

We came back home with no eyes,
we came back home with no arms,
with strange foreign complaints,
and a strange foreign pain in our hearts.

И в пыли на базаре сели
И победные песни запели:
– Подавайте нам, инвалидам!
Мы сидим с искалеченным видом,
Пожалейте нас, победителей,
Поминаючи ваших родителей.

1946, 1953, Калуга

Now for the marketplace throngs
we sing our victory songs:
– Spare some change for us, amputees,
we're all war cripples, as you can see,
for the sake of your departed parents,
take pity on us, conquering heroes!

1946, 1953 Kaluga

Вспоминая войну

The War
Remembered

ДАВИД САМУИЛОВИЧ САМОЙЛОВ

Samoilov was in the original IFLI poetic brotherhood. He served as an infantry officer, was wounded and decorated. He became recognized as a major poet for the philosophic and coolly ironic poems he wrote in the 1960s and 1970s about the War and what it meant in the context of Soviet history and Russian culture.

Сороковые

Сороковые, роковые,
Военные и фронтовые,
Где извещенья похоронные
И перестуки эшелонные.

Гудят накатанные рельсы.
Просторно. Холодно. Высоко.
И погорельцы, погорельцы
Кочуют с запада к востоку...

А это я на полустанке
В своей замурзанной ушанке,
Где звездочка не уставная,
А вырезанная из банки.

Да, это я на белом свете,
Худой, веселый и задорный.
И у меня табак в кисете,
И у меня мундштук наборный.

И я с девчонкой балагурю,
И больше нужного хромаю,
И пайку надвое ломаю,
И все на свете понимаю.

DAVID SAMOILOV

One of Samoilov's main subjects was the fate of his generation, young soldiers who fought in the War. He wrote: 'we were convinced that only we, the front-line veterans, witnessed the tragedy of war, and we believed this tragedy to be poetry's main subject.'

The Forties

The forties, fateful,
warring, frontline,
with funeral notices,
clattering trains.

The hum of the rails.
All is cold, high, and barren.
Their houses have burned –
they're heading east.

That's me at the station
in my scraggy wool cap.
The star's not standard issue –
It's cut from a can.

Yes. Here I am in the world,
Skinny, happy, carefree.
I've got tobacco in my pouch –
I have a stash of rolling papers.

I joke with the girls,
and limp a little overmuch.
I break my rationed bread in half,
and I know everything on earth.

Как это было! Как совпало –
Война, беда, мечта и юность!
И это все в меня запало
И лишь потом во мне очнулось!..

Сороковые, роковые,
Свинцовые, пороховые...
Война гуляет по России,
А мы такие молодые!

1961

Imagine! What coincidence –
war, horror, dreams and youth!
And all that sank deep inside me...
and only later did it wake.

The forties, fateful,
Lead and gun smoke...
War wanders through the land
and we are all so young!

1961

Samoilov saw the War as the redeeming moment in Soviet history. Aside from the national self-sacrifice that helped destroy Nazism, he felt there was little cause for collective pride, but much cause for collective guilt.

'Если вычеркнуть войну...'

Если вычеркнуть войну,
Что останется – не густо.
Небогатое искусство
Бередить свою вину.

Что ещё? Самообман,
Позже ставший формой страха.
Мудрость – что своя рубаха
Ближе к телу. И туман...

Нет, не вычеркнуть войну.
Ведь она для поколенья –
Что-то вроде искупленья
За себя и за страну.

Простота её начал,
Быт жестокий и спартанский,
Словно доблестью гражданской,
Нас невольно отмечал.

Если спросят нас юнцы,
Как вы жили, чем вы жили?
Мы помалкиваем или
Кажем шрамы и рубцы.

Словно может нас спасти
От упреков и досады
Правота одной десятой,
Низость прочих девяти.

The poem was not published during Samoilov's lifetime because of its underlying claim that there was never any freedom in the Soviet Union, other than briefly during the war. It was published only in 1990.

'Let's Say We Cross Out the War...'

Let's say we cross out the war.
What remains? The pitiful art
of stirring guilt up in our hearts.
Mainly that. Anything more?

Murk, that's all... And self-deceit,
which became a form of fear.
That old standby – I don't care
if it's not happening to me.

No, we can't cross out the war.
It became our generation's
nearest thing to expiation –
for our country and ourselves.

Its essentials were so stark,
daily life so harsh and Spartan,
as if all who played a part in it
got a civic courage mark.

If the youngsters come and ask,
how we lived and what we lived by,
we stay silent in reply,
or else show our battle scars.

We pretend that all is fine –
we're safe from pain and shame,
as if that one tenth's rightful fame
trumps the other shameful nine.

Ведь из наших сорока
Было лишь четыре года,
Где нежданная свобода
Нам, как смерть, была близка.

поздние 1950ые–ранние 1960ые

We had forty years, no less
but of them just four in sum,
when unexpected freedom,
was as close to us as death.

early 1950s–late 1960s

Samoilov felt that he spoke for his generation. The actor Zinovy Gerdt, said, 'every line of his verse is written about me. Maybe that's because we're of the same generation, maybe because the Great Patriotic War was the main thing in both our lives... Samoilov expresses my inner life, my worldview.'

'Пью водку под хрустящую капустку...'

Пью водку под хрустящую капустку.
В окне луна. Снаружи слышен хруст
Задумчивых шагов по первопутку.
Всё это вместе навевает грусть.

Пью. Наливаю. По второй, по третьей.
Шаги затихли. Вечер снова тих.
И опыт четырёх десятилетий
Понуро и печально входит в стих.

Я понимаю, если бы не юмор,
Зарезаться бы надо огурцом.
Но если вышло так, что ты не умер, –
Сиди и пей с потерянным лицом.

Пью. Наливаю. Пятую. Шестую.
Закусываю, глядя на Луну.
И всё живу. И всё же существую.
А хорошо бы снова на войну.

1966

In the first two years of the War, when the Soviet Union experienced devastating losses, State controls over its citizens became more relaxed. The hope that this quasi-liberalization would be extended was soon crushed and left many disillusioned and cynical.

'I've Got Some Vodka and Some Cabbage...'

I've got myself some vodka and some cabbage.
The moon is shining. Someone's pensive steps
crunch loudly on the fresh snow outside.
This winter scene could hardly be more sad.

I down a shot. I pour another. Then a third.
The footsteps fade. Now nothing stirs.
And all I lived in four long decades
glumly goes into lines of verse.

At least there's such a thing as humour,
it's clear that without humour I'd be toast,
but if death skipped you, what's there to do
except to sit and drink here, feeling lost.

And so I drink. A shot. A fifth. A sixth.
I look out at the moon and eat some more.
But I keep living. And, it seems, existing.
You know, I'd rather go back to the war.

1966

БОРИС АБРАМОВИЧ СЛУЦКИЙ

Slutsky, another member of IFLI's poetic brotherhood and a close friend of Samoilov, enlisted and was wounded and decorated. He began to publish only in the late-1950s, aided by Ehrenburg. Many considered Slutsky the greatest poet of the postwar era. Joseph Brodsky said that Slutsky 'almost singlehandedly changed the sound of postwar Russian poetry.'

Госпиталь

Еще скребут по сердцу 'мессера',
еще
  вот здесь
    безумствуют стрелки,
еще в ушах работает 'ура',
русское 'ура-рарара-рарара!' –
на двадцать
    слогов
      строки.
Здесь
  ставший клубом
     бывший сельский храм,
лежим
  под диаграммами труда,
но прелым богом пахнет по углам –
попа бы деревенского сюда!
Крепка анафема, хоть вера не тверда.
Попишку бы лядащего сюда!

Какие фрески светятся в углу!
Здесь рай поет!
    Здесь
     ад
      ревмя
       ревет!

BORIS SLUTSKY (1919–1986)

Slutsky said that this poem had played a seminal role in his poetic development and that he learned how to write poetry while working on it. He wrote the poem in 1945 and then kept rewriting it over several years, the first of his many ballads. It was first published in 1957.

Hospital

The Messerschmitts still tear one's heart
Still,
   even here,
      the firing raves.
Still in our ears the cheering sounds
The repeated Russian 'rah-rah-rah!'
Twenty
     syllables
        a line.
In a village club
   that used to be
        a church
We lie
   under wall charts of labour figures,
But the smell of the dead god hangs on in corners –
Surely the village priest ought to be here!
Anathema is strong, though faith infirm.
If we had a sniveling parson here!

What frescoes flow in corners!
Here heaven sings –
      here
        sinners
          squeal
            in hell.

На глиняном нетопленом полу
лежит диавол,
   раненный в живот.
Под фресками в нетопленом углу
Лежит подбитый унтер на полу.

Напротив,
   на приземистом топчане,
кончается молоденький комбат.
На гимнастерке ордена горят.
Он. Нарушает. Молчанье.
Кричит!
   (Шепотом – как мертвые кричат.)
Он требует как офицер, как русский,
как человек, чтоб в этот крайний час
зеленый,
   рыжий,
     ржавый
       унтер прусский
не помирал меж нас!
Он гладит, гладит, гладит ордена,
оглаживает,
   гладит гимнастерку
и плачет,
   плачет,
     плачет
       горько,
что эта просьба не соблюдена.

А в двух шагах, в нетопленом углу,
лежит подбитый унтер на полу.
И санитар его, покорного,
уносит прочь, в какой-то дальний зал,
чтобы он
   своею смертью черной
нашей светлой смерти
     не смущал.
И снова ниспадает тишина.

On the unheated earthen floor,
Hit in the stomach,
 a prisoner groans.
Under the frescoes, in a freezing corner
He lies, a wounded *unteroffizier.*

Opposite, on a low field stretcher
 A young colonel is dying.
Decorations shine on his tunic.
He... breaks... the silence.
He shouts
 (in whispers, as the dying shout)
Demanding, as an officer, as a Russian –
As a human being, that in that final hour
The green-faced
 red-haired
   rusty
     Prussian *unter*
Should not die among us!
Fingering, fingering his medals
Smoothing
 and smoothing his tunic
He weeps –
 weeps
  bitterly
   that
    this
Demand, this plea of his is not fulfilled.

On the floor two steps away, in his unheated
Corner, lies the wounded NCO –
And an orderly drags him out, submissive,
Into some further room,
So that
 his black dying
shall not smirch
   Our glorious death.
And silence falls again.

И новобранца
          наставляют
               воины:
– Так вот оно,
          какая
               здесь
                    война!
Тебе, видать,
          не нравится
               она –
попробуй
     перевоевать
          по-своему!

1957

And old hands
        to the new recruit,
                in witness:
That's it –
        that's what it's like,
                the war
                        here.
You don't
        like
            it?
Then try
        to win it
                your way!

1957

Few poets wrote about women on the frontlines with the same measure of understanding and compassion as Slutsky. Some of his most moving poems are about young girls and women who fought, were wounded, and died on the front, all the while facing challenges unknown to men soldiers.

Волокуша

Вот и вспомнилась мне волокуша
и девчонки лет двадцати:
ими раненые волокутся,
умирая по пути.

Страшно жалко и просто страшно:
мины воют, пули свистят.
Просто так погибнуть, зряшно,
эти девушки не хотят.

Прежде надо раненых выволочь,
может, их в медсанбате вылечат,
а потом чайку согреть,
а потом – хоть умереть.

Натаскавшись, належавшись,
кипяточку поглотав,
в сыроватый блиндажик залезши,
младший крепко спит комсостав.

Три сержантки – мала куча –
вспоминаются нынче мне.
Что же снится им?
Волокуша.
Тянут раненых и во сне.

Vladimir Kornilov wrote, 'poets of my generation and much younger, robbed Slutsky blind in their poems. But... more important is the fact that he is really a poet of tragedy... of the mountain and the abyss.' This poem is one of thousands discovered after Slutsky's death.

The Stretcher

I just thought of it now – a stretcher,
and those lassies still in their teens,
whose job was casualty fetching
(some died before they were seen).

Dreadful detail and very dirty:
howling landmines and whining lead.
To die before doing their duty
didn't enter those lassies' head.

The wounded they wanted to succour,
– a chance that life might survive, –
and then they could have a cuppa,
after that, maybe, they could die.

They'd drive themselves to prostration,
swallow some water down,
crawl into their damp-earth station,
and their junior-rank sleep would be sound.

Pretty maids in a row, three three-stripers
I remember, stretched out on their backs.
And their dream?
That stretcher. Sleeping,
they're still carrying the casualties back.

Slutsky, a law student, was a soldier, then a political officer on the front (he regularly went on reconnaissance missions); he also had to serve as a judge on the tribunals that dealt with soldiers who 'reneged on their duties.' The experience seared him and he kept returning to it in his poems.

Расстреливали Ваньку-Взводного

Расстреливали Ваньку-взводного
за то, что рубежа он водного
не удержал, не устерёг.
Не выдержал. Не смог. Убёг.

Бомбардировщики бомбили
и всех до одного убили.
Убили всех до одного,
его не тронув одного.

Он доказать не смог суду,
что взвода общую беду
он избежал совсем случайно.
Унёс в могилу эту тайну.

Удар в сосок, удар в висок,
и вот зарыт Иван в песок,
и даже холмик не насыпан
над ямой, где Иван засыпан.

До речки не дойдя Днепра,
он тихо канул в речку Лету.
Всё это сделано с утра,
Зане жара была в то лето.

During the War, Soviet war tribunals condemned 284,344 members of Soviet armed forces to death by execution. In many cases this was substituted by service in a penal battalion.

'Vanya, the Troop Leader, Was Stood Against the Wall...'

Vanya, the troop leader, was stood against the wall –
for the riverbank that he failed to hold,
failed to guard it properly, he simply let it slip.
Couldn't do it. Lost his nerve. So he chose to split.

Bomber planes howled through the air,
killing all the soldiers there.
Killing each and every one,
sparing only him alone.

He couldn't explain to the tribunal
how he escaped the fate communal
of his whole troop – how he was saved.
He took that secret to his grave.

A shot to the chest, a shot to the head –
to make sure Ivan was really dead.
Now he's buried in the sand
with nothing there to mark his end.

Failing to reach the river Dnieper,
he crossed the Styx that day.
All over by mid-morning,
before the heat got in the way.

Баллада о догматике

Slutsky, like many of his generation, internalized the dogma he was taught, and tried to harmonize it with his experiences. Slutsky never did resolve the contradictions: he saw the flaws of the Soviet model, but hoped it could be reformed, questioning it only privately in the many poems meant for the desk drawer.

– Немецкий пролетарий не должон! –
Майор Петров, немецким войском битый,
ошеломлен, сбит с толку, поражен
неправильным развитием событий.

Гоним вдоль родины, как желтый лист,
гоним вдоль осени, под пулеметным свистом
майор кричал, что рурский металлист
не враг, а друг уральским металлистам.

Но рурский пролетарий сало жрал,
а также яйки, млеко, масло,
и что-то в нем, по-видимому, погасло,
он знать не знал про классы и Урал.

– По Ленину не так идти должно! –
Но войско перед немцем отходило,
раскручивалось страшное кино,
по Ленину пока не выходило.

По Ленину, по всем его томам,
по тридцати томам его собрания.
Хоть Ленин – ум и всем пример умам
и разобрался в том, что было ранее.

Когда же изменились времена
и мы наперли весело и споро,
майор Петров решил: теперь война
пойдет по Ленину и по майору.

A Ballad About a Dogmatist

This is a rewrite of the first poem Slutsky wrote while recovering from wartime injuries. The war demonstrated, in practice, that there were problems with the theory Slutsky was taught and preached himself as a political officer about class consciousness, the brotherhood of the proletariat, and the course of the war.

'The German proletariat cannot!!!' –
to Major Petrov things just don't make sense,
he's shocked, bewildered, and distraught
at such a strange progression of events.

Swept by the Germans like an autumn leaf,
swept through the land, under machine gun roar,
Petrov declared all metal-workers friends,
no matter from the Urals or the Ruhr.

But the Rhine-Ruhr proletariat just stuffed its face
with bacon, eggs, milk, and butter,
and it's not clear what was the matter –
it seemed to lack all consciousness of class.

'That's not the way that Lenin said it'd go!' –
the Germans came, the army beat retreat,
it all unfolded like a horror show,
nothing worked out in Lenin's way just yet.

Not in the way Lenin outlined in his tomes,
the thirty volumes of his collected works,
even though Lenin was a brain and all,
and figured out how history works.

But when the tide had finally turned –
we routed them and sent them packing,
Major Petrov decided that the war
would now go as foretold by him and Lenin.

Все это было в марте, и снежок
выдерживал свободно полоз санный.
Майор Петров, словно Иван Сусанин,
свершил диалектический прыжок.

Он на санях сам-друг легко догнал
колонну отступающих баварцев.
Он думал объяснить им, дать сигнал,
он думал их уговорить сдаваться.

Язык противника не знал совсем
майор Петров, хоть много раз пытался.
Но слово 'класс' – оно понятно всем,
и слово 'Маркс', и слово 'пролетарий'.

Когда с него снимали сапоги,
не спрашивая соцпроисхождения,
когда без спешки и без снисхождения
ему прикладом вышибли мозги,

в сознании угаснувшем его,
несчастного догматика Петрова,
не отразилось ровно ничего.
И если бы воскрес он – начал снова.

1960

That was in March, the snows still deep
but light and suited for sled running.
And Major Petrov, like Ivan Susanin,
got set to make his dialectical leap.

Alone, driving a horse and sled,
he caught up with the retreating Germans
He thought he could explain, expound,
and get them to surrender with his sermons.

Now, Petrov didn't speak the German tongue,
though many times he tried to study it,
but the word *class* is understood by all,
and so is *Marx*, and so is *proletariat*.

They took off Major Petrov's boots
(his social origin was never queried);
then, without feeling, without hurry,
bashed in his skull with rifle butts.

Yet not an element of what transpired
impacted his extinguished brain.
Poor dogmatist Petrov expired,
but if revived, he'd do it all again.

1960

This poem was first published in 1965, the year that Victory Day (9 May) was restored as a national holiday.

Шестое небо

Любитель, совместитель, дилетант –
Все эти прозвища сношу без гнева.
Да, я не мастер, да, я долетал
Не до седьмого – до шестого неба.

Седьмое небо – хоры совершенств.
Шестое небо – это то, что надо.
И если то, что надо, совершил,
То большего вершить тебе не надо.

Седьмое небо – это блеск, и лоск,
И ангельские, нелюдские звуки.
Шестое небо – это ясный мозг
И хорошо работающие руки.

Седьмое небо – вывеска, фасад,
Излишества, колонны, все такое.
Шестое небо – это дом, и сад,
И ощущенье воли и покоя.

Шестое небо – это взят Берлин.
Конец войне, томительной и длинной.
Седьмое небо – это свод былин
Официальных о взятии Берлина.

Сам завершу сравнения мои
И бережно сложу стихов листочки.
Над «и» не надо ставить точки. «И»
Читается без точки.

1965

When the poem was first published it was without the fifth stanza. It was published in full only in 1988.

The Sixth Heaven

I have been called an amateur, a dabbler,
Jack of all trades. These names don't bother me.
A master I am not. I've only ever made it
To the sixth heaven, never to the seventh.

The seventh heaven has a perfect choir,
Whereas the sixth one gives you what you need.
There is no need to set the world on fire
Once you've achieved what needs to be achieved.

The seventh heaven, with its brilliance and shine,
Is full of otherworldly songs.
The sixth one favours clarity of mind
And cleverness of working hands.

The seventh heaven is a glossy signboard,
A grand façade with columns, extras, frills.
The sixth one is a house and garden,
A place to feel at home, at peace and free.

The sixth one is the taking of Berlin,
Ending a never-ending war.
The seventh heaven is a compilation
Of stately ballads, honouring the taking of Berlin.

I will consider my comparisons complete
And put away the pages of my poems.
No need to put too fine a point upon it,
No need to dot my 'i's' or cross my 't's'.

1965

АЛЕКСАНДР ПЕТРОВИЧ МЕЖИРОВ

Mezhirov, an outstanding soldier poet, continued to ponder the war's meaning throughout his long poetic career. 'In the first postwar years,' he said, 'the war appeared in my poems as something separate from life. Later, I began to think that certain aspects of the war repeat in normal life as well.'

Прощай Оружие!

В следующем году было много побед.
Э. Хемингуэй

Ты пришла смотреть на меня.
А такого нету в помине.
Не от вражеского огня
Он погиб. Не на нашей мине
Подорвался. А просто так.
Не за звонкой чеканки песню,
Не в размахе лихих атак
Он погиб. И уже не воскреснет.
Вот по берегу я иду.
В небе пасмурном, невысоком
Десять туч. Утопают в пруду,
Наливаясь тяжелым соком,
Сотни лилий. Красно. Закат.
Вот мужчина стоит без движенья
Или мальчик. Он из блокад,
Из окопов, из окружений.
Ты пришла на него смотреть.
А такого нету в помине.
Не от пули он принял смерть,
Не от голода, не на мине
Подорвался. А просто так.
Что ему красивые песни
О размахе лихих атак, –
Он от этого не воскреснет.
Он не мертвый. Он не живой.

ALEXANDER MEZHIROV (1923–2009)

One of Mezhirov's main themes was the way that war destroys even those who manage to survive physically. Many years after the war, he wrote, in two separate poems, 'I went through that war/and that war went right through me,' and 'I live on the verge of collapsing/unable to break with the war.'

A Farewell to Arms

The next year there were many victories.
E. Hemingway

You came to gaze upon me.
But there is no trace of such a person.
He died not from enemy fire.
He was blown up not by
One of our mines. It just happened.
He died not for the silver tones of a song,
Not in the sweep of daring attacks.
And he will not rise again.
I walk along the shore.
In the low, mournful sky are
A dozen clouds. Hundreds of lilies,
Juicy with heavy sap,
Float in the pond. Red. Sunset.
Here stands a man motionless
Or a boy. He is from the blockades,
From the trenches, the encirclements.
You came to gaze at him.
But there is no trace of such a person.
He took death not from a bullet.
Not from starvation. Was not blown up
By a mine. It just happened.
What do pretty songs about the sweep of daring attacks
Mean to him –
These will not resurrect him.
He is not dead. Not alive.

Не живет на земле. Не видит,
Как плывут над его головой
Десять туч. Он навстречу не выйдет,
Не заметит тебя. И ты
Зря несешь на ладонях пыл.
Зря под гребнем твоим цветы –
Те, которые он любил.
Он от голода умирал.
На подбитом танке сгорал.
Спал в болотной воде. И вот
Он не умер. Но не живет.
Он стоит посредине Века.
Одинешенек на земле.
Можно выстроить на золе
Новый дом. Но не человека.
Он дотла растрачен в бою.
Он не видит, не слышит, как
Тонут лилии и поют
Птицы, скрытые в ивняках.

Does not live on earth. Does not see
A dozen dark clouds floating above his head.
He will not go out to greet you.
Will not even see you.
In vain you bring ardor on outstretched palms,
In vain you wear flowers in your hair,
Those which he loved.
He is all of those who died of starvation,
Burned up in disabled tanks.
Slept in swampy water. And still
He did not die. But he does not live.
He towers amidst our century,
Entirely alone on earth.
A new house can be built
From ashes. But not a man.
He was totally spent in battle.
He does not see, does not hear
The lilies floating and the birds
Singing, hidden in the willow beds.

Among the many things Soviet poets had to avoid when writing about the war was the topic of collateral damage and friendly fire. These taboo areas, often those experienced by the poets themselves while fighting on the front, were also dangerously evocative of the State's repressions and persecutions of its veterans and civilians after the war.

'Мы под Колпином скопом стоим…'

Мы под Колпином скопом стоим.
Артиллерия бьёт по своим.
Это наша разведка, наверно,
Ориентир указала неверно.

Недолёт, перелёт, недолёт.
По своим артиллерия бьёт.

Мы недаром присягу давали,
За собою мосты подрывали.
Из окопов никто не уйдёт.
По своим артиллерия бьёт.

Мы под Колпином скопом лежим,
Мы дрожим, прокопчённые дымом.
Надо всё-таки бить по чужим,
А она – по своим, по родимым.

Нас комбаты утешить хотят,
Говорят, что нас родина любит.
По своим артиллерия лупит.
Лес не рубят, а щепки летят.

1956

This poem couldn't be published for many years. Yevtushenko recited it publicly in 1956, after which he was expelled from Moscow's Literary Institute. In order to protect Mezhirov, Yevtushenko announced that it was written by a soldier killed in the war. Mezhirov, moved by the reading, told Yevtushenko afterwards, 'Yes... Essentially, we were all killed in that war.'

'We are Huddled in a Crowd...'

We are huddled in a crowd before Kolpino.
Under the fire of our own artillery.
It's probably because our reconnaissance
Gave the wrong bearings.

Falling short, overshooting, falling short again...
Our own artillery is shooting at us.

It wasn't for nothing we took an oath,
Blew up the bridges behind us.
No one will escape from these trenches.
Our own artillery is shooting at us.

We're lying in a heap before Kolpino.
We're trembling, saturated with smoke.
They should be shooting at the enemy,
But instead they're shooting at their own.

The commanders want to console us.
They say the motherland loves us.
The artillery is thrashing its own.
They're not making an omelette, but they're breaking eggs.

1956

Most young frontline poets, who were raised to believe in the moral superiority of the Soviet system, in Stalin's genius and benevolence, and in the glorious future of mankind under the Soviet aegis, fought for these beliefs in the War and were bitterly disillusioned in the decades that followed.

'Что ж ты плачешь, старая развалина...'

Что ж ты плачешь, старая развалина, –
Где она, священная твоя
Вера в революцию и в Сталина,
В классовую сущность бытия...

Вдохновлялись сталинскими планами,
Устремлялись в сталинскую высь,
Были мы с тобой однополчанами,
Сталинскому знамени клялись.

Шли, сопровождаемые взрывами,
По всеобщей и ничьей вине.
О, какими были б мы счастливыми,
Если б нас убили на войне.

1971

*Mezhirov became famous for his 1945 poem 'Communists, Forward!'
written in response to a request from another frontline poet to write
a poem commemorating those killed in the War. What he saw after
the War, however, made him rethink, and then eventually lose his
faith in everything that he held sacred before and during the War.*

'So Why Are You Crying, Old Wreck?'

So why are you crying, old wreck?
Has your sacred faith taken a fall?
How you trusted the Revolution and Stalin,
the class struggle that underlies all...

We were once both inspired by Stalin's plan,
Stalin's goals were our one-way track.
We fought in the same division,
and swore allegiance to Stalin's flag.

We marched under heavy bombardment
never knowing what lay in store.
All blameless, all bearing the blame –
how I wish we'd been killed in that war...

1971

ВАЛЕРИЙ ПЕРЕЛЕШИН

Pereleshin, the greatest poet associated with the Russian émigré community in China, moved to Harbin in 1920. He was active in Churaevka, a circle of literary Russian émigrés, as a poet and translator. He eventually moved to Brazil and wrote poetry in Portuguese.

Утешение

Мне говорят: «Софист обманчивый,
Всегда бывавший всех правее,
Ненужной песни не заканчивай,
Посторонись, да поживее!

Умри, как жил: цветком беспочвенным,
Окраинным, больным и странным,
Напрасной страстью притороченным
К болотным лунам и туманам.

Тебя, кувшинку бледнолицую,
Не приласкают, не оценят:
Тебя осанистой пшеницею,
Овсом питательным заменят.

Уместно ли стихам лирическим
Звучать, больным и бесполезным,
В тысячелетьи металлическом,
В столетьи угольно-железном?

Ты ненавидишь муравьенышей,
И муравьев, и Муравейник, –
Умри же, догматы затронувший
Изгой, чужак, несовременник!

VALERY PERELESHIN (1913–1992)

Pereleshin's view of the future was decidedly a dark one. He hardly wrote any poems about war. This poem, forecasting a nuclear holocaust (of which the world got a taste at the end of the War at Hiroshima and Nagasaki), is an exception.

Consolation

They're telling me: 'Deceitful Sophist,
who's always righter than the rest,
don't bother finishing your song –
out of the way, and fast!

Die as you lived: a rootless flower,
a sickly marginal, a loon,
bound by a useless passion
for mists and swampy moons.

Who needs you, common waterlily,
pathetic and pale-faced –
with stately wheat, nutritious oats
you'll quickly be replaced!

Why would you go on writing poems,
so wan and useless they appal,
in our metallic hard millennium,
this age all iron-coal?

You hate all ant-like beings, you tell us,
the ants and the Antheap they made,
then die, now that you've challenged dogma,
you alien, outcast, retrograde!

Ни сына от тебя, ни дочери,
Ни песни воинской, ни клича:
Так в первую погибни очередь,
Забвенья верная добыча!»

Но в день, когда весь мир низринется
В безумие войны последней,
Утешится душа-пустынница,
Заулыбается победней:

Отрадно быть ни с кем не связанной,
Ни перед кем не виноватой
В час, ею же самой предсказанный, –
На красном празднике Гекаты!

Ей будет некого и нечего
Терять в смерчах атомной бомбы:
Ни фунта мяса человечьего
Поэт не внес для гекатомбы!

1948

You've never sired son nor daughter,
composed no martial song –
so now you'll be the first to perish,
oblivion won't take long!'

But when the world will plunge headlong
into the final maddening war,
the hermit-soul will be consoled,
and smile at the score.

How sweet not be tied to anyone,
not to feel guilty in the least,
that hour the soul herself foretold
of Hecate's scarlet feast!

She won't be losing anyone or anything
in the tornadoes of the atom bomb:
there's not a single pound of human flesh
this poet offered for the hecatomb!

1948

НИКОЛАЙ ВАСИЛЬЕВИЧ ПАНЧЕНКО

Panchenko, soldier, poet, writer, and editor, briefly believed during Khrushchev's Thaw that all aspects of the War could be discussed openly. He wrote a series called 'Obelisks: A Soldier's Poems' and published them in a journal he founded. It was shut down immediately.

'Девчонка Парикмахершей Работала...'

Девчонка парикмахершей работала,
Девчонку изнасиловала рота:
Ей в рот портянки потные совали,
Ласкали непечатными словами,
Сорвали гимнастёрку с красной ленточкой:
была девчонка ранена в бою.
Девчонку мы в полку прозвали «деточкой» –
невенчанную женщину мою.

Не для стихов дела такого рода –
Но это была власовская рота.
Мы женщину забыли в отступлении.
В пяти верстах догнала злая весть.
Хоть в петлю лезь –
не будет подкрепления.
Полсотни душ –
был полк разбитый весь.
Бежали мы,
летели мы над вёрстами.
В село ворвались сомкнутыми горстками.
Нет – кулаками, быстрыми и жесткими!
не биться и не меряться – карать!
И где-то бабы всхлипывали: «Господи!
Откуда эта праведная рать?!»
Колёсный гул,
разрывы, вопли, громы.

NIKOLAI PANCHENKO (1924–2005)

This poem is one of the few written on the taboo topic of wartime rape of army personnel. Here the rapists are soldiers from Vlasov's army, who fought alongside the Germans. Panchenko faced a torrent of outrage for this poem and didn't publish it again.

'The Girl Worked in Our Unit as a Barber...'

The girl worked in our unit as a barber.
The girl got raped by an entire squadron.
They gagged her with their fetid footcloths.
They talked filth as they mauled her.
They stripped her army shirt with its red badge
(the badge was for being wounded).
Our unit used to call her 'babyface' –
my untouched woman.

These things are not the stuff of poems –
the girl was raped by Vlasov's squadron.
We had forgotten her in our retreat;
three miles off, we got the evil news.
We could go hang ourselves,
there'd be no extra troops.
We were just fifty men
left of our wiped-out unit.
We ran,
we raced over the miles,
we burst into that village in tight fistfuls.
Not fistfuls – fast, hard-hitting fists!
Not there to fight or to contend – to smite!
And we could hear the village women weeping:
'Good Lord! Who sent this righteous might?!'
The din of wheels.
Explosions, howls, and shots.

Я штык согнул
и растерял патроны.
Добили мы их в рытвине, за баней,
хватали у своих из-под руки:
я этими вот белыми зубами
откусывал, как репы, кадыки.

Девчонка задремала под шинелью.
А мы, глотнув трофейного вина,
сидели, охраняли, не шумели,
как будто что-то слышала она.
Был вымыт пол,
блиндаж украшен, убран,
как будто что-то видела она.

...За эту операцию под утро
прислали нам из штаба ордена.
Мы их зарыли в холмик,
вместе с нею.
Ушли вперёд,
в Литовские края.

Чем дальше в жизнь,
тем чище и яснее,
невенчанная женщина моя.

1961

My bayonet was bent,
my bullets lost.
We got them in the hollow by the banya,
each of us fought to kill as many as we could.
With these white teeth
I bit through Adam's apples.

The girl dozed off under a greatcoat.
We drank some wine we found
and sat there, guarding her in silence,
as if she could hear anything at all.
The floor was washed,
the dugout cleaned and tidied,
as if she could see anything at all.

...And for that operation, in the morning,
the HQ sent us medals, one and all.
We dug them down into a hillock
right beside her.
Lithuania was next, we had to move on.

The more I live,
the brighter and more pure she seems,
my untouched woman.

1961

АЛЕКСАНДР АРКАДЬЕВИЧ ГАЛИЧ

Galich was one of the three great Soviet-era poet-singers in the sixties, banned and eventually exiled. He was declared unfit for military service and spent the War entertaining troops and the wounded. His poem-songs about the War address the injustices faced by returning soldiers and the way post-war Soviet life made a mockery of their sacrifices.

Вальс Посвященный Уставу Караульной Службы

Поколение обреченных!
Как недавно – и ох как давно, –
Мы смешили смешливых девчонок,
На протырку ходили в кино.

Но задул сорок первого ветер –
Вот и стали мы взрослыми вдруг.
И вколачивал шкура-ефрейтор
В нас премудрость науки наук.

О, суконная прелесть устава –
И во сне позабыть не моги,
Что любое движенье направо
Начинается с левой ноги.

А потом в разноцветных нашивках
Принесли мы гвардейскую стать,
И женились на разных паршивках,
Чтобы все поскорей наверстать.

И по площади Красной, шалея,
Мы шагали – со славой на «ты», –
Улыбался нам Он с мавзолея,
И охрана бросала цветы.

ALEXANDER GALICH (1918–1977)

Later, in exile, Galich wrote about the scandalous treatment of homecoming soldiers, the 'prison trains jam-packed with those same war heroes about whom we were singing... [while] the newly restored archives of the [NKVD] were swelling with the files of former and future prisoners of the labour camps.'

Waltz Dedicated to the Regulations for Guard Duty

Generation of the accursed!
Only recently, so long ago,
We had fun with our giggling girlfriends,
And we packed every cinema show.

'41 came along, blowing icy,
And we suddenly had to grow wise;
We were drilled in the science of sciences
By a bastard in corporal stripes.

Oh, that coarse-woven joy, regulations –
Even sleeping, don't ever forget
That a move in a rightward direction
Begins with a step to the left.

And then in our bright medal ribbons
We puffed out our chests and walked tall,
We got married to any old scrubber
Just to make up for time we had lost.

We strode over Red Square in triumph,
Full of glory, the men of the hour;
On the podium He stood there smiling,
With his bodyguards throwing flowers.

Ах, как шаг мы печатали браво,
Как легко мы прощали долги!..
Позабыв, что движенье направо
Начинается с левой ноги.

Что же вы присмирели, задиры?!
Не такой нам мечтался удел.
Как пошли нас судит дезертиры,
Только пух, так сказать, полетел.

– Отвечай, солдат, как есть на духу!
Отвечай, солдат, как есть на духу!
Отвечай, солдат, как есть на духу!
Ты кончай, солдат, нести чепуху:
Что от Волги, мол, дошел до Белграда,
Не искал, мол, ни чинов, ни разживу...
Так чего же ты не помер, как надо,
Как положено тебе по ранжиру?!

Еле слышно отвечает солдат,
Еле слышно отвечает солдат,
Еле слышно отвечает солдат:
– Ну, не вышло помереть, виноват.
Виноват, что не загнулся от пули,
Пуля-дура не в того угодила.
Это вроде как с наградами в ПУРе,
Вот и пули на меня не хватило!

– Все морочишь нас, солдат, стариной?!
Все морочишь нас, солдат, стариной!
Все морочишь нас, солдат, стариной –
Бьешь на жалость, гражданин строевой!
Ни деньжат, мол, ни квартирки отдельной,
Ничего, мол, нет такого в заводе,
И один ты, значит, вроде идейный,
А другие, значит, вроде Володи!

Oh, our marching steps rang so blithely,
We so easily wrote off our debts;
We forgot that a move the right must
Always start with a step to the left.

What's become of your courage, you skivers,
Was this really the dream in your eyes?
Those deserters got going with their trials,
It was then the fur started to fly.

'Answer, soldier boy, what's eating you up?
Answer, soldier boy, what's eating you up?
Answer, soldier boy, what's eating you up?
Soldier, soldier, let's have less of that crap!
Fought your way, you say, from Volga to Vistula,
And you didn't look for rank or easy number?
You're not dead – why not? I want to know the reason,
By the figures, you should be six feet under!'

What the soldier said could barely be heard,
What the soldier said could barely be heard,
What the soldier said could barely be heard,
'I just happened not to die, 'scuse me, sir!
Please forgive me for not catching a bullet,
Looks as if those bullets hadn't eyes to see, sir,
Just like medals for political merit,
There just didn't seem to be one for me, sir!'

'Let's have less old soldiers' yarns, soldier boy!
Let's have less old soldiers' yarns soldier boy!
Let's have less old soldiers' yarns soldier boy!
You're a citizen, and it's pity you want?
You've no money, and no flat for your family?
And the king of thing we're after's unknown here?
You're the only loyal man in this factory?
And the others are a load of old scroungers?'

Ох, лютует прокурор-дезертир!
Ох, лютует прокурор-дезертир!
Ох, лютует прокурор-дезертир!
Припечатает годкам к десяти!

Ах, друзья ж вы мои, дуралеи, –
Снова в грязь непроезжих дорог!
Заколюченные параллели
Преподали нам славных урок –

Не делить с подонками хлеба,
Перед лестью не падать ниц
И не верить ни в чистое небо,
Ни в улыбку сиятельных лиц.

Пусть опять нас тетешкает слава,
Пусть друзьями назвались враги, –
Помним мы, что движенье направо
Начинается с левой ноги!

1965/66

The deserter-procurator raves and rants,
The deserter-procurator raves and rants,
The deserter-procurator raves and rants,
And his sentence is – ten years in the camps!

Oh, my friends, you poor suffering idiots,
Back again to the slime of new roads;
But those barbed-wire frontiers and limits
They have taught us a lesson of gold:

Don't go sparing a crust for a scrounger,
Don't let flattery lead you astray,
Don't believe in a sky blue and cloudless,
Or the smile on a fat shining face.

Maybe fame has come back now to pet us,
And our enemies call themselves friends,
But a move to the right, – we'll remember, –
Always starts with a step by the left.

1965/66

In Galich's broadcasts on Radio Liberty in the late seventies, he spoke about the way post-war life had a way of turning wartime heroes into cowards.

Больничная цыганочка

А начальник всё, спьяну, про Сталина,
Все хватает баранку рукой,
А потом нас, конечно, доставили
Санитары в приемный покой.
Сняли брюки с меня и кожаночку,
Все мое покидали в мешок,
И прислали Марусю-хожалочку,
Чтоб дала мне живой порошок.

А я твердил, что я здоров,
А если ж, печки-лавочки,
То в этом лучшем из миров
Мне все давно до лампочки,
Мне все равно, мне все давно
До лампочки!

Вот лежу я на койке, как чайничек,
Злая смерть надо мною кружит,
А начальничек мой, а начальничек,
Он в отдельной палате лежит.
Ему нянечка шторку повесила,
Создают персональный уют,
Водят к гаду еврея-профессора,
Передачи из дома дают!

А там икра, а там вино,
И сыр, и печки-лавочки!
А мне – больничное говно,
Хоть это и до лампочки,
Хоть все равно, мне все давно
До лампочки!

Galich frequently wrote about the way the Soviet system corroded people and relationships. Here, two soldiers who fought together in the War fare differently after the war.

Hospital Jig

Piss-drunk, my boss started up about Stalin,
grabbed my steering as he ranted and roared,
and the very next thing I remember
is waking up at the emergency ward.
My pants and my jacket were stripped off,
all my stuff had been stuffed in a sack,
and Marusia the Nurse tried to make me
pop some pills while I lay on my back.

And I kept saying that I was fine,
but if that was it and all the rest,
then, in this best and perfect world,
I really couldn't care much less.
It's all the same, whatever the game,
I can't care less.

So there I lay on a cot like some psycho,
the Grim Reaper was sizing me up,
and my good old boss got a private room,
ruffled curtains and that sort of stuff.
The nurse prettied everything up for him,
so the bastard was cozy and warm.
got a Jewish professor to see him,
brought him fresh lunches from home.

He had his caviar and wine
and fancy cheese and all the rest,
while I got to eat the hospital shit
even if I couldn't care much less!
Even if it's all the same and whatever the game
I can't care less!

Я с обеда для сестрина мальчика –
Граммов сто отолью киселю,
У меня ж ни кола, ни калачика,
Я с начальством харчи не делю!
Я возил его, падлу, на «Чаечке»,
И к Маргошке возил, и в Фили,
Ой, вы добрые люди, начальнички!
Соль и гордость родимой земли!

Не то он зав, не то он зам,
Не то он печки-лавочки,
А что мне зам! Я сам с усам,
И мне чины до лампочки,
Мне все чины да ветчины
До лампочки!

Надеваю я утром пижамочку,
Выхожу покурить в туалет,
И встречаю Марусю-хожалочку, –
Сколько зим, говорю, сколько лет!
Доложи, говорю, обстановочку,
А она отвечает не в такт –
Твой начальничек дал упаковочку –
У него получился инфаркт! –

На всех больничных корпусах
И шум, и печки-лавочки,
А я стою – темно в глазах,
И как-то всё до лампочки,
И как-то вдруг мне всё вокруг
До лампочки...

So I saved up a bit for my sister's kid
of that sweet sop they fed us for lunch.
see, I don't own a share of my boss's pie,
and it's not like I've got very much...
I just drive him round in the limo,
to his sluts and then out on the town.
They're the salt of the earth, our bosses,
our heroes won't let us down!

He's right on top or just below,
the guy in charge and all the rest,
but rank won't make me piss my pants,
in fact, I couldn't care much less!
A VIP don't impress me!
I can't care less!

So I pull on my hospital PJs
and I go for a smoke in the john,
when I see Nurse Marusia come scurrying.
'Hey,' I stop her, 'what's going on?'
'Got your marching orders?' I ask her,
but her answer threw me off track,
'That boss of yours is no more,' she says,
'He just died of a heart attack!'

And all around the hospital wards
there are cries and shouts and all the rest
while I just stand there totally stunned,
what happens now, I couldn't care less.
What happens now – odd, but somehow,
I can't care less!

Да, конечно, гражданка гражданочкой,
Но когда воевали, братва,
Мы ж с ним вместе под этой кожаночкой
Ночевали не раз и не два,
И тянули спиртягу из чайника,
Под обстрел загорали в пути...
Нет, ребята, такого начальника
Мне, наверно, уже не найти!

Не слезы это, а капель,
И всё, и печки-лавочки,
И мне теперь, мне всё теперь
Фактически до лампочки,
Мне всё теперь, мне всё теперь
До лампочки!

1963

See, civilian life is separate story,
but at the front, with our lives on the line,
there were times all we had to keep warm
was this old bomber jacket of mine.
And we drank our booze from a kettle,
cooled our heels as the shelling raged on,
no, I don't think I'll ever be able
to replace the boss that is gone.

These are not tears but raindrops,
and that is it and all the rest,
and as for me, well, as you see,
I really couldn't care much less.
Whatever comes, whatever comes,
I can't care less!

1963

ЕВГЕНИЙ АЛЕКСАНДРОВИЧ ЕВТУШЕНКО

Yevtushenko was nine in 1941. He said and wrote many times that the most important thing about his generation, was that each had all seen the War through the eyes of a child.

Военные Свадьбы

А. Межирову

О, свадьбы в дни военные!
Обманчивый уют,
слова неоткровенные
о том, что не убьют...
Дорогой зимней, снежною,
сквозь ветер, бьющий зло,
лечу на свадьбу спешную
в соседнее село.
Походочкой расслабленной,
с челочкой на лбу
вхожу,
плясун прославленный,
в гудящую избу.
Наряженный,
взволнованный,
среди друзей,
родных,
сидит мобилизованный
растерянный жених.
Сидит
с невестой – Верою.
А через пару дней
шинель наденет серую,
на фронт поедет в ней.

350

YEVGENY YEVTUSHENKO (1932–2017)

Yevtushenko called wartime weddings 'his first civil trauma': 'tragic weddings, often collective ones... Even now there are decrepit old women in Siberia, considered saints... They didn't even get to spend their wedding nights with their husbands, but still remained faithful to those who had left.'

Wartime Weddings

to A. Mezhirov

O, those old wartime weddings,
complete with put-on cheer
and toasts to coming home safe,
that sound so insincere!
...The winter wind is vicious,
but down the road I fly –
to a last-minute wedding
in a village nearby.
I'm looking good,
I've got the moves,
you couldn't ask for more –
I am the dazzling dancer
they've all been waiting for.
The place is crammed with people,
the groom is centre stage,
decked-out,
worked-up,
and mobilized –
they're calling up his age.
He sits
with his bride, Vera,
but in a day or so,
he'll put on his new uniform
and off to war he'll go.

с винтовкою пойдет,
Землей чужой,
не местною,
под пулею немецкою,
быть может, упадет.
В стакане брага пенная,
но пить ее невмочь.
Быть может, ночь их первая –
последняя их ночь.
Глядит он опечаленно
И – болью всей души
мне через стол отчаянно:
'А ну давай, пляши!'
Забыли все о выпитом,
все смотрят на меня,
и вот иду я с вывертом,
подковками звеня.
То выдам дробь,
то по полу
носки проволоку.
Свищу,
в ладоши хлопаю,
взлетаю к потолку.
Летят по стенкам лозунги,
что Гитлеру капут,
а у невесты
слезыньки
горючие
текут.
Уже я измочаленный,
уже едва дышу...
'Пляши!..' –
кричат отчаянно,
и я опять пляшу...
Ступни как деревянные,
когда вернусь домой,
но с новой свадьбы
пьяные являются за мной.

A rifle on his shoulder,
he'll walk in
distant lands,
who knows,
a German bullet
might prove to be his end.
He doesn't drink the homebrew,
though it's the very best –
he's thinking that their first night
might prove to be their last.
His heart is nearly broken
by their sorrowful romance,
then he shouts wildly at me,
'You! Go ahead and dance!'
The guests forget their drinking,
they too have heard the groom –
I start my fancy footwork
and circle round the room.
I do a rapid tap dance
then slow it down a notch,
I whoop,
and leap,
and clap my hands –
they all can't help but watch.
The room is hung with slogans
that we will stop the Hun,
but the bride
just keeps on crying,
her tears are streaming down.
I'm pretty wiped already,
I'm just about to drop...
'Dance on!'
they're shouting wildly
and so I mustn't stop.
I finally get home,
my feet are feeling numb,
but there's
another wedding:
they're asking me to come.

Едва отпущен матерью,
на свадьбы вновь гляжу
и вновь у самой скатерти
вприсядочку хожу.
Невесте горько плачется,
стоят в слезах друзья.
Мне страшно.
Мне не пляшется,
но не плясать –
нельзя.

2 Октября 1955

My mother lets me go again –
more weddings, what'd you know...
I do my fancy footwork
and round the room I go...
The bride is crying bitterly,
her friends are crying too,
I'm frightened.
I don't want to dance,
but that's
what I must do.

2 October 1955

ГЛЕБ АЛЕКСАНДРОВИЧ ГЛИНКА

A poet, writer, and literary critic of the second wave of emigration, Glinka was a member of the literary group 'Pereval,' repressed by the authorities in the 1930s. He was spared and taught literature and poetic theory. After the war, he became a sculptor, then returned to teaching literature and writing poetry.

На чужбине

Ведь мне немного надо:
Хотел бы тишины.
Восставшему из ада
Забавы не нужны.

С любимыми своими
Я тут живу давно,
Не с прежними – с другими;
Что ж, это все равно.

Что было, то уплыло.
Но след остался там,
Где смерть за мной ходила,
Как нянька, по пятам.

Лишь ты меня не мучай,
С укором не смотри,
Когда сушу, на случай
Ржаные сухари.

Не мудрено, не мудро
Жить с горем пополам.
Сейчас в России утро
И где-то, где-то там...

195?

GLEB GLINKA (1903–1989)

Glinka who enlisted in 1941, became a POW, stayed in various prisoner camps, and was eventually liberated by the allies. His wife and daughter were first told that he was missing in action, later, that he was dead. Fearing reprisals, Glinka couldn't let his family know his real fate. He eventually remarried and emigrated to the US.

In a Foreign Land

No, I don't need a lot now:
some quiet and I'm done.
When you return from hell,
you won't be wanting fun.

I've lived here for some years
with those I love so dear.
Not those I loved before –
but really now, who cares?

What was before has vanished,
but there is still a trace,
where death, just like a nursemaid,
once tracked my every step.

So now don't you torment me,
look with reproach, or ask
why is it that I'm drying
old rye bread into rusks.

No wisdom helps life's sorrows,
this life is yours to bear.
It's morning now in Russia
and somewhere... somewhere there...

195?

ВЛАДИМИР СЕМЕНОВИЧ ВЫСОЦКИЙ

Vysotsky, one of the top unofficial Soviet singer–songwriters, was three years old in 1941, but he never forgot the air-raids and the shelters. He spoke at length about his generation's war trauma and wrote many songs about the war. His songs about life on the frontlines were so convincing, that many ex-soldiers believed he was one of them.

Братские могилы

На братских могилах не ставят крестов,
И вдовы на них не рыдают, –
К ним кто-то приносит букеты цветов,
И Вечный огонь зажигают.

Здесь раньше вставала земля на дыбы,
А нынче – гранитные плиты.
Здесь нет ни одной персональной судьбы –
Все судьбы в единую слиты.

А в Вечном огне – видишь вспыхнувший танк,
Горящие русские хаты,
Горящий Смоленск и горящий рейхстаг,
Горящее сердце солдата.

У братских могил нет заплаканных вдов –
Сюда ходят люди покрепче,
На братских могилах не ставят крестов...
Но разве от этого легче?!

1963

VLADIMIR VYSOTSKY (1938–1980)

Vysotsky first performed this in 1963, on the birthday of his father, a veteran of the War. He considered it the first song of his extensive war cycle. It became nationally popular in 1966 after it was sung by both Vysotsky and Mark Bernes in Victor Turov's film I Come From Childhood, *about children who are waiting for the end of the War.*

Soldiers' Mass Graves

There are no crosses on these graves,
and widows don't come here to mourn.
If you'll come around bring some flowers,
and watch the eternal flame burn.

Once this ground reared up and buckled,
now granite is holding it down,
there are no singular fates here –
all the fates have merged into one.

Deep in the flame you'll see tanks blown to pieces,
and Russian villages smoulder,
flaming Smolensk, burning Reichstag,
the blazing heart of a soldier.

Widows don't weep on these graves –
those who come are of stronger stuff.
They don't put up crosses here –
but does that make it any less tough?

1963

In many of his poem-songs about the War, Vysotsky spoke on behalf of those who were not given a voice in the official Soviet narratives of the war. The soldiers who fought and died in the penal units defending Stalingrad and in other famous battles, were not mentioned in most accounts of Soviet wartime victories.

Штрафные батальоны

Всего лишь час дают на артобстрел.
Всего лишь час пехоте передышки.
Всего лишь час до самых главных дел:
Кому – до ордена, ну, а кому – до вышки.

За этот час не пишем ни строки.
Молись богам войны – артиллеристам!
Ведь мы ж не просто так, мы – штрафники.
Нам не писать: Считайте коммунистом.

Перед атакой – водку? Вот мура!
Свое отпили мы еще в гражданку.
Поэтому мы не кричим ура!,
Со смертью мы играемся в молчанку.

У штрафников один закон, один конец –
Коли-руби фашистского бродягу!
И если не поймаешь в грудь свинец,
Медаль на грудь поймаешь За отвагу.

Ты бей штыком, а лучше бей рукой –
Оно надежней, да оно и тише.
И ежели останешься живой,
Гуляй, рванина, от рубля и выше!

Считает враг – морально мы слабы.
За ним и лес, и города сожжены.
Вы лучше лес рубите на гробы –
В прорыв идут штрафные батальоны!

Soviet penal battalions were formed in 1942. It is estimated that over 400,000 Soviet soldiers served in penal units, for reasons ranging from relatively minor infractions during military service to serious crimes. They died at a rate six times that of regular troops, but many who survived were decorated and rejoined the regular army.

Penal Battalions

There's just an hour set aside for shelling.
An hour for infantry to catch its breath.
An hour left until the main event:
Some will get medals, others – death.

You won't find us reaching for a pen.
We put our faith in gods of war – artillerymen!
We're penal troops, it's not for us to write:
'Count us all communists, if this is the end!'

Swig vodka before battle? Hell, what for?!
We drank our fill back in the civil war.
We don't hurrah – we play a game with Death.
Let's see who breaks the silence: us or her!

There's just one law for penal troops – you learn it fast:
Snuff out the Nazi scum, forget the rest!
And if your chest won't end up full of lead,
You'll get a medal on your chest, instead.

Use bayonets, or better, use your hands –
It's more secure and there's less mess.
And if you come out of this job alive,
Then live it up, while you still got the chance!

The Nazis think that we're about to crack.
Burned towns and forests lie behind their backs.
They better chop those forests down for coffins:
The penal troops are heading for attack!

Вот шесть ноль-ноль, и вот сейчас – обстрел.
Ну, бог войны! Давай – без передышки!
Всего лишь час до самых главных дел:
Кому – до ордена, а большинству – вышки.

1963

It's six-o-o – and now the shelling starts.
Go at 'em, gods of war, don't let 'em rest!
There's just an hour to the main event:
Medals for some, for most – it's certain death.

1963

ВЛАДИМИР АЛЕКСАНДРОВИЧ ЛИФШИЦ

Lifshits was a war correspondent; he fought in the Finnish War and in the Second World War when he was wounded and decorated for military valour.

Отступление в Арденнах

Ах, как нам было весело,
Когда швырять нас начало!
Жизнь ничего не весила,
Смерть ничего не значила.
Нас оставалось пятеро
В промозглом блиндаже.
Командованье спятило
И драпало уже.
Мы из консервной банки
По кругу пили виски,
Уничтожали бланки,
Приказы, карты, списки,
И, отдаленный слыша бой,
Я – жалкий раб господен –
Впервые был самим собой,
Впервые был свободен!
Я был свободен, видит бог,
От всех сомнений и тревог,
Меня поймавших в сети.
Я был свободен, черт возьми,
От вашей суетной возни
И от всего на свете!..
Я позабуду мокрый лес,
И тот рассвет, – он был белес, –
И как средь призрачных стволов
Текло людское месиво,

Vladimir Lifshits (1913–1978)

Lifshits had to invent James Clifford, a British poet-soldier, killed in the War, in order to express his own thoughts about the war. This poem is a supposed translation from Clifford.

The Retreat

Oh, if you knew what fun we had,
when we were written off as dead,
when life was of no value,
and death was meaningless...
The five of us were left behind
down in the freezing bunker.
The high command had taken off –
those yellow-bellied plonkers!
We drank the whiskey from a tin,
destroying all that we could see:
the lists, the orders, maps and forms,
were torn apart and scattered.
I heard the distant battle roar,
and I felt free – so help me, Lord!
Yes, I was free to be myself,
and that is all that mattered!
And for the first time in my life,
I stood there free of inner strife,
free of the doubts and worries
that held me on a tether.
Yes, I was free of your intrigues,
your scurrying and pulling strings –
the whole mess altogether!
I will forget those woods, that dawn,
the hordes of people streaming down,
but I'll remember till I'm dead,

Но не забуду никогда,
Как мы срывали провода,
Как в блиндаже приказы жгли,
Как всё крушили, что могли,
И как нам было весело!

1964

trashing the bunker when all fled,
watching the orders burn unread,
tearing the wires off the wall,
and in that final free-for-all,
just how much fun we had!

1964

ОЛЬГА ФЕДОРОВНА БЕРГГОЛЬЦ

Although the relationship between Berggolts and Akhmatova was complex, there was a closeness brought about by their work together on the Leningrad radio station during the siege of Leningrad. Berggolts publicly supported Akhmatova after Zhdanov's attack in 1946.

Анна Ахматова в 1941 году в Ленинграде

У Фонтанного дома, у Фонтанного дома,
у подъездов, глухо запахнутых,
у резных чугунных ворот
гражданка Анна Андреевна Ахматова,
поэт Анна Ахматова
на дежурство ночью встает.
На левом бедре ее
тяжелеет, обвиснув, противогаз,
а по правую руку, как всегда, налегке,
в покрывале одном,
приоткинутом
над сиянием глаз,
гостья милая – Муза
с легкою дудочкою в руке.
А напротив, через Фонтанку, –
немые сплошные дома,
окна в белых крестах. А за ними ни искры,
ни зги.
И мерцает на стеклах
жемчужно-прозрачная тьма.
И на подступах ближних отброшены
снова враги.
О, кого ты, кого, супостат, захотел
превозмочь?
Или Анну Ахматову,
вставшую у Фонтанного дома,
от Армии невдалеке?

OLGA BERGGOLTS

Akhmatova lived in the former Sheremetiev Palace on Fontanka.
When the siege began, she was on watch at her building as part of the
anti-fire and anti-gas squads. She is cast here as a symbol of poetry,
who withstood not only the Nazi invaders but also the post-war State
repressions.

Anna Akhmatova in Leningrad, 1941

By the house on Fontanka, that house on Fontanka,
with boarded-off entrances,
and ornate iron gates,
the citizen Anna Andreevna Akhmatova,
the poet Anna Akhmatova,
rises for night duty with the patrol brigade.
On her left hip sags the heavy gas mask,
and to her right, travelling light,
clad in little more than a veil
raised above shining eyes,
is her sweet guest – the Muse,
slender reed pipe in hand.
Across from them,
on the other side of Fontanka,
nothing but silent buildings,
their windows taped over with white crosses.
Behind the windows, it's pitch black,
not even a glimmer.
The window panes shimmer
with pearly translucent darkness.
The enemy was fought back again
at the approaches to the city.
Oh, who was it, who was it
that you, evil rogue, had tried to defeat?
Was it Anna Akhmatova,
on guard by the house on Fontanka,
the army fighting nearby?

Или стражу ее, ленинградскую эту бессмертную
белую ночь?
Или Музу ее со смертельным оружьем,
с легкой дудочкой
в легкой руке?

1970 или 1971

Or her sentry – this immortal
Leningrad white night?
Or her Muse, with her deadly weapon,
a slender reed pipe
held in slender hand?

1970 or 1971

ЮЛИЯ ВЛАДИМИРОВНА ДРУНИНА

Drunina, a frontline poet who became famous after the war, had difficulties accepting the harshness and soullessness of post-Soviet society of the nineties. The death of her husband was also a terrible blow. She committed suicide, writing in her suicide note about the impossibility of living in this 'horrible backbiting world, made for pushy dealers.'

'Я опять о своем, невеселом...'

Я опять о своем, невеселом, –
Едем с ярмарки, черт побери!..
Привыкают ходить с валидолом
Фронтовые подружки мои.
А ведь это же, честное слово,
Тяжелей, чем таскать автомат...
Мы не носим шинелей пудовых,
Мы не носим военных наград.
Но повсюду клубится за нами,
Поколеньям другим не видна –
Как мираж, как проклятье, как знамя –
Мировая вторая война...

1967

YULIA DRUNINA

The postwar trauma of combat soldiers and civilians on the home front was barely acknowledged in the postwar years. The State wanted its citizens to stop dwelling on the horrors of the war and to start rebuilding for the future. The need to rebuild was, indeed, great, but those traumatized by the war were traumatized still further by being silenced.

'I'm Still on the Same Gloomy Topic...'

I'm still on the same gloomy topic –
we're all way over the hill...
The girls who fought on the frontlines,
now carry angina pills.
And that's much harder, believe me,
than to lug a machinegun around...
We don't wear our old army greatcoats,
or the medals we got at the front.
But it's always trailing behind us,
latecomers don't have a clue,
like a curse, a mirage, or a flag –
World War Two...

1967

ЛИДИЯ ДАВЫДОВНА ЧЕРВИНСКАЯ

Chervinskaya's family emigrated to France after the Revolution. In the 1930s, she was an extravagant and scandal-prone member of the Parisian émigré literary scene.

1939

Помню жестокие женские лица.
Жар иссушающий. Страх.
Как человек, поседела столица
в несколько дней, на глазах.

Долго над ней догорали закаты.
Долго несчастью не верил никто...
Шли по бульварам толпою солдаты –
в куртках, в шинелях, в пальто.

Не было в том сентябре возвращений
с моря и гор загорелых людей.
Сторож с медалью, в аллее осенней,
хмуро кормил голубей.

В каждом бистро, обнимая соседа,
кто-нибудь плакал и пел.
Не умолкала под песню беседа –
родина, слава, герои, победа...

Груды развалин и тел.

195?

LYDIA CHERVINSKAYA (1907–1988)

Chervinskaya worked for the Resistance, but was put on trial after the War for leaking classified information to her lover, who worked for the Gestapo.

1939

Lodged in my mind are the harsh women's faces.
Withering heat, and the fear.
Like an old man, all of Paris turned grey
in a matter of days, it appeared.

Long were the sunsets that faded above her.
Long did nobody believe in her woes...
Down her long boulevards soldiers came marching –
tunics, and greatcoats and cloaks.

Never did people come back that September,
Tanned from the hills and the sea.
Wearing a medal, a watchman tossed feed to the
birds in the autumnal street.

Inside the cafés, embracing their neighbours,
people in tears singing tunes.
Under their chorus continued their stories –
victory, motherland, heroes and glory...

Mountains of bodies and ruins.

195?

НИКОЛАЙ ФЕДОРОВИЧ ДОМОВИТОВ

Domovitov, a Leningrad poet, fought on the Leningrad front and was twice wounded. Recovering in hospital, he was arrested and sent to the Gulag. There he continued to write poetry; his poems, put to music, were popular with the Gulag inmates. After rehabilitation, he worked in the Donbass mines.

Витька

Десять лет мы с Витькою дружили.
Неплохой был вроде паренек.
Никогда уроков не зубрили,
Хоть и строг был старый педагог.
Беспокойно было в нашем мире...
Чтоб о днях грядущих не гадать,
Мы с дружком учились в школьном тире
По врагам без промаха стрелять.
А когда без шума, без обмолвки
Вдруг на нас обрушились враги,
Получил в каптерке я обмотки,
Витька в трибунале – сапоги.
Получил я старую винтовку,
Витьке дали новенький наган.
Как в обмотках тяжко и неловко
Мне бежать в смертельный ураган!
Скоро жизнь прервется молодая.
Все смешалось, будто бы в аду.
А потом, кого-то проклиная,
Я метался в тягостном бреду.
И, на жизнь мою поставив точку,
На исходе мартовского дня
С госпитальной койки – в одиночку
Увезли «сотрудники» меня.
Я этапа ждал на пересылке.
Эшелоны гнали за Урал.
А дружок мой в бритые затылки

NIKOLAI DOMOVITOV (1918–1996)

Domovitov was arrested because when he added up the figures of enemy dead provided by Pravda *he exclaimed, 'So who are we fighting with, if all the Nazis have been killed?*

Victor

Ten long years I was buddies with Victor,
and he seemed to be a decent lad.
The two of us never did homework,
though it made our old teacher mad.
The whole world was becoming uneasy,
days ahead felt uncertain and dark,
so we practiced at our school's gun club
to hit foes without missing the mark.
But when the foe finally struck us
(and he didn't hold back or stall),
I got footcloths at the army depot,
Victor got boots at the Tribunal.
I was issued an old army rifle,
Victor got a new handgun.
How clumsy I felt in my footcloths,
when we had to attack on the run!
I knew my young life was over,
everything turned upside down,
and I found myself in a hospital bed,
delirious and cursing someone.
Then, things got even grimmer:
that March, just as evening fell,
'operatives' took me from that bed
straight into a solitary cell.
And while I waited in jail for my transfer
on Ural-bound trains, it was said –
my old friend in Stalin's dungeons,

В подземельях сталинских стрелял.
Жизнь, как прежде, встречами богата,
Избежать и этой я не смог.
Что ж, здорово, Витька Куропатов!
Здравствуй, ворошиловский стрелок!

shoot prisoners in the back of their heads.
Life is rife with unexpected meetings,
this one too fell to my lot –
so, hullo there, Victor Kuropatov!
Well met, Voroshilov's crack shot!

СЕРГЕЙ СЕРГЕЕВИЧ НАРОВЧАТОВ

Narovchatov fought in the Finnish War and in the Second World War. Many accused him of becoming a functionary, especially when he attacked the young poets of the 1960s.

О главном

Не будет ничего тошнее, –
Живи ещё хоть сотню лет, –
Чем эта мокрая траншея,
Чем этот серенький рассвет.

Стою в намокшей плащ-палатке,
Надвинув каску на глаза,
Ругая всласть и без оглядки
Всё то, что можно и нельзя.

Сегодня лопнуло терпенье,
Осточертел проклятый дождь, –
Пока поднимут в наступленье,
До ручки, кажется, дойдёшь.

Ведь как-никак мы в сорок пятом,
Победа – вот она! Видна!
Выходит срок служить солдатам,
А лишь окончится война,
Тогда-то, главное, случится!..

И мне, мальчишке, невдомёк,
Что ничего не приключится,
Чего б я лучше делать смог.
Что ни главнее, ни важнее
Я не увижу в сотню лет,
Чем эта мокрая траншея,
Чем этот серенький рассвет.

1970

SERGEI NAROVCHATOV (1919–1981)

Narovchatov was one of the bright hopes of Moscow's prewar IFLI. Like many of his generation, he came to believe that the War was the most significant part of his life.

The Greatest Thing

You won't see a thing more dreary,
even if you live on and on,
then this waterlogged trench,
and this pallid grey dawn.

I'm standing in my sodden cape,
my helmet pushed down low,
cursing a heartfelt blue streak
at the whole of it, tip to toe.

Today I've finally had it!
Can't stand the bloody rain!
They stall with orders to attack
till you could go insane.

Isn't this nineteen forty-five?
It's almost Victory! We won!
Our soldiers' job is nearly over,
and once the war is done,
all the great things will come!

I didn't know back then, I was a kid –
there won't be anything at all,
where I could outdo what I did.
I never saw anything greater
even as I lived on and on,
then that waterlogged trench,
and that pallid grey dawn.

1970

БУЛАТ ШАЛВОВИЧ ОКУДЖАВА

As the child of an 'enemy of the people' Okudzhava was especially keen to enlist when the War began. He served as a mortar gunner, was wounded and decorated. The Taman Peninsula is in the Northern Caucasus.

Тамань

Год сорок первый. Зябкий туман.
Уходят последние солдаты в Тамань.

А ему подписан пулей приговор.
Он лежит у кромки береговой,
он лежит на самой передовой:
ногами – в песок,
            к волне – головой.

Грязная волна наползёт едва –
приподнимется слегка голова;
вспять волну прилив отнесет –
ткнется устало голова в песок.

Эй, волна!
      Перестань, не шамань:
            не заманишь парня в Тамань...

Отучило время меня дома сидеть.
Научило время меня в прорезь глядеть.
Скоро ли – не скоро, на том ли берегу
я впервые выстрелил на бегу.

Отучило время от доброты:
атака, атака, охрипшие рты...
Вот и я гостинцы раздаю-раздаю...
Ты прости меня, мама, за щедрость мою.

1958

BULAT OKUDZHAVA (1924–1997)

One of originators of the poet-bard movement, Okudzhava said that most of his poems and songs 'have something to do with the war... My memories keep trailing after me.'

Taman

It's nineteen forty-one. Cold fog shrouds the land.
The last few soldiers cross into Taman.

But one met a bullet that sealed his fate.
Down on the shore, by the water he'll stay,
right where the fighting raged that day;
his legs in the sand,
        his head in the bay.

The muddy wave creeps over the dead,
ever so slightly lifting his head;
then it turns back, all spent,
sending his head back onto the sand.

Stop your conjuring, wave!
    Stop rousing the man –
       you won't lure him into Taman...

The times said to me: no more sitting around.
The times said to me: learn to fire a gun.
Was it on that same shore – was it there, was it then
that I took my first shot on the run?

The times said to me: there's no use being kind.
Endless attacks, pay those bastards no mind.
I let them all have it, I give them their fill...
My kind-hearted mother – forgive me my zeal.

1958

Okudzhava later wrote: 'I enlisted right after I finished grade nine, in 1942. I enlisted not because I wanted adventure, but because I wanted to fight the Nazis. I was a patriot, but I romanticized everything too. The romanticism dissipated quickly, within a few days: it turned out that war was a difficult and bloody business.'

Бумажный солдат

Один солдат на свете жил,
красивый и отважный,
но он игрушкой детской был:
ведь был солдат бумажный.

Он переделать мир хотел,
чтоб был счастливым каждый,
а сам на ниточке висел:
ведь был солдат бумажный.

Он был бы рад – в огонь и в дым,
за вас погибнуть дважды,
но потешались вы над ним:
ведь был солдат бумажный.

Не доверяли вы ему
своих секретов важных,
а почему? А потому,
что был солдат бумажный.

В огонь? Ну что ж, иди! Идешь?
И он шагнул однажды,
и там сгорел он ни за грош:
ведь был солдат бумажный.

1959

'The Paper Soldier' is one of Okudzhava's early poem-songs. It quickly became immensely popular as a poem and as a song. Okudzhava's depiction of a brave and vulnerable young soldier consumed in the fires of the war was antithetical to the official representation of Soviet soldiers as heroic conquerors.

The Paper Soldier

There was a handsome soldier lad –
there weren't any braver,
but he was just a children's toy,
and he was made of paper.

He wanted to bring joy to all –
turn life into a caper,
but he was hanging by a thread,
that soldier made of paper.

He would've gone through hell for you,
he would've never wavered,
but all you did was laugh at him,
'cause he was made of paper.

You never shared your schemes with him,
no, he was never favoured...
And why is that? Because he was
a soldier made of paper.

Through hell, you said? Alright, let's go!
And so he went, the scraper,
and died for nothing in the flames,
that soldier made of paper.

1959

АРСЕНИЙ АЛЕКСАНДРОВИЧ ТАРКОВСКИЙ

After the war, Tarkovsky was silenced by the authorities, and he wrote poetry for the desk-drawer, publishing only his translations. During Khruschev's Thaw, he began to publish his poetry again, including new poems about the war.

Полевой Госпиталь

Стол повернули к свету. Я лежал
Вниз головой, как мясо на весах,
Душа моя на нитке колотилась,
И видел я себя со стороны:
Я без довесков был уравновешен
Базарной жирной гирей.

    Это было
Посередине снежного щита,
Щербатого по западному краю,
В кругу незамерзающих болот,
Деревьев с перебитыми ногами
И железнодорожных полустанков
С расколотыми черепами, чёрных
От снежных шапок, то двойных, а то
Тройных.

    В тот день остановилось время,
Не шли часы, и души поездов
По насыпям не пролетали больше
Без фонарей, на серых ластах пара,
И ни вороньих свадеб, ни метелей,
Ни оттепелей не было в том лимбе,
Где я лежал в позоре, в наготе,
В крови своей, вне поля тяготенья
Грядущего.

ARSENY TARKOVSKY (1907–1989)

Tarkovsky was declared unfit for military service, but he kept trying to enlist. Finally, after many attempts, he managed to go to the front as a war correspondent. Two years later, he was wounded, gangrene set in, and he had to have a series of progressive amputations, losing his leg in the process and surviving by a miracle.

Field Hospital

They turned the table to the light. I lay
upside down, like meat slapped onto a scale;
my soul swayed, dangling on a string,
I saw myself from the side:
balanced without makeweights,
against a fat mass from the market.

                              This was
in the middle of a snow shield,
chipped along its western edge,
surrounded by icy swamps,
by trees on broken legs,
and railroad halts with their skulls
cracked open, looking black
beneath their snowy caps, some double,
and some triple.

                  Time stopped that day,
clocks didn't run – the soul of trains
no longer flew along the mounds,
lightless, on grizzled fins of steam.
No gatherings of crows,
no blizzards, no thaws inside that limbo
where I lay naked in disgrace,
in my own blood, outside the pall
of future's gravity.

Но сдвинулся и на оси пошёл
По кругу щит слепительного снега,
И низко у меня над головой
Семёрка самолетов развернулась,
И марля, как древесная кора,
На теле затвердела, и бежала
Чужая кровь из колбы в жилы мне,
И я дышал как рыба на песке,
Глотая твёрдый, слюдяной, земной,
Холодный и благословенный воздух.

Мне губы обметало, и ещё
Меня поили с ложки, и ещё
Не мог я вспомнить, как меня зовут,
Но ожил у меня на языке
Словарь царя Давида.

               А потом
И снег сошёл, и ранняя весна
На цыпочки привстала и деревья
Окутала своим платком зелёным.

1964

But then it shifted, circling on its axis –
the shield of blinding snow.
A wedge of seven airplanes
turned low above me. And the gauze,
like tree bark, stiffened on my body,
while someone else's blood now ran
into my veins out of a flask, and I
breathed like a fish tossed on the sand,
gulping the hard, earthy, mica-like,
cold, and blessed air.

My lips were chapped, and then,
they fed me with a spoon, and then,
I couldn't recall my name,
while King David's lexicon
awoke upon my tongue.

     Then
snow melted away, and early spring
stood on her toes and wrapped
the trees with her green kerchief.

1964

ЛЕВ АДОЛЬФОВИЧ ОЗЕРОВ

Ozerov, a poet, translator, literary scholar, and editor, was born in Kiev and moved to Moscow to enrol in the famous IFLI before the War. He published his first book of poems in 1940. He was a war correspondent during the War. He faced repressions as a Jew during the postwar anti-cosmopolitan campaign, but was reinstated after Stalin's death.

Отрывок из 'Гудзенко' (Портреты без Рам)

На войну он ушел из ИФЛИ,
Как потом написал об этом.
Сперва был слагателем стихов,
Потом на войне стал поэтом.
Я встретил его на Маросейке –
Перебинтованного, неузнаваемого,
После ранения.
Обнялись, условясь о встрече.
Он ушел в военную газету.
Он и меня позвал в газету
«Победа за нами».
– Писал пейзажи – пиши заметки,
Лозунги, подтекстовки,
А захочешь – поэмы.
Да, очерки о солдатах,
О памятных датах.
Иногда Семен говорил:
– Кажется, ты умеешь... –
Младший хвалил старшего.

Семена ранили.
В госпитале он не вылежал.
«Я был пехотой в поле чистом,
В грязи окопной и в огне,
Я стал военным журналистом
В последний год на той войне».

LEV OZEROV (1914–1996)

Ozerov knew Gudzenko from their shared childhood in Kiev. Ozerov's unforgettable portrait of Gudzenko is part of his 'encyclopedia of Soviet life,' a collection of free verse poems, Portraits Without Frames.

from 'Gudzenko' *(Portraits Without Frames)*

...He went from the institute
straight to the front,
as he recounted later.
He'd written verse before,
but it was the war made him a poet.
I ran into him in Moscow, on Maroseyka,
bandaged, unrecognizable.
We embraced and agreed upon a time and place
we could meet again.
He went to work for an army newspaper,
Victory Shall Be Ours, and asked me to join him:
'You wrote idylls,now you must write articles,
slogans, captions –
even poems, if you like –
and stories about soldiers,
great battles in history.'
Sometimes, Semyon would say,
'I think you've got it...'
The freshman praising the senior.

Semyon had been severely wounded
and had left the hospital too early.
'I was a soldier fighting with my comrades
in muddy trenches, under fire;
Then I became a frontline correspondent
to cover the war's last year.'

Красив, непоседлив, удачлив,
Он возникал то тут, то там,
С армией шел, по ее пятам,
В глазах азарт,
Презренье к смерти.

Handsome, restless – he seemed so lucky,
showing up everywhere,
going forward with the first of our soldiers,
a spark of daring in his eyes,
and a contempt for death.

РАСУЛ ГАМЗАТОВИЧ ГАМЗАТОВ

Gamzatov, a Soviet Dagestani poet, wrote 'Cranes,' his meditation on war, death, and memory, in 1965. The poem's translation caught the eye of Mark Bernes who, with the composer Yan Frenkel, turned it into a song (the last one Bernes recorded before his death).

Журавли

Мне кажется порою, что солдаты,
С кровавых не пришедшие полей,
Не в землю нашу полегли когда-то,
А превратились в белых журавлей.

Они до сей поры с времен тех дальних
Летят и подают нам голоса.
Не потому ль так часто и печально
Мы замолкаем, глядя в небеса.

Летит, летит по небу клин усталый,
Летит в тумане, на исходе дня.
И в том строю есть промежуток малый,
Быть может, это место для меня.

Настанет день, и с журавлиной стаей
Я поплыву в такой же сизой мгле,
Из-под небес по-птичьи окликая,
Всех вас, кого оставил на земле...

1965, 1969

RASUL GAMZATOV (1923–2003)

Although Gamzatov said 'Cranes' is about soldiers in all wars, it became almost exclusively associated with the Second World War. Lines from 'Cranes' as well as the image of flying cranes figure on many war memorials, and the song is a staple at concerts dedicated to the remembrance of the War.

Cranes

Sometimes I think that soldiers, who have never
come back to us from the blood-covered plains,
escaped the ground and didn't cross the River,
but turned instead into white screeching cranes.

And since that time the flock is flying, narrow
or wide, or long – and maybe that is why
so often and with such a sudden sorrow
we stop abruptly, staring at the sky.

On flies the wedge trespassing every border –
a sad formation, ranks of do-re-mi,
and there's a gap in their open order:
it is the space they have reserved for me.

The day will come: beneath an evening cloud
I'll fly, crane on my right, crane on my left,
and in a voice like theirs, shrill and loud,
call out, call out to those on earth I've left.

1965, 1969

СЕМЁН ИЗРАИЛЕВИЧ ЛИПКИН

Lipkin, whose poetry was admired by Akhmatova and Brodsky, was best-known as a translator of poetry. He enlisted as a war correspondent in in the War and took part in the Battle of Stalingrad. He was later instrumental in sending Vasily Grossman's manuscript of Life and Fate *to the West.*

Зола

Я был остывшею золой
Без мысли, облика и речи,
Но вышел я на путь земной
Из чрева матери – из печи.

Еще и жизни не поняв
И прежней смерти не оплакав,
Я шел среди баварских трав
И обезлюдевших бараков.

Неспешно в сумерках текли
«Фольксвагены» и «мерседесы»,
А я шептал: «Меня сожгли.
Как мне добраться до Одессы?»

1967

SEMYON LIPKIN (1911–2003)

Lipkin wrote many poems about the tragedy of the Holocaust, a tragedy that he saw firsthand. He emphasized the interconnectedness of those who were killed and those who survived.

Charred

and ashen I whisper *I've been cremated*
in deserted barracks on Bavarian grasslands.
I think *I'm blind confounded*
my palate has claimed my tongue.

When Mercedes Benz' and Volkswagens
course silently through evening autobahns
I ask *how do I find my way to Odessa?*
Born burnt I can't yet mourn

what it means to be alive or dead.
My cold embers won't light a flame

1967

Lipkin served with the Kalmyk Cavalry Division in the War. The deportation depicted here is the Kalmyk deportations of 1943, when more than 93,000 Kalmyks were forcibly relocated to Siberia for forced labour, as collective punishment because some Kalmyks fought on the side of the Nazis.

Отрывок из 'Техника–Интенданта'

– За Родину! За Сталина! –
Это навстречу бронемашинам ринулся в степь
Командир обескровленного эскадрона,
Стоявшего насмерть в вишневых садах.
Ты вспомнил его: Церен Пюрбеев,
Гордость политработников, образцовый кавалерист,
У которого самое смуглое в дивизии лицо,
У которого самые белые зубы и подворотнички,
У которого под пленкой загара
Круглятся скулы и движутся желваки.
Маленький, в твердой бурке, он ладно сидит верхом,
Хотя у него неуклюжей формы
Противотанковое ружье.
Он стреляет в бортовую часть бронемашин.
Ему стыдно за нас, за себя, за свое племя,
За то материнское молоко,
Которое он пил из потной груди,
Он хочет верить, что поднимет бойцов,
Но все бегут, бегут.
И только ты как зачарованный смотришь, ты видишь:
Голова Пюрбеева в желтой пилотке
Отскакивает от черной бурки,
Лошадь вздрагивает, а бурка
Еще продолжает сидеть в седле...
Время! Что ты есть – мгновение или вечность?
Племя! Что ты есть – целое или часть?
Грамотная его сестра в это утро
Читает отцу в улусной кибитке
Полученный от Церена треугольник.
Безнадежно больной чабан с выщипанной бородкой
Кивает в лад

Lipkin considered 'Lieutenant Quartermaster' his most important work, and was proud that Akhmatova wept over it in 1961. The punitive deportation of the Kalmyks (as of other nationalities during the War) was a taboo topic.

from 'Lieutenant Quartermaster'

...The bled-white squadron's tiny remnant
Hears their Commander scream, 'Fight on
For Motherland, Stalin, your lives –
It's not over...' They see him rush
Toward the steppe, confront the tanks.
Remember him Tseren Pyurbeev
Our best comrade fighter,
The darkest-faced of the division
With the whitest teeth,
The cleanest undercollars,
The roundest cheekbones,
The most resolute jaw, clenched
Under its taught film of sunburnt skin,
Small, in his stiff felt cloak,
Steady in his saddle
Despite the heft of his
Anti-tank gun which he fires
Ashamed of us, himself,
His tribe, the milk he drank
From his mother's sweaty breast,
He wants to believe he'll raise the troops
But they just run. And I watch gripped,
See Pyurbeev's head, in his yellow field cap,
Bounce off his black felt cloak,
His horse flinches.
His cloak stays in the saddle –
Time, what are you, a moment, eternity?
Tribe, what are you, an ingredient, everything?
Tseren Pyurbeev's sister, Nina,
Read the letter that had just arrived

Учтиво, хорошо составленным словам сына,
А голова сына катится по донской траве.
Настанет ночь под новый, сорок четвертый год.
Его сестру, и весь улус, и все калмыцкое племя
Увезут на машинах, а потом в теплушках в Сибирь.
Но разве может жить без него степная трава,
Но разве может жить на земле человечество,
Если оно не досчитается хотя бы одного,
Даже самого малого племени?
Но что ты об этом знаешь, техник-интендант?
Ты недвижен, а время уносит тебя, как река.
Ты останешься жить, ты будешь стоять,
Не так, как теперь, в безумии бегства,
А в напряженном деловом ожидании,
Сырым, грязным, зимним утром
На сгоревшей станции под Сталинградом.
Ты увидишь непонятный состав, конвойных.
Из узкого, тюремного окна теплушки,
Остановившейся против крана с кипятком,
На тебя посмотрят косого разреза глаза,
Цвета подточенной напильником стали.
Такими глазами смотрят породистые кони,
Когда их в трехтонках, за ненадобностью,
Увозят на мясокомбинат,
Такими глазами смотрит сама печаль земли,
Бесконечная, как время
Или как степь.
Быть может, это смотрит сестра Церена,
Образованная Нина Пюрбеева,
Всегда аккуратная учительница,
Такая длиннокосая и такая тоненькая,
С твердыми понятиями о любви,
О синтаксисе, о культурности.
В ее чемодане, –
А им разрешили взять
По одному чемодану на человека –
Справка о геройской звезде
Посмертно награжденного брата,
Книга народного, буддийского эпоса,

From the front
This morning, in their nomad's tent
To her illiterate father.
As the sickly man's fingers
Slid down his sparse chin hair,
He kept time, nodded at each
Of his son's courteous, elegant phrases,
Now Pyurbeev's head rolls on the grass of the Don steppe,
And on the last night of 1943 – New Year's eve,
Pyurbeev's sister, their whole village, every Kalmyk tribe
Will be taken, first by truck then cattle train, to Siberia –
Can the Don steppe's grass survive when the last are gone,
Can mankind live on earth
If even one, even the smallest tribe
Is missing?
But what do I, Lieutenant Quartermaster, know about this?
I'm washed by time, like a river washes rock around its flows
I'll stay alive, stand,
But not like I do now, stunned by the retreat, it's insanity,
I'll stand anxious, expectant, in front of the
Platform's water taps, one hot one cold,
At a burnt-out station near Stalingrad,
On a dirty winter's morning.
Watched by long, steel-grey eyes
Which look out from the narrow prison windows
Of the box-car of a strange train, under army escort,
Eyes which plead like those of old horses
Loaded into huge slaughterhouse lorries,
Eyes which look like earth's sadness,
Old as time,
Endless as the steppe –
Maybe Tseren's sister
Will be one of them.
She was so modern
So neat, with her long braids,
So trim – a teacher,
With solid notions of love,
Syntax, culture.
She'll be allowed one suitcase,

Иллюстрированная знаменитым русским художником,
Кое-что из белья и одежды,
Пачка плиточного чая
И ни кусочка хлеба, чтобы обмануть голодный желудок,
Ни травинки, ни суслика,
А бывало,
Покойные родители и суслика бросали в казан.
В той же самой теплушке –
Круглая, крепкая, с налитыми ягодицами –
Золотозубая Тегряш Бимбаева,
Еще недавно видный профсоюзный деятель,
Мать четырех детей и жена предателя,
Полицая, удравшего вместе с немцами.
Она-то понимала, что ее непременно вышлют,
Она-то к этому заранее подготовилась,
В ее пяти чемоданах полно союзнических консервов,
Есть колбаса, есть концентраты.
От всего сердца
Она предлагает одну банку своей подруге,
Она предлагает одну банку сестре героя,
Но та не берет.
– Бери! Бери! – кричат старухи, –
Мы же одного племени, одной крови! –
Но та не берет.
– Бери! Бери! – кричат плоскогрудые молодые женщины, –
Разве она отвечает за мужа?
Что же ты стоишь, техник-интендант?
(Впрочем, ты уже будешь тогда капитаном.)
Видишь ты эту теплушку?
Слышишь ты эти крики?
Останови состав с высланным племенем:
Поголовная смерть одного, даже малого племени,
Есть бесславный конец всего человечества!
Останови состав, останови!
Иначе – ты виноват, ты, ты, ты виноват!

1960–1961

She'll take the certificate which attests
To her brother's posthumous Hero's Star,
A Buddhist folk epic – illustrated,
By a well-known Russian artist,
Underwear and clothes, a brick of tea
But not even the smallest piece of bread
To deceive a starved stomach,
Nor blade of grass, nor squirrel,
Which in her late parents' time
Would have been meat for the pot.
Maybe the fat, round, strong,
Fleshy buttocked, gold toothed,
Mother of four,
Trade-unionist head,
Tegryash Bimbaeva will be there,
Married to a traitor Politzei
Who'd run off with the Germans,
She'll know she's going to be reported,
She'll prepare cases of foreign tinned foods,
She'll offer Nina a can, which Nina will refuse,
'Take them, take them!' An old woman will shout,
'We're one tribe, one blood!' –
But Nina won't,
'Take them, take them!'
The bud-breasted adolescent girls will shout,
'You can't blame her for her husband!'
Why do you stand still, Lieutenant Quartermaster,
(Though, by then you'll be a Captain),
Do you see this box car,
Hear those screams,
Will you stop the train which exiles the tribe?
Killing any tribe, even a small one,
Is the shameful end of humanity,
Stop the train, stop the train,
If you don't, you're guilty, you, you're to blame.

1961–1963

АРКАДИЙ АКИМОВИЧ ШТЕЙНБЕРГ

Shteynberg's early poems enjoyed good reviews from both Mandelshtam and Mayakovsky. When his poetry couldn't be published, he worked as a translator. He was arrested in 1937. When his sentence was overturned, he enlisted in 1941 and served until 1944, when he was arrested again.

'Я День Победы праздновал во Львове...'

Я День Победы праздновал во Львове.
Давным-давно я с тюрьмами знаком.
Но мне в ту пору показалось внове
Сидеть на пересылке под замком.

Был день как день: баланда из гороха
И нищенская каша магара.
До вечера мы прожили неплохо.
Отбой поверки. Значит, спать пора.

Мы прилегли на телогрейки наши,
Укрылись чем попало с головой.
И лишь майор немецкий у параши
Сидел как добровольный часовой.

Он знал, что победителей не судят.
Мы победили. Честь и место – нам.
Он побеждён. И до кончины будет
Мочой дышать и ложки мыть панам.

Он, европеец, нынче самый низкий,
Бесправный раб. Он знал, что завтра днём
Ему опять господские огрызки
Мы, азиаты, словно псу швырнём.

ARKADY SHTEYNBERG (1907–1954)

Shteynberg was arrested following a denunciation, sent to Lvov from Bucharest under guard, by foot, and was in a Lvov transit jail on V-Day. After a three-year investigation, he was found guilty and sentenced to eight years in the Gulag.

'I Celebrated V-Day Down in Lvov...'

I celebrated V-Day down in Lvov.
By then I knew jails inside out.
But that day felt like my first one
inside a transfer jail, locked up.

It was a regular day: we got pea soup
and *magara* – a poor man's gruel.
We did alright, then it was night,
and lights out after roll call.

We laid ourselves down on our jackets
and covered up with our heads, to a man.
All but the German Major – like some guard,
he sat himself beside the piss can.

He knew that victors are not judged.
Ours was the glory, we were tops.
His side just lost. And till he died,
he'd smell the piss and get worst jobs.

A European – he was now a nothing.
He knew that, come tomorrow,
we, lowly Asians, would treat him like a dog,
and throw him our leftovers.

Таков закон в неволе и на воле.
Он это знал. Он это понимал.
И, сразу притерпевшись к новой роли,
Губ не кусал и пальцев не ломал.

А мы не знали, мы не понимали
Путей судьбы, её добро и зло.
На досках мы бока себе намяли.
Нас только чудо вразумить могло.

Нам не спалось. А ну засни попробуй,
Когда тебя корёжит и знобит
И ты листаешь со стыдом и злобой
Незавершённый перечень обид,

И ты гнушаешься, как посторонний,
Своей же плотью, брезгуешь собой—
И трупным смрадом собственных ладоней,
И собственной зловещей худобой,

И грязной, поседевшей раньше срока
Щетиною на коже впалых щёк...
А Вечное Всевидящее Око
Ежеминутно смотрит сквозь волчок.

1965

That is the law both in and out of jail.
He understood. He knew the score.
So he adjusted to his role at once,
and didn't wring his hands in sorrow.

We neither knew nor understood
the good and evil hands dealt out by fate.
We tossed all night on our bed-boards.
Only a miracle could set us straight.

We couldn't sleep. How could we sleep,
so angry, so ashamed, in such disgrace,
as we went through the endless list
of all the grievances we'd faced?

And we were sickened by our flesh,
disgusted like some strangers
by the carrion stench of our own palms,
and our emaciation,

the dirty stubble on our sunken cheeks,
gone grey before its time...
while the Eternal and All-seeing Eye
was looking through the peephole.

1965

ВСЕВОЛОД НИКОЛАЕВИЧ НЕКРАСОВ

During the War Nekrasov was evacuated as a child with his family to Kazan with his family. His father died of pellagra, and he himself almost died of dystrophy. Nekrasov's minimalist poems about the war challenged the Soviet and post-Soviet packaging of its remembrance.

из Дойче Бух

уже и споры пошли
кто же был
хуже

гитлер сталин здесь
стаин гитлер там
сталин гитлер здесь
       там
гитлер это сталин тогда
сталин это гитлер сейчас
и в то же время
гитлер это сталин сейчас
сталин это гитлер тогда же
и даже так
stalin ist hitler dort
заслуженный сталинист гитлер
hitler ist stalin hier
заслуженный гитлерист сталин
stalin hitler hier
stalin dort
да черт

гитлер
это сталин вчера
а сталин
черт это
это гитлер сегодня
сталин и гитлер и сталины гитлеры

VSEVOLOD NEKRASOV (1934–2009)

Nekrasov visited Germany in 1989 and 1992. This poem was an attempt to define and clarify his relationship to Germany and to ask what Soviet victory really meant.

from Doiche Bukh

the debates are already on
who was
worse

hitler stalin here
stalin hitler there
stalin hitler here
       there
hitler is stalin then
stalin is hitler now
and at the same time
hitler is stalin now
stalin is hitler back then
and even like
stalin ist hitler dort
the notorious stalinist hitler
hitler is stalin hier
the distinguished hitlerite stalin
stalin hitler hier
stalin dort
blast it

hitler
is stalin yesterday
but stalin
that bastard
is hitler today
stalin and hitler and stalins and hitlers

сапоги мозги гитлеры это сталины
вчера
сегодня
и завтра

мерзавцы они мерзавцы мерзавцами
а мы не мерзавцы у нас мерзавцы
мерзавцами и не называются

кто хуже был
кто это нам
теперь скажет-то
кто был хуже

поспорим лучше кому
хуже

на что спорим
спорим на будущее
спорим же
что нам тут
хуже пришлось
больше досталось

жили хуже кто
наверно уж мы
хуже жили
пострадавшие кто
тоже ведь мы
больше

/хотя понятно
поляки в польше
и того больше
всё   из-за той же
сталин-гитлер-гипер-гитлер-ост-вест-
джугашвили-шикльгрубер-политике/

boots brains hitlers are stalins
yesterday
today
and tomorrow

villains they are villains among villains
but we are not villains we have villains
but our villains are not called villains

who was worse
but who'll
tell us
now who was worse

what're the
stakes

staking the future
staking the claim
that we here
have it worse
took on more

who lived worse
well probably we
lived worse
who are the victims
we are again
more

/though we know
the poles in poland
took it even harder
all   because of that same
stalin-hitler-hyper-hitler-ost-vest-
Dzhugashvili-schicklgruber-politics/

и мы-то и победили
бедовали бедовали

действительно
и

но
как

за каждого
из ихних
своих наших
троих
если не четвертых
положив

и хорошо если двух
в живых оставив
из каждых ста
от звонка
до звонка
отвоевавших
так
какая же тогда это победа

победа победа победа победа
победа победа победа победа
победа победа победа победа
победа победа победа побед а
победа победа победа победа
победа победа победа победа
победа победа победа победа
победа победа победа побед а
победа победа победа победа
победа победа победа победа
победа победа победа победа
победа победа победа победа

and were the ones who won
woeful woeful

really
and

but
how

for every one
of theirs
of our own
three
if not four
laid down

and lucky if two
stayed alive
from every hundred
from start
to finish
all those spent in fighting
so
then how the hell is that victory

victory victory victory victory
victory victory victory victory
victory victory victory victory
victory victory victory victory
victory victory victory victor yes
victory victory victory victory
victory victory victory victory
victory victory victory victory
victory victory victory victor yes
victory victory victory victory
victory victory victory victory
victory victory victory victory

5 лет
10 лет
15
и 20
и 25 лет
и 30
и 40
и скоро 55 лет
победа победа победа побед –

до
последнего

да после этого
что ли для победы война
да она
подлая
если
для чего-то была
то
для одного

чтоб
ее
не было

подобная победа уже
похоже
ужо себе
похуже будет
выходит
и по дорожке выйти может
быть
и потяжелей
другого типа уже
и поражения

        5 years
        10 years
        15
and 20
and 25 years
and 30
and 40
and soon 55 years
victory victory victory victor –

to
the last

yes after that
what for victory is war
yes it's
base
if
it was for something
then
only for this

that
it
not exist

this kind of victory already
seems a woe
to ye
it'll be worse
and dearer
it could well
be
and harder
a different kind now
and defeats

нет
а мы-то
в войне-то мы
победить-то мы в войне победили
то-то и оно
   но

разгромить
в мире

так
как это они нас разгромилиа

милые мои

вы только взгляните

◊ *

1990, 1991

no
but we now
in war we
know victory in war we were victorious
well maybe
   but

to wreck
the world

like that
what they're the ones who wrecked us

my dears

just take a look

◊ *

1990, 1991

ВАДИМ ВИКТОРОВИЧ КОВДА

Kovda was five years old when Germany attacked the USSR. Memories of his wartime childhood and post-war adolescence, the fate of war veterans and the aftermath of the war are the focus of many of his poems.

На дружеской встрече ветеранов

Фриц морщинистый, прыткий, поджарый,
малость выпил – его не унять:
– Нет-нет-нет!! Мне не снятся кошмары.
Но хочу я хоть что-то понять.

– Мы вас били... Но всё потеряли...
Я ведь помню... Я в здравом уме.
Это как же мы ВАМ! проиграли?
Вон у вас всё доныне в дерьме!

– Мусор, ямины, грязь и вонища
среди тучной и щедрой земли.
ЗДЕСЬ у вас до сих пор пепелище,
словно танки недавно прошли!

– Сколько лиц, измождённых и пьяных!
Как мутна в вашей речке вода...
Это мне не понятно и странно,
что мы вас не добили тогда...

– Как мы шли! И как пели крылато!
Вот уж Химки!! Нам скоро домой...
Проиграли бы Англии..., Штатам...
Ну а ВАМ-то... – ах, Боже ты мой...!

А наш Ваня – дышал перегаром.
Улыбался... И слёзы из глаз.
Фриц сосал дорогую сигару
и угрюмо косился на нас...

2002

VADIM KOVDA (1936–)

Kovda visited Germany in the late 1990s, seeking treatment for a devastating illness. He settled there and continued to write poems about post-war realities.

At a Veteran Get-together

A spry old Fritz knocked back a few,
now there's no holding him back:
'No, no! I don't have any nightmares –
there's one problem that I just can't crack.

We were winning... Then it was over...
I remember... I'm mentally fit.
How is it that we lost to YOU then?
Look around – you're still drowning in shit!

This country could have been heaven –
but the trash, the potholes, the stink...
It's a pigsty, as if we had only
just now rolled through in our tanks!

All those faces, haggard and drunken!
All those rivers flowing with waste...
I can't figure out how we failed then –
we should have crushed you posthaste!

How we marched! How our voices soared proudly!
We'd take Moscow in no time flat...
If we'd lost to the Brits or the Yanks... Well...
But to YOU? No... No sense in that!'

Our old Ivan with booze on his breath,
just smiled, his eyes full of tears,
while the Fritz sucked his fancy cigar
and threw us all sullen stares.

2002

ЮРИЙ ДАВИДОВИЧ ЛЕВИТАНСКИЙ

Levitansky was called a poet 'of private despair' by Samoilov. He enlisted in the beginning of the War and was demobilized only in 1947.

'Ну что с того, что я там был...'

Ну что с того, что я там был.
Я был давно, я все забыл.
Не помню дней, не помню дат.
И тех форсированных рек.
Я неопознанный солдат.
Я рядовой, я имярек.
Я меткой пули недолет.
Я лед кровавый в январе.
Я крепко впаян в этот лед.
Я в нем как мушка в янтаре.

Ну что с того, что я там был.
Я все забыл. Я все избыл.
Не помню дат, не помню дней,
названий вспомнить не могу.
Я топот загнанных коней.
Я хриплый окрик на бегу.
Я миг непрожитого дня,
я бой на дальнем рубеже.
Я пламя вечного огня,
и пламя гильзы в блиндаже.

Ну что с того, что я там был.
В том грозном быть или не быть.
Я это все почти забыл,
я это все хочу забыть.
Я не участвую в войне,
война участвует во мне.
И пламя вечного огня
горит на скулах у меня.

YURI LEVITANSKY (1922–1996)

Although Levitansky published poems in army newspapers, he avoided writing about the War after it was over. This famous poem is an exception.

'So What if I Was There Back Then?'

So what if I was there back then?
It's long forgotten, it's all spent.
I don't recall the days, the dates,
the rivers crossed in the attacks.
I'm the dead they couldn't trace.
I'm rank and file, I'm soldier X.
I'm a bullet's undershot.
I'm slabs of bloody ice in winter –
I'm frozen in that icy spot,
suspended, like a fly in amber.

So what if I was there back then?
I've lived out all that I can stand.
I don't recall the dates, the days,
I can't recall the names of towns.
I'm horses galloping in a daze.
I'm shouts of warning on the run.
I'm the moment of an unlived day,
I'm the frontier's desperate fight.
I'm the fire of the eternal flame
and of the dugout's makeshift light.

So what if I was there back then –
in that grim to-be-or-not-to-be...
I had forgotten all I can,
I'd like to forget all I've seen.
I didn't *take part* in the war,
the war became a part of me.
The blaze of the eternal flame
scorches my cheekbones to this day.

Уже меня не исключить
из этих лет, из той войны.
Уже меня не излечить
от тех снегов, от той зимы.
И с той зимой, и с той землей,
уже меня не разлучить.
До тех снегов, где вам уже
моих следов не различить.

You can't expel me anymore
out of those years and from that war.
And you can't heal me anymore
after that winter and those storms,
and from that winter and that land
you cannot part me anymore.
Until that final snowfall comes –
turning my footsteps to a blur.

ИВАН ВЕНЕДИКТОВИЧ ЕЛАГИН

Elagin was in Kiev during the Nazi Occupation. He and his wife Olga Anstei left Kiev with the retreating Germans, stayed in a DP camp, then emigrated to the USA, where Elagin taught Russian literature and published his poetry.

Наплыв

Мы выезжали из Чикаго,
А может быть, из Конотопа,
Из Киева, из Магадана,
И, как в атаку из окопа,
Кидался ветер из оврага
И налетал на нас нежданно.

Мы выезжали из Чикаго.
Нас было четверо в машине.
Тот день был днем последним года.
Шоссе белело, как бумага,
Стояла зимняя погода,
Но снега не было в помине.

Но память не дает мне спуску,
Переставляет то и это
По собственному произволу.
(Вот по Андреевскому спуску
Мчит Скорой помощи карета
По направлению к Подолу.)

Мы выезжали из Чикаго.
Катились мы по автостраде.
Ветров могучая ватага
Нас била спереди и сзади,
Ветров свирепая орава
Нас била слева, била справа.

IVAN ELAGIN (1918–1987)

Elagin enrolled on a German-run medical course in Kiev in order to avoid deportation to Germany. In this poem, the memory of driving a dying soldier to hospital under shelling is superimposed on a car accident he had years later in Chicago.

Fadeout

We drove out of Chicago
(or Konotop, or Kiev,
or maybe Magadan?)
and were abruptly ambushed
by the ravine-based winds
that lunged at our sedan.

We drove out of Chicago.
The year was on its last day,
and we were four in all.
The road spread pale as paper,
and it was winter weather
without a trace of snow.

But memory cuts me no slack,
it switches things around,
true to its own intent.
(An ambulance is speeding
toward the Podol district
down Andreev's Descent.)

We drove out of Chicago
and rolled along the highway.
A mighty squad of winds
hit us both front and back;
they slammed us left and right,
that crew of blustery fiends.

Мы выезжали из Чикаго.
(А может быть, из Куреневки
Мы ехали на хутор Грушки.
Забылся раненый, бедняга.
За городом без остановки
Переговаривались пушки.)

Мы выезжали из Чикаго,
Мы не заметили, что в трансе
Мы очарованно застыли,
Что мы не сделали ни шагу,
Что едем в том автомобиле
Во времени, а не в пространстве.

Мы выезжали из Чикаго.
Над озером кричали птицы.
Мы в путь пустились на рассвете.
(Еще далеко до больницы.
Очнулся раненый в карете,
На нем шинель, пилотка, фляга.)

Мы выезжали из Чикаго.
Оставленные небоскребы
Вдали затягивались дымом.
Мгновенье – как земная тяга,
Мгновенье нам дается, чтобы
Остаться в нас неистребимым.

(Трясло карету на пригорке.
Его шатало и бросало,
Но он держался, молодчага,
И только попросил устало
Свернуть закрутку из махорки.)
Мы выезжали из Чикаго

We drove out of Chicago.
(Or was it Kurenevka?
We drove to Grushki hamlet,
the wounded man passed out.
The guns, just out of town,
kept up their endless racket.)

We drove out of Chicago,
not knowing we're entranced,
enchanted, in a daze.
We hadn't gained a single inch,
because our car was driving
through time and not through space.

We drove out of Chicago,
The birds screeched at the lake.
We left at crack of dawn.
(The hospital was far away,
the wounded man awoke,
wedge cap and greatcoat on.)

We drove out of Chicago.
The skyscrapers behind us
were covered up by smoke.
A moment is like gravity,
its pull is indestructible,
it stays within us locked.

(Uphill, the ambulance juddered,
and he got knocked and battered;
but hung on even so,
just asking us if someone
could roll him some tobacco.)
We drove out of Chicago,

Или из даты новогодней?
Из календарного порядка?
Из часового циферблата?
Из потускневшего сегодня?
Мы двинулись в «давно когда-то»,
У нас на звездах пересадка.

(А из дорожного зигзага
Еще не вырвалась карета,
Ухабам отдана на милость.
Мне, может быть, тогда приснилось,
Что я за океаном где-то,
Что выезжаю из Чикаго.

И может быть – еще мне снится
Иль кажется, по крайней мере,
Что клиника за поворотом.
Но раненного минометом
Не довезли мы до больницы –
Скончался от кровопотери.)

Ну как угомониться слабым,
Войной чудовищною смятым,
Моим издергавшимся нервам?
Я думал, в семьдесят девятом,
А оказалось – в сорок первом
Еще я еду по ухабам!..

(Я снова в Киеве военном,
Я с коченеющим солдатом
Лечу по спускам и подъемам,
А день расплавился закатом
По этим, с детства мне знакомым,
Кирпичным желтоватым стенам.)

or was it out of New Year's –
or did we leave the calendar,
or the hours on our clock,
or our tarnished present?
We headed for 'long-time-ago' –
stopover at the stars.

(But the ambulance still rode
that snaking road, careening
over bumps high and low.
And maybe I was dreaming
that, way across the ocean,
I drove out of Chicago.

And maybe I was dreaming,
or else it seemed to me,
that the hospital was near.
But the man hit by the mortar,
had suffered too much blood loss,
and never made it there.)

How can I calm my feeble nerves,
brutally crushed
by that horrific war?
I thought I was in 'seventy-nine,
instead, I was in 'forty-one,
my pedal to the floor!..

(I am again in wartime Kiev,
speeding along the hilly streets
together with the stiffening soldier.
The day had melted into sunset,
upon these walls of yellow brick
familiar since childhood.)

А мне казалось – из Чикаго
Я выехал в автомобиле.
(Но вот пошла дорога криво,
И мы с трудом заколесили,
И около универмага
Нас бросило волною взрыва.

Но уцелела всем на диво
Разболтанная колымага.
Вослед за этим взрывом третье
Уже прошло десятилетье) –
Мы по дороге из Чикаго
От этого взлетели взрыва!

Машина сумасшедшей птицей
На сосны кинулась с откоса
И загремела вдоль оврага,
И на дороге из Чикаго
Я с переломанной ключицей,
Я с кровью, хлынувшей из носа.

Колен разорванные связки
И переломанные ребра,
Десятки синяков и ссадин.
Я очень скоро буду найден,
И, как Иван-царевич в сказке,
Я буду по кусочкам собран.

Меня положат на носилки,
И вежливые санитары
Перенесут меня в карету,
И, несмотря на боль в затылке,
На переломы, на удары,
У них спрошу я сигарету.

And here, I thought, it was Chicago
that I was leaving in my car...
(The road went sideways fast,
we zigzagged but kept going,
and right by the department store
got sideswiped by a blast.

But the broken-down jalopy
survived to our amazement.
More than three decades passed
since that store-side explosion) –
still, on the road out of Chicago
we were launched by that blast!

Like some crazed bird, our car
plunged down the pine-lined gorge,
and flew across the slopes.
And near the road out of Chicago
I lay with a cracked collarbone,
blood gushing from my nose.

My knee ligaments were torn,
and many ribs were broken;
I was full of scrapes and scratches.
But very soon they'd find me,
and piece me back together,
just like Ivan-Tsarevich.

The polite paramedics
would put me on a stretcher,
and carry me aloft.
And lying in the ambulance,
despite the pain and fractures,
I'd ask them for a smoke.

В карете на носилках лежа,
Затягиваюсь струйкой дыма,
Я понимаю, что мне плохо,
Что жизнь моя непоправима,
И с чем-то очень давним схожа
Сегодняшняя суматоха,
Сегодняшняя передряга,
Что я живу уже сверх плана,
Что существую рикошетом,
Что, видимо, по всем приметам
Не существует ни Чикаго,
Ни Киева, ни Магадана,
Ни Конотопа, ни вселенной,
А только есть одна дорога,
А на дороге катастрофы...

And lying on that stretcher,
and taking in a drag,
I'd know I'm in a bad way,
that my life can't be fixed
and that the day's ordeal,
all of the day's commotion,
were strangely reminiscent of
of something long ago,
and that I've been alive too long,
I was living on a rebound,
and it seemed there's no Chicago,
no Kiev, no Magadan,
no Konotop, no universe –
there was a single road
lined with catastrophes...

ИРИНА ВИКТОРОВНА МАШИНСКАЯ

Irina Mashinski, born in Moscow, is a bilingual poet, translator, editor, author of ten books of poetry and translation. She emigrated to the US in 1991.

В Югендстиле. Браунау-Ам-Инн

Ночевала тучка золотая
        на груди у Гитлера младенца.
    Кружева слегка приподымались
все еще далекой занавески.
Улыбалось ласковое чрево
    мира, прогибавшегося к югу,
    улетала чудо-занавеска.
    То ей захотелось восвояси,
        то скользила внутрь, на подоконник
        налегала, словно это мама
        гладила, скользя по одеялу
        алою атласною ладонью.
            Месяц нам какой апрель достался –
            утренний, летящий, изумрудный,
            Климт червленый, и Бердслей червивый –
            ядовитая пыльца балкона
            Как живые, движутся обои,
            как живые легкие картины,
            кружево ласкает подбородок –
        Кто зияет в дыры золотые?
    Солнце, словно радио, играло,
с нами ни за что не расстается...
Ночевала тучка где попало,
    а проснулась – радио играет,
        песни распевает из колодца.

2000

IRINA MASHINSKI (1958–)

This poem written at the turn of the millennium, during the Second Chechen War, is arguably the most chilling of the entire anthology, a darkly foreboding contemplation of baby Hitler.

In Jugendstil. Braunau Am Inn

A golden cloud
on baby Hitler's chest
Laced curtain far away —
where that light is – bright
bulges the world outside cambers
and curves towards the East –
Breeze – and the curtain
flies away, then suddenly steps in
leaning on the window sill
– like Mutter, strokes unrippled blanket
with her scarlet satin palm.
Late April trembles on the
wallpaper, sweeps to the door in one move
– like pictures in the magic lantern –
its greenish patterns.
Sleep! little sheep sing
their quiet *Donna, donna*
look how they amble down. Sleep,
Klimt shines in gilded windows,
and Beardsley's railing snakes
and meanders on balconies.
Who shows through the golden gaps?
Healthy evening Sun plays
like a radio
spinning its wired waltzes.

2000

ВЕРА АНАТОЛЬЕВНА ПАВЛОВА

Pavlova, born in Moscow, has published 22 books and written several opera libretti. She lives in Moscow, New York and Toronto.

'Дед Матвей вернулся с войны...'

Дед Матвей вернулся с войны
на немецком велосипеде
раньше, чем из братской страны
располневший дедушка Федя.
Дед Матвей привёз пистолет,
сапоги, несушку в корзине,
а у Феди трофеев нет –
он уже тогда был разиней!

1998

VERA PAVLOVA (1963–)

This poem, an ironic reworking of the canonical 'soldier's return home' theme, is based on Pavlova's two grandfathers' return home after the War. One, a political instructor, ended the war as a Major. The other, an illiterate private, returned to his native village in September 1945; his family didn't know that the War was over.

'Grandpa Matvey Returned from War...'

Grandpa Matvey returned from the front
riding a trophy German bike,
long before Grandpa Fedia came back
all plumped up, at a higher rank.
Grandpa Matvey brought back a gun,
boots, and a basket with a laying hen,
but Grandpa Fedia brought back nothing –
    a loser even then!

1998

ВИТАЛИЙ ВЛАДИМИРОВИЧ ПУХАНОВ

Pukhanov, a Moscow-based poet, writer and editor, graduated from the Maxim Gorky Literary Institute shortly after the fall of the Soviet Union. He has written four books of poetry.

'В эвакуации под Саратовом...'

В эвакуации под Саратовом маме давали в школе кусочек хлеба
в обед.
Мама хлеб не съедала, заворачивала в исписанную на уроке
газету.
Тогда чистописанием занимались не в тетради, а на газетах
В пробелах между строк передовиц.
Мама несла хлеб в чужой дом, приютивший беженцев,
Где ждала трёхлетняя сестра, стояла у дверей и ждала хлеб.
Спустя семьдесят пять лет сестра возит маме через весь город
еду.
Мама не выходит из дома, потому что ей много лет,
Как сестра не выходила из дома в эвакуации, потому что ей
было мало лет.
А потом было долгое возвращение в освобожденный Крым,
И сразу депортация из Крыма в Соликамск.
Мама сбежала в пути, возвращалась ночью через обезлюдевшие
села,
Постучалась в окно родственницы, женщина была замужем за
русским, ее не стали высылать.
«Уходи, девочка» – добрым голосом сказала женщина и закрыла
дверь.
И мама пошла в ночь, шла и шла, и еще шла,
И выросла большая, и стало всё у мамы хорошо.
Но в семье не принято было вспоминать о прошлом,
Не принято делиться горем,
Не принято обнимать и гладить по голове,

VITALY PUKHANOV (1966–)

While Pukhanov's father and both his grandfathers were in the army,
his grandmother and her four daughters were forcibly deported from
the Crimea, because they were Bulgarian.

'During the Evacuation, Near Saratov...'

During the evacuation, near Saratov, my mom would get a small
piece of bread for lunch.
Mom never ate the bread but wrapped it into the newspaper she
wrote on during the lesson.
Back then you practiced writing not in a notebook, but on the
newspaper page,
In the white spaces between the lines of the front-page stories.
Mom brought the bread to a house that took in the refugees,
Where her three-year-old sister stood by the door and waited for
bread.
Seventy-five years later, the sister brings my mom food from across
the city.
Mom doesn't leave the house now, because she is too old.
Just as her sister didn't leave the house during the evacuation,
because she was too little.
Then there was the long return to the Crimea, liberated from the
Germans,
And then a deportation from the Crimea to Solikamsk.
Mom ran away on route, travelling at night through villages without
people,
She knocked on the window of a relative, a woman married to a
Russian, and so, not deported.
'Go away, little girl,' – the woman said in a kind voice and closed the
door.
So mom walked off into the night, and walked and walked,
Then mom grew up and everything worked out just fine.
But we didn't talk about the past in our family,
We didn't share sorrows,
We didn't hug or stroke each other's hair,

Целовать в лоб и жалеть.

Но я учусь по самоучителю с вырванными страницами.
Пусть объятия мои медвежьи, а поцелуи мокрые,
Добрые слова не всегда искренние, а будто с подъёбкой.
Но я хотя бы пытаюсь,
Я пытаюсь.

2016

Or kiss each other on the forehead, or empathize.

But I'm learning how to, even though the self-help book has pages
missing.
Even though my embraces are clumsy, and my kisses sloppy,
And my kind words sound mocking and not always sincere.
But at least I'm trying,
I'm trying.

2016

ПОЛИНА ЮРЬЕВНА БАРСКОВА

Barskova is a poet, writer, and scholar with a special interest in the siege of Leningrad, her birth city. She debuted a poet at a precociously young age and has since published eleven books of poetry, as well as several books about the siege. She lives and teaches in the USA.

'Старуха Гиппиус брезгливых кормит птиц...»

Старуха Гиппиус брезгливых кормит птиц
Под ней шатается скамейка
А на скамейке, сбоку от неё
Все, кто ушёл по льду, по илу
В самопроклятие, в безвидное житьё –
В посмертия воздушную могилу.
Кого блокада и голодомор
Вскормили чистым трупным ядом,
Кто убежав нквдшных нор
Исполнил заданное на дом:
Избыть свой дом, не оставлять следов,
Переменить лицо-привычку,
Среди послевоенных городов
В анкете ставить жирный прочерк/птичку
Приманивать: мы ниоткуда, мы
Никто, мы – выбравшие плохо
Мы двоечники в строгой школе тьмы
И чистоплюйская эпоха
Нас подотрёт как пыль – до одного
Чтоб следующим не было повадно
Рассматривать и плакать существо,
Чумные на котором пятна.

2017

POLINA BARSKOVA (1976–)

This recent poem tries to place the War in the context of other events of the Soviet epoch, and contemplates the postwar reality for people who lived through the various 'plagues' of the twentieth century and those who remain only as shadows in the memories of the aged survivors.

'Old Lady Gippius Feeds the Squeamish Birds...'

Old lady Gippius feeds the squeamish birds
the park bench wobbles underneath her
and by her side, on that same bench,
sit all who trudged the ice and sludge
to self-damnation, to a dead-end domicile –
to the aerial graves of afterlife.
Those whom the Siege and Holodomor
fed unalloyed cadaver poison,
who finished all their prescribed chores,
after escaping the NKVD's warrens:
left home, leaving behind no trace,
changed face and habit, amid postwar cities
filled out all forms by writing in the space
a bold dash – inviting a check: see,
we're nobodies from nowhere, fools,
whose choices weren't sage,
we're failures of darkness's strict school,
and our neat-freak age
will wipe us off as dust, seeing
to it that all avoid the big mistake:
to look upon and cry over a being
who bears stigmata of the Plague.

2017

Notes

Pavel Kogan, *A Letter*
Triangular postmarks were stamped on letters sent from so-called evacuation hospitals that treated soldiers evacuated from the battlefield.

Georgy Ivanov, *'Immortal Music Tells the Story...'*
Tchaikovsky's *1812 Overture* (1880) celebrated Russia's victory over Napoleon's armies at the battle of Borodino. 'Lads, isn't Moscow behind us?' is a famous line from Mikhail Lermontov's poem 'Borodino' (1837); it was supposedly used as a rallying cry by the 28 guardsmen of the Panfilov Division who held off the German attack on Moscow at the price of their own lives.

Justina Kruzenshtern-Peterets, *Russia*
Kitezh is a mythological Russian holy city that, according to legend, still goes on with its day-to-day life under the waters of a lake, where it was divinely submerged to save its inhabitants from the Golden Horde. In some versions of the myth, the city occasionally rises up to the surface of the lake. It can be seen only by the holy and the pure of heart.

Marina Tsvetaeva, *O, I Refuse*
On 15 March 1939, German troops occupied the rest of Czecho-slovakia. Tsvetaeva was writing to her friend and correspondent, Ariadna Berg.

Konstantin Levin, *And Our Own Artillery Buried Us*
Yuri Fayer (1890–1971) was the chief ballet conductor at the Bolshoi Theatre from 1923–1963. Olga Lepeshinskaya (1916–2008) was a famous ballerina who was a part of the Bolshoi Front Brigade and performed numerous times for troops stationed close to front lines.

Boris Slutsky, *A Ballad about a Dogmatist*
Ivan Susanin was a seventeenth-century Russian national hero, famous according to legend, for tricking the enemies of Russia to follow him deep into the forest, where they all froze to death.

Alexander Mezhivov *Farewell to Arms*

Ernest Hemingway was avidly read in the USSR during the war; Ehrenburg read excerpts from *For Whom the Bell Tolls* at an open meeting of the Russian Theatrical Society in 1942, as the Germans were approaching Stalingrad. That same year, Akhmatova chose lines from *Farewell to Arms* as her initial epigraph to the epilogue of *Poem Without A Hero*.

Valery Pereleshin. *Consolation*

The capitalized Antheap is a reference to Dostoevsky's *Notes from Underground* (1864), where the Underground Man condemns the Socialist collective as an antheap.

Vladimir Vysotsky, *Penal Battalions*

Penal battalions were for officers, penal companies were for soldiers. Stalin famously called artillery 'the god of war.' The phrase 'If I die, consider me a Communist,' was commonly found as a last request in the papers of Soviet soldiers who were not members of the Communist party and who were going into combat.

Acknowledgements

This anthology exists only because of Andy Croft's vision and persistence. He had asked me to compile and translate a selection of Russian poems from the War; was incredibly patient when other obligations and various unexpected events made me put it off repeatedly; and was remarkably open-minded when the book developed differently than both he and I envisioned at the start. I'm very grateful to him for getting me involved in this project and for putting up with me throughout its tortuous progress.

The success of a bilingual poetry anthology rests largely on the quality of its translations. This anthology has benefitted enormously from the work of translators past and present, and includes some of the finest examples of the translator's art (as, for instance, Arseny Tarkovsky's 'Field Hospital,' translated by Boris Dralyuk and Irina Mashinski, which won the Joseph Brodsky/Stephen Spender Prize). I am grateful to all the translators who put their hearts and talents into the translation of these remarkable poems, particularly to those who translated poems specifically for this anthology: Bryan Karetnyk who scouted and translated several brilliant Russian émigré poems; Yvonne Green, for her work on a selection from Semyon Lipkin's extraordinary long poem *Lieutenant Quartermaster*; Veniamin Gushchin, for his translation of Olga Berggolts's chilling poem, 'The Road to the Battle Front'; and Mary Jane White, for her translation of Marina Tsvetaeva's 'O, I Refuse.'

My own translations in this anthology and, indeed, all my literary productions of the past seven years, have been inspired, guided, and endlessly improved by my three heroes: Robert Chandler, Boris Dralyuk, and Irina Mashinski. Over the seven years that I have been enormously lucky to know them, they have been endlessly supportive, generous, and giving of their time, their advice, and their friendship. There could be no better comrade-in-arms, whether the battlefront is translation, poetry, or life itself. I won't even try to express here how much I appreciate their unwavering support of me and of my efforts throughout this impossible project.

The Translators

All the translations are by Maria Bloshteyn, apart from the following:

Anna Akhmatova, *Первый дальнобойный в Ленинграде* translated by Lyn Coffin; *Мужество* translated by Nancy K. Anderson; *Отрывок из 'Эпилога' (Поэма без героя)* translated by Nancy K. Anderson.

Anna Alekseeva, *Одиночество* translated by Caroline Walton; *'Мы плывем на нашем обстрелянном судне...'* translated by Boris Dralyuk and Maria Bloshteyn.

Olga Berggolts, *Разговор с соседкой* translated by Daniel Weissbort; *Дорога на фронт* translated by Veniamin Gushchin; *'На собранье целый день сидела'* translated by Robert Chandler.

Lydia Chervinskaya, *1939* translated by Bryan Karetnyk.

Ilya Ehrenburg, *Возмездие* translated by Gordon Mcvay.

Alexander Galich *Вальс посвященный уставу караульной службы* translated by Gerald Stanton Smith.

Rasul Gamzatov, *Журавли* translated by Irina Mashinski.

Semyon Gudzenko, *Перед атакой* translated by Gordon Mcvay; *Мое поколение* translated by Katharine Hodgson.

Vera Inber, *Отрывок из заря в блокадном Ленинграде* translated by Jack Lindsay.

Mikhail Isakovsky, *Враги сожгли родную хату* translated by Peter Tempest.

Georgy Ivanov, *'Все на свете пропадает даром...'* and *'Рассказать обо всех мировых дураках...'* translated by Bryan Karetnyk; *Лунатик в пустоту глядит...'* translated by Robert Chandler.

Semyon Lipkin, *Зола* and *Отрывок из 'Техника-интенданта'* translated by Yvonne Green.

Mikhail Lukonin, *Приду к тебе* translated by Walter May.

Irina Mashinski, *В Югендстиле. Браунау-Ам-Инн* translated by Irina Mashinski.

Alexander Mezhirov, *Ладожский лед* translated by Deming Brown; *Прощай оружие!* and *'Мы под Колпином скопом стоим...'* translated by Deming Brown.

Sergei Narovchatov, *В те годы* translated by Dorian Rottenberg.

Vsevolod Nekrasov, *Из Дойче Бух* translated by Ainsley Morse and Bela Shayevich.

Lev Ozerov, *Отрывок из 'Гудзенко' (Портреты без рам)* translated by Boris Dralyuk.

Boris Pasternak, *Одесса* translated by Maria Bloshteyn and Boris Dralyuk.

David Samoilov, *Бандитка* and *Сороковые* translated by Boris Dralyuk.

Ilya Selvinsky, *Тамань* translated by Peter Tempest.

Konstantin Simonov, *Жди меня, 'Я, перебрав весь год, не вижу...'* and *Ты помнишь, Алеша, дороги Смоленщины* translated by Mike Munford; *Убей его!* translated by Vladimir Markov and Merrill Sparks.

Boris Slutsky, *Госпиталь* translated by J. R. Rowland; *Волокуша* translated by Gerald Stanton Smith: *Шестое небо* translated by Yulia Kartalova O Doherty.

Yaroslav Smelyakov, *Судья* translated by Simon Franklin and Albert C Todd.

Vadim Strelchenko, *Промельк,* translated by Boris Dralyuk.

Alexey Surkov, *В землянке* translated by Dorian Rottenberg.

Arseny Tarkovsky, *Полевой госпиталь* translated by Boris Dralyuk and Irina Mashinski.

Marina Tsvetaeva, *'О слезы на глазах...'* translated by Mary Jane White.

Alexander Tvardovsky, *Смерть и воин* translated by James Womack.

Thanks are due to the editors of the following publications, where some of these translations first appeared:

Yuri Andreyev (ed) *Soviet Russian Literature 1917–1977, Poetry and Prose* (Progress Publishers, 1980)

Polina Barskova (ed) *Written in the Dark: Five Poets in the Siege of Leningrad* (Ugly Duckling Presse, 2016)

Lyn Coffin (ed) Anna Akhmatova, *Poems* (Norton, 1983)

Nancy K Anderson, *The Word That Causes Death's Defeat* (Yale University Press, 2004)

Nikolai Bannikov (ed) *Three Centuries of Russian Poetry* (Progress Publishers, 1980)

Robert Chandler, Boris Dralyuk, and Irina Mashinski (eds) *The Penguin Book of Russian Poetry* (Penguin, 2015)

Robert Chandler and Boris Dralyuk (eds) Lev Ozerov, *Portraits Without Frames* (NYRB, 2018)

Alexander Galich, *Dress Rehearsal* (Slavica Press, 2008)

Alexander Galich, *Songs and Poems* (Ardis, 1983)

Yvonne Green, *After Semyon Izailevich Lipkin* (Smith/Doorstop, 2011)

Max Hayward and Albert C Todd (eds) *20th Century Russian Poetry, Silver and Steel* (Doubleday, 1993)

Katharine Hodgson (ed) *A Journey in Five Postcards: Russian Poetry from the 20th Century* (*Rossica,* special issue 2011)

VN Kornilov, *While Readers Weep Over Poems... A Book About Russian Lyrical Poetry* (Akademia, 1997)

Lazar Lazarev, *Notes of an Elderly Man: A Book of Memoirs* (Vremia, 2005)

Jack Lindsay (ed) *Russian Poetry 1917–1955* (Bodley Head, 1957)

Vladimir Markov and Merrill Sparks (eds) *Modern Russian Poetry* (Bobbs-Merrill, 1967)

Vsevolod Nekrasov, *I Live, I See/Selected Poems* (Ugly Duckling Press, 2013)

Vladimir Ognev and Dorian Rottenberg (eds) *Fifty Soviet Poets* (Progress Publishers, 1969)

GS Smith (ed), Boris Slutsky, *Things That Happened* (Glas, 1999)

Alexander Tvardovsky, *Vasili Tyorkin* (Smokestack Books, 2020)

Caroline Walton, *The Besieged: A Story of Survival* (Biteback Publishing, 2011)

Muse Under Fire:
The Second World War and Russian Poetry

The Battle of Stalingrad. The Battle of Kursk. The Battle of Smolensk. The Siege of Leningrad. These names resonate grimly and thrillingly in all the states of the former Soviet Union, a country that lost twenty-seven million dead in the war,[1] both military and civilian – more than any other country involved. Politically and culturally, the war has been and continues to be analysed, commemorated, and used in a variety of strategic ways in Russia, the other countries of the FSU, and former members of the Warsaw Pact. Sometimes, it feels like the war is still lurking just beneath the surface. To this day, construction of roads and even a casual walk in the woods in the areas where the heaviest fighting took place can lead to an unsettling encounter with the past – a skeleton of a soldier lying beneath the moss, still holding a rifle, with an antipersonnel mine (in working order) right beside him. To this day, a chance conversation can set off an explosion of painful memories for those who witnessed the war themselves or who grew up on stories of what happened to their parents, grandparents, and great-grandparents – an intergenerational trauma that shows no signs of abating.

If the devastating battles that took place on Russian soil have reshaped the landscape in both direct and indirect ways (one thinks of the thirteen-month long battle for Rzhev, which leveled the ground and created so-called valleys of death, where the corpses of the soldiers were piled three or four deep, attracting birds of prey that permanently changed the fauna of the area), the war also altered the landscape of Russian poetry. For decades, the understanding of what the War meant was defined and circumscribed by the multitude of official poetry anthologies published in the Soviet Union both during and after the war. These anthologies began simply as collections of Soviet poetry written in 1941–1945, but broadened over the years to include poems written by frontline poets well after the war, and then poems written by poets who were children during the war. Separate books were dedicated to the poetry of the many frontline poets who were killed in the war. All of these anthologies focussed on celebrating the Soviet victory over Nazi Germany (they were typically published in anniversary years) and the poems they included were usually those published earlier by officially recognized poets. The anthologies themselves were understood either as memorials to those who fought in the war, a rendering of national debt to those who shed their blood for the country, or, more universally, as testaments to the suffering endured – the enormous price of national victory. After the fall of the Soviet Union, anthologies of war poetry have continued to come out regularly, and expanded their scope to include later generations of poets who wrote about the war, while largely following the pattern of Soviet-era publications.

The present anthology is, among other things, an attempt to look at the Russian poetry of the War through a wider lens, while questioning some of the assumptions that have informed the canon since its inception.

'The Great War' and Official Soviet Russian Poetry

Readers coming to any anthology of Russian poetry about the War from an Anglophone perspective will have to make considerable mental readjustments. To begin with, the cultural importance of the War vis-à-vis the First World War was reversed in Soviet Russia. In Russia the Great War is not the war of 1914–18, with its horrific new weapons and carnage, disillusionment, moral outrage, and loss of innocence, and, of course, its great poetic legacy, but the Great War of Soviet Russian cultural memory. There are several reasons why the First World War is dwarfed into insignificance for Russians. First of all, the Soviet losses in the Great Patriotic War were greater than the losses of all sides fighting in the First World War combined. If only on the scale of destruction, the War outweighed anything that preceded or followed it. Secondly, the First World War was written off in the Soviet Union as an imperialist war that was historically important only as a precursor of the October Revolution; The war of 1941–45, on the other hand, was the first major war fought by the Soviet State. Finally, the significant poetic legacy of the Russian poets of the First World War was largely inaccessible, because the State banned the poems and – as in the case of Nikolai Gumilyov – executed the poets.[2]

It is common knowledge that people could be killed for writing poetry in the Soviet Union, where poetry was often perceived to be a weapon by the State. What is less understood is the grand scale on which poetry was utilised and mobilised by the Soviet government during the War. The first two poems of the Great Patriotic War (as the war was immediately named in the Soviet press by analogy with the Patriotic War of 1812) were published in *Pravda*, on 23 June 1941, together with the declaration of war. The poems were 'We

Pledge Victory' by Alexey Surkov on the second page of the newspaper, and 'Victory Will be Ours' by Nikolai Aseev on the third page; they opened the floodgates to tens of thousands of war poems written by hundreds upon hundreds of poets in the next four years.[3]

War poems were published both in the civilian press (national and regional newspapers, literary journals, factory newspapers, anthologies, books by individual poets) and in the military press, which by 1942 consisted of *Krasnaia Zvezda* (the newspaper of the Soviet Ministry of Defence), four main military newspapers, 13 Front newspapers, 93 army and field corps newspapers, several hundred divisional newspapers, and 70 newspapers of the navy; by 1944 there were about 800 military newspapers with an output of three million issues in all. In addition to that, there were poems in the informational leaflets distributed to the soldiers (sometimes the information itself was presented in the form of a poem), poems on propaganda posters and poems in partisan newspapers published on German-occupied territory (270 of them by 1944). Poems were read to soldiers during political education meetings. Poems were read on the radio and in concert halls and various venues across the country, often on makeshift stages at the front, by visiting poets and actors. Poems were put to music, performed by the most popular singers and orchestras, and sung in dugouts and trenches. They were issued on records that were played on portable record players at home and on the front. All of these platforms created a demand for wartime poetry that was unprecedented and unparalleled not only in the Soviet Union but in any other country.

There were more than 120 languages spoken in the Soviet Union. Legally, all of them had equal status. Translations of poems from many of these languages into Russian were regularly published (there were also military newspapers published in the main regional languages). In practice, however, it was the Russian language, the language of the 'elder brother' in the Soviet family of nations, and Russian literary culture that were given a special status and privileged by the State. The prodigious demand for wartime poetry was thus specifically a demand for Russian poetry or, at the very least, for poetry translated into the Russian language.

Who delivered on the wartime poetry mandate in the Soviet Union? It would be fair to say that all poets responded to the national emergency. Even children's poets like Agniya Barto and Samuel Marshak contributed; Barto with poems of children in the war, Marshak with his wildly popular satirical poetic slogans and four-line poetic captions for the propaganda posters of *Okna TASS*. Poems were written by veteran members of the Soviet Writers Union and by young aspiring poets, by soldiers at the front, workers in factories, teachers and school-children. A special role in all of this was played by war correspondents.

Verse on the Battlefront: Propaganda vs Poetry

Following an order of 24 June 1941 from the Main Administration of the Political Propaganda and Agitation of the Red Army, thirty-one members of the Soviet Writers Union were called up from the reserves to active service as writers attached to various military publications. At the same time, many poets and writers who were exempt from combat for reasons of age or health, enlisted as war correspondents. It is estimated that over a thousand members of the Writers Union eventually worked as war correspondents. This was the beginning of the network of Soviet war correspondents that would soon span the entire Eastern Front.

War correspondents were so close to the action that they frequently took part in the fighting themselves. For this reason, among many others, war correspondents became official members of the Soviet Armed Forces in 1942, with ranks and specific duties, which included being

> 'exemplars of discipline, bravery, and tireless industry... ready to do battle at a moment's notice,' and providing material that 'sheds light on a) the military experience of the [Red Army] in the Patriotic War... against the German-Fascist invaders... b) the local population's efforts...to assist the Red Army c) the atrocities... perpetrated by the German-Fascist invaders against the civilian population... and, most importantly, [strives] to depict the resolution, dedication, and discipline of [Soviet] soldiers and officers.'[4]

The job of a war correspondent was to get as close as possible to the fighting and write about what he saw (the vast majority of war correspondents were men) in prose or poetry for his paper, in order to rouse the soldiers and raise the morale of the troops and of the civilian population. Poems were especially welcome. According to the editorial secretary of one military newspaper, 'already in the first months of the war, frontline poetry became "the queen of the newspaper page". In our newspaper, as in others, it had shown superior battle readiness.' Nikolai Tikhonov, a poet and writer who worked in the Political Administration of the Leningrad Front, put it more bluntly: 'a poem didn't take long to write, didn't take up much newspaper space, and was immediately useful.'

The most famous propaganda poem of the War was Konstantin Simonov's 'Kill Him', written at the Bryansk Front in July 1942 after witnessing the devastating losses and retreats of the Soviet army (Stalin's famous order #227, popularly known as 'Not a Step Back!' came out later that same month, forbidding retreat, as well as creating penal battalions and barrier troops). Simonov's poem was published on the 18 July 1942 in *Krasnaia Zvezda* on the second day of the battle for Stalingrad. The next day it was reprinted in the civilian *Komsomolskaia Pravda*. The day after that, two stanzas from the poem came out as a poster in *Okna TASS* designed by the Kukryniksy artists. After that, the poem was read on the radio. Then it became a leaflet, printed by the millions and dropped from planes. It was translated into a number of other languages, reprinted countless times in national and regional and military newspapers, and read at political meetings and concerts. The poem, it was said, 'killed more Nazis than the most famous sniper.'

It would be a mistake, however, to conclude that poems written by war correspondents had value only as propaganda. Even Simonov's 'Kill Him,' while clearly a propaganda piece, was full of genuine outrage, pain and palpable hatred of the invaders, and was so immensely moving that it continued to be in demand long after the War was over (renamed 'If Your House is Dear to You.'). It wasn't only the young bloods of Soviet poetry who served as war correspondents, but experienced poets like Mikhail Svetlov, Arseny Tarkovsky and Semyon Kirsanov. The latter, who wrote a poetic series during the war called, *Wise Words from Foma Smyslov, a Seasoned Russian Soldier* – an informative soldier's pamphlet that was distributed in the millions – explained at the Soviet Writers' Congress in 1944, 'this isn't some cheap entertainment or dumbed-down literature for the unsophisticated... I've never exerted this much effort on any other project. I've invested it with all my skill and mastery.'

Alexander Tvardovsky, who served as a war correspondent for a number of military newspapers, wrote the most famous poetic series of the War, about a fictional Russian soldier called Vasily Tyorkin. The cheerful and resourceful Tyorkin was extremely popular at home and at the front, where soldiers memorized stanzas from the poems and saw Tyorkin as a model for their own conduct. While an obvious success from the propaganda angle (although, notably, neither Stalin nor the Communist Party are ever mentioned in any of the Tyorkin poems), the series garnered high praise from the Nobel Prize-winning writer and poet Ivan Bunin: 'a truly rare book: what freedom, what wonderful bravado, what exactitude, what precision in everything, and what extraordinary folk and soldier vernacular! Everything is pitch perfect – there's not a single word that rings false, not a single word that's a prefabricated literary vulgarity!' When Boris Pasternak was asked in 1945, what he thought was the best thing written about the War, he replied simply 'Tyorkin!'

Alexander Tvardovsky, Konstantin Simonov, Ilya Selvinsky and Mikhail Svetlov each wrote poems that provided vital insights into the nature of war and personal sacrifice that continue to stand the test of time. Even more importantly, it was from the hell of the fighting – the rough drafts of war correspondents, the notebooks of soldiers who began to write poetry in earnest on the frontlines or shortly thereafter – that the new voices of Russian poetry emerged, bringing new words, new rhythms, new intolerance for jingoism, new demand for telling things as they are. Semyon Gudzenko, Lev Ozerov, Alexander Mezhirov, Yulia Drunina, Boris Slutsky and David Samoilov were all part of the frontline generation of Soviet Russian poets (known in Russian as *poety frontoviki*) who helped to change the face of Russian poetry in the decades following the war.

Together with the bone-chilling, heart-rending poetry coming out of blockaded Leningrad, from writers like Olga Berggolts and Vera Inber, and with the poetry of Boris Pasternak and Anna Akhmatova, whom the State finally allowed to publish during the first harrowing years of the war, these poets sent an overarching message of unity to the Soviet readership that was more powerful than any propagandistic exhortations. The Germans, who were, ironically, trying to use Russian poetry for their own ends (mainly in collaborationist publications, to bolster their popularity in the conquered Russian-speaking territories), were well aware of the danger this unified poetic front represented in rallying the people.

The crisis of the first two years of the Great Patriotic War with its catastrophic losses and the looming threat of defeat, meant that after the repressions and purges of the late 1930s and the silencing of the great poets, the State was willing to use any means available to mobilise the people. Most importantly, Soviet readers were once again allowed to seek out their poets, and even semi-banned Soviet poets were once again allowed to reach their readers.

Russian Émigré Poetry and the War

The military situation in the Soviet Union was closely watched by Russian poets abroad. Hundreds of thousands of Russians had left Russia after the Revolution of 1917, during the so-called first wave of Russian emigration, settling in Berlin, Paris, Riga, Prague, Harbin and Shanghai. As the 1930s progressed, with the rise of Fascism and Japanese Imperialism, there were further relocations. In the far East, Russians moved from Japanese-occupied Harbin to Shanghai, and then further away (some as far as Australia and South America) when the Japanese occupied Shanghai in 1937. In Europe, as Fascism grew in strength, Russian émigrés moved from Berlin and Prague, to Paris and New York (or Argentina, Chile, and Uruguay). By 1939, the only significant centres of émigré life – places where Russian prose and poetry was still in some demand, and where Russian-language journals were being published – were Paris, Shanghai, and New York.

The émigré poet, writer, and literary critic Yuri Terapiano, who lived in Occupied Paris, later recalled: 'In 1941, in hungry Paris, occupied by the Germans, in the midst of a remarkably cold winter... the Russian [émigré] literary circles were all disconnected and overwhelmed by the problems of everyday life. There were no longer any Russian newspapers in Paris...' Many Russian-Jewish émigré intellectuals were taken to concentration camps, where they were killed (the fates of Yuri Mandelshtam, Elizaveta Kuzmina-Karavaeva, and Yuri Felzen). Others fought against the Nazi Occupation, like Boris Vildé, who joined the French Resistance (and who, in fact, came up with the term 'Resistance').

First-wave Russian émigré poets and intellectuals had a very different relationship with the 1914–18 war than their Soviet counterparts. While the Soviets separated themselves from the experience of the imperialist war, the Russian émigrés were constantly reminded of it, if only by the large émigré veterans contingent who enshrined it as the great 'Lost Cause' and the link with the idealized past in imperial Russia. If the poets of Soviet Russia were by and large encountering war with fresh eyes, first-wave Russian émigré poets were not only fully connected with that legacy, but had created a large portion of it themselves.

For émigré poets like Vyacheslav Ivanov, Georgy Ivanov, Zinaida Gippius, Teffi and Igor Severianin who had written so many defining texts about and during the 1914-18 war, it was difficult to think about the War as anything but a sequel, and to write about it without repeating what they had written twenty years previously. Very few of them wrote about the War directly.

This is not to say that first-wave Russian émigré poets were indifferent to the progress of the war – their own lives, after all, were at stake, as well as the future of Russia and of the world itself. Their perception of the war, however (both of the older and the younger poets) was complicated by their personal experience of and attitude toward the Soviet state. The emigration was divided into *porazhentsy* (Defeatists) and *oborontsy* (Defenders); the former felt that anyone who attacked the Soviet Union had to be supported, irrespective of what the attacker stood for; the latter believed that while Russia was still a part of the Soviet state, it had to be defended, irrespective of who was at its helm. Sometimes, the divisions happened in the same family: Zinaida Gippius was reportedly horrified when her spouse, the philosopher, novelist, and poet Dmitry Merezhkovsky, went on the German radio in the summer of 1941, comparing Hitler to Jeanne D'Arc, and extoling his crusade against the Soviet Union.

In practice, however, most first-wave Russian émigré intellectuals were anti-Nazi during the war (the majority of Merezhkovsky's and Gippius's friends and associates turned away from the couple after the pro-Hitler speech). Some, like the poet and novelist Vladimir Nabokov, who escaped to the United States with his Jewish wife and son at the beginning of the war, could support neither the Nazis nor the Soviets, though his heart was breaking for the Russian losses:

No matter how the soul dissolves in pity,
I will not bend, I will not cease
Loathing the filth, brutality and boredom
Of silent servitude.

The younger generation of first-wave émigré poets like Mikhail Volin, Irina Knorring and Nikolai Turoverov, were also writing moving poems about the fate of Russia and the horror they saw around them. Others, like Georgy Ivanov, for whom the War only confirmed his dark predictions about mankind's impending doom, saw the war from the position of nihilistic despair, whereby no renewal was possible, whoever claimed victory. The poems that Georgy Ivanov wrote during the War about what it was like to live during that desperate time, had a striking new simplicity about them, a new energy, and a new resonance, quite different from the poems he wrote in his youth (which he sarcastically described as 'hurrah, hurrah, hurrah for the Russian Tsar'). His wife, the poet, writer, and memoirist Irina Odoevstseva, wrote that it was the privations and the pain he experienced during the War, 'not only for himself but for Russia and its fate that turned him a into a true poet.'

Throughout all of this, the émigré community was watching nervously how the fate of Russia would unfold in the war – Bunin was one of many who recorded the progress of the war and his fears in his diary. The Russian émigrés were also reading the poetry that was coming out of Russia, and were particularly moved by Konstantin Simonov's 'Remember Alyosha, the Roads of Smolenshchina...' with its crosses, blessings, and old villages with their cemeteries – evoking concepts of Russian Orthodoxy and Russian folk traditions. The poem was Stalin-sanctified, of course, and expressed a shift in Soviet State policy that ultimately led to Stalin's permission for the election of a new Patriarch of the Russian Orthodox Church in 1943, but for the émigrés Simonov was a hero who dared say things that no one had said out loud before in the Soviet Union. It is not accidental that Stalin sent Simonov to Paris after the war to meet with the émigré writers and poets to try to convince them to repatriate.

The Great Patriotic War, the State and Poetry

There was a point in the War when it seemed that the Soviet regime was too concerned for its own survival to oppress its citizens in the manner of the late 1930s. The horror of invasion, the shocking German successes, and the obvious bewilderment of the Soviet leaders, resulted in a relaxation of controls. The historian and philosopher, Mikhail Gefter, who enlisted in 1941 and was wounded twice, remembered the liberating atmosphere of the early war period:

> Even though 1941 and 1942 were the blackest years of the war, they were also the freest... This was a period of *spontaneous de-Stalinization*. We were in full crisis. Stalin's totalitarian system had fallen apart in the face of the invasion and occupation. People were suddenly forced to make their own decisions, to take responsibility for themselves. Events pressed us into becoming truly independent human beings.

In his novel *Life and Fate*, Vasily Grossman wrote, 'Stalingrad had a soul – and its soul was freedom.' His words were amplified by Lazar Lazarev, also a decorated war veteran, editor, and literary critic: 'for many of us, those first two years of the war coincided with a spontaneous de-Stalinization, a true emancipation. We felt that everything depended on us personally, and that gave us an extraordinary feeling of freedom.'[5]

This unforgettable experience of personal freedom is evoked repeatedly in wartime poems (only to be subsequently either removed by censorship, or attacked by Soviet critics). Semyon Gudzenko exclaims in a poem written toward the end of the war, 'What freedom have I known! / Hands off the memory!' (these lines were promptly excised by the censors). In 1942, Olga Berggolts imagined herself in the future, looking back at herself, living through the siege: 'We breathed such unbridled freedom / that our grandchildren will envy us.'

Marietta Chudakova has suggested that before Khrushchev's Thaw, there were actually two earlier 'micro-Thaws' that were suppressed by the State: in 1941–1943 and in 1946. The first one was directly connected to the massive defeats of the first years of the war and the unbelievable sacrifices made by the Soviet people to turn back the enemy – all of which created if not a sense of entitlement, then certain expectations within Soviet society. Chudakova explains that the 'hopes of a renewal were heightened in the [first] years of the war, especially in the turning-point year of 1943. Mikhail Zoshchenko's *Before Sunrise* and Boris Pasternak's long poem *Nightglow* began publication, but were stopped. Pasternak was even advised not to finish the poem.'[6] The second micro-Thaw was occasioned by the victory over Nazi Germany and the return home of the victorious Soviet troops – once again expectations were raised about social changes in the Soviet Union. The State reacted with another, harsher, clampdown in 1946.

According to Ilya Ehrenburg, writer, poet, essayist, and the most widely-read Soviet war correspondent of the War, 'in 1943, the clouds began to gather that five years later covered the entire sky. But the enemy was still occupying our land. Our people fought staunchly, and in their heroism there was such power, that you could still live honestly and out loud, ignoring much else. I firmly believed that after victory all would change immediately. Now, looking back, I find myself having to constantly admit to my naivety and blindness...'[7]

But if 1941 and 1942 represented a taste of freedom for some Soviet citizens, it was freedom only by comparison with what preceded and followed it. A glimpse at blockaded Leningrad during those years, for example, shows that all the systems of repression were in place and functioning even under the extreme conditions of the siege. The State system of informants was very much in working order. When in 1942 Olga Berggolts's father, a respected military surgeon, refused to work for the NKVD, he was forced to leave blockaded Leningrad as punishment. The eminent linguist and scholar Victor Zhirmunsky was arrested as a German spy in early autumn of 1941, because of his earlier contacts with German linguists. Many of those arrested on similarly trumped-up charges died in Leningrad jails. There were even cases when Gulag inmates were brought into the blockaded city to be confronted by their accusers. Those suspected of sympathizing with the enemy because of their ethnic origin were sent out of the blockaded city and deported to the Far East; in the course of three days in 1942, those Leningraders who had German or Finnish family names were taken out of the city 'in inhuman conditions. Many perished, those who survived became invalids.'[8] The system of misinformation was also as active as ever; it was forbidden to report how terrible the situation was in the city. When Berggolts briefly left Leningrad for Moscow in 1942, she was shocked that the Muscovites she met had no idea that Leningrad was starving. Berggolts kept a secret diary where she wrote what she couldn't say or write openly. And, as far as poetry is concerned, many Leningrad poets wrote all their poems for the desk drawer as matter of course, not even dreaming of publication (for example, the nonconformist siege poets in Paulina Barskova's extraordinary collection were published only after the fall of the Soviet Union).[9]

But the clampdown that came when the military situation began to turn in Soviet favour in 1943 made the early period of the war seem positively libertarian. When Ilya Selvinsky, who had distinguished himself in the fighting in Crimea, was called back to Moscow in 1943, he thought he was going to be commended for his heroism and for his popular poetry. Instead, he was put on the carpet for his 'pernicious' and 'inartistic' poems and forced to leave the army.

Two more clampdown measures can be noted here, because their impact was so palpable and wide-reaching. First, many civilians who lived 'under the German' in the territories liberated by the Soviet troops, and most Soviet soldiers who had been captured by the enemy and either escaped or were liberated, were subjected to internment in the special NKVD camps for 'screening and filtration.' Many of these people were later released but some were sent to the Gulag.

It should be noted that a large contingent of Russians who were taken to Germany to provide free labour, or who left with the retreating German troops because of concerns that they would be accused of collaborating with the enemy (some, with good cause), had no interest in returning to the Soviet Union, and made their way through war-torn Europe, eventually becoming the second-wave of Russian emigration. This wave included the poets Olga Anstei, Nikolai Morshen, Yuri Ivask and Ivan Elagin, all of whom ended up settling in the USA.

Secondly, although incidents of collaboration happened within almost every ethnicity living in the Soviet Union, several ethnicities were singled out for punitive measures, accused of collaborating with the Germans, and relocated to other parts of the Soviet Union. These punitive transfers were done to the Chechen-Ingushes, the Crimean Tatars, Kalmyks, and several others ethnic minorities. The conditions during these forced deportations were extremely harsh and many people died both on route and in the areas of resettlement. The Kalmyks whom Semyon Lipkin wrote about were rehabilitated and allowed to return only in 1956; in 1989, during Perestroika, the Supreme Soviet declared the forced national deportations of Kalmyks and others a 'barbaric act of the Stalin regime.' Moreover, these filtrations and deportations were not publicized internally or outside the Soviet Union, so it was still possible to avert one's eyes from what was happening. As the poet-singer Alexander Galich later remembered:

> We knew only too well of the humiliating interrogations... that were inflicted upon the old men and children who lived 'under the Germans,'... We also knew what fate awaited Soviet officers and soldiers who were taken prisoner, managed to survive the hell of the Nazi caps, and were then liberated... We knew about the fate of Russified Germans of the Volga Region, of the Crimean Tatars, of the Chechens and the Ingushes... We knew but... [prevented ourselves] from hearing, thinking, seeing, and remembering anything that could disturb... our communal joy [at the impending victory] even for a moment.'[10]

The dissident writer Grigory Svirsky, who was first a military pilot and then a war correspondent, called 1946 'a year when Russia began to recover from fear.' The victorious Soviet army was returning home, having seen much in the four years of fighting. 'We knew a lot, too much,' wrote Svirsky, 'we knew not only about how people lived under "the yoke of Capitalism"... Every war vet witnessed many times how soldiers perished because of the idiocy of the military leaders, because of their heartlessness, their total indifference to the common man.'[11] But the change in the returning soldiers was even more profound. Soviet citizens had lived their lives as if surrounded by iron walls, cut off from the rest of the world. The returning soldiers had learned that their previous isolation was not a given. This was a major psychological shift in perspective. The returning soldiers were expecting change because they now knew for a fact that change was possible, that isolation was artificial, and that seemingly impermeable borders could be penetrated by both people and ideas.

Altogether, the returning men and women who sacrificed and experienced so much, were expecting a different life, with greater freedoms. Back in 1944, the poet Nikolai Aseev, in a private conversation reported to the authorities, expressed the thoughts of many when he said 'demobilization will bring back... people who had seen everything. These people will bring a new measure of things... I don't know what that time will be like. I believe, however, that it will be a time of freedom for poetry.'[12]

The first set of measures was a tsunami of arrests across the country. People were arrested for joking, for something they had written or said years earlier, for acting suspiciously, for having lived in German-occupied territories, for being taken prisoner during the war, for having been arrested earlier. Former Soviet prisoners of war who have been already 'filtrated,' cleared, and released were re-arrested. In his memoirs Ehrenburg remembered Olga Berggolts asking him prior to the crackdown, 'Do you think that we could have a repeat of year 1937 or is it impossible now?' Ehrenburg answered that he didn't think the purges could happen again. 'Your voice sounds uncertain,' Berggolts wryly commented. A few months before his arrest in 1948 for 'storing anti-Soviet literature,' the playwright Alexander Gladkov wrote in his diary, 'I was travelling [to Moscow]. In the train I was attacked by fear, and not without reason either. I'm not one to panic, but after summer of 1937 and spring of 1939, I've never felt this way [till now].'[13]

There was an economic aspect to the mass arrests as well: according to the opera singer Galina Vishnevskaya, whose father was arrested right after the war for telling a joke about Stalin, 'the country lay in ruins – what was needed was unpaid slave labour... a new slave army... after the war, under [Stalin's] leadership... his henchmen crammed the Gulag to bursting with men and women, explained it all by politics and – there you go, at least ten years worth of free labour.'[14]

Second, the War was, in the words of Evgeny Dobrenko, relegated from the realm of experience to memory and from memory to history, history being easier to shape at will than either individual experience or its memory.[15] Immediately after the War, Stalin let it be known that military memoirs were not welcomed, and in February of 1946, he announced that 'Victors can and should be judged. They should be criticized and tested... [so that] they'll be less arrogant and more modest.' Many famous generals and heroes of the War were demoted, including the Marshal of the Soviet Union, Georgy Zhukov himself. Only two years after the war, Victory Day lost the status of a national holiday. Simultaneously, war veterans stopped receiving allowances for their medals and decorations.

Possibly the most brutal measures were directed at disabled war veterans, whom the State had already denied visibility (beginning in 1945, photographs of disfigured or crippled veterans were excised from private letters by the censors). According to eyewitness accounts, one day in May of 1948, disabled veterans who were already reduced to begging at the marketplace because they had no other means of financial support, were rounded up along with other vagrants to be taken away from Kiev and other big cities.

Third, in a move straight out the late-1930s, the State began a public campaign against an internal enemy, the agent of the powerful and devious external foe. The campaign against 'rootless cosmopolitans' appeared to flow out smoothly from an earlier campaign, directed against 'servility before the West,' but this time had a more specific target – Soviet Jews, as agents of world Zionism. According to the historian Irina Zubkova, Jews 'were not only spread throughout the territory of the Soviet Union, but many of them belonged to the Soviet scientific and cultural elite and held responsible government positions. Furthermore, Soviet Jews had their own organization of volunteers (the Jewish Anti-Fascist Committee, to which, if necessary, the role of a 'nationalist centre' could be assigned). Organizers of the anti-Semitic campaign also took into consideration the factor of latent popular anti-Semitism, still present in various strata of Russian society.'[16] Furthermore, several prominent Soviet Jews, like the actor Solomon Mikhoels, worked hard throughout the War to drum up support for the Soviet cause among world Jewry – at the request of the Soviet leadership. They thus had strong and demonstrable ties with the West. Also, Stalin himself had issues with Jews in general; a number of statements he made over the years were demonstrably antisemitic.

In many ways, the campaign was an intensification of something that so many Jewish soldiers had already experienced during the war years. In 1943, Ehrenburg was told that he shouldn't be writing about the heroic exploits of Jewish soldiers at the front. By 1944, after Stalin's meeting with Party, army and national security officials to discuss 'the Jewish problem,' followed by a memo from Georgy Malenkov to Party officials, listing which positions should not be held by Jews, Jewish soldiers and officers knew that they were being denied official recognition, often despite their superiors' recommendations. Ion Degen wrote and talked about Jewish soldiers and officers who were put forward for a medal but were denied, or given a lesser decoration, because of their obviously Jewish family name. He himself was twice put forward for the 'Hero of the Soviet Union' medal, which he didn't get because he was Jewish. Degen, Konstantin Levin, and many other Jewish combatants, repeatedly wrote about their constant need to show bravery to counter the prevalent stereotype of the cowardly Jew, the bad Jewish soldier. The battle with cosmopolitanism led to the murder of Mikhoels, the destruction of the Jewish Anti-Fascist Committee, and the notorious Doctors' Plot, which was stopped only with Stalin's death.

Finally, and perhaps most cynically, the State went after those same poets and writers who only recently, during the critical days of the war, were treated as valuable allies and – in the Russian tradition – moral compasses in the fight against Nazism. In August of 1946, Stalin instructed Andrei Zhdanov, the face of Soviet cultural policy after the war, to attack Anna Akhmatova, Mikhail Zoshchenko and the journals *Zvezda* and *Leningrad*. Zhdanov did so with enthusiasm, savaging everyone concerned. Grigory Svirsky, who witnessed all of this as a young writer and recently demobilised soldier, later wrote, 'on that day the intoxicating feeling of victory vanished.' Zhdanov attacked Akhmatova for her 'measly, narrow private life, with its paltry dramas and religiously-mystical eroticism,' referring to her wartime poems as 'junk' that was infinitely removed from Soviet life, reminding everyone that she was evacuated from Leningrad during the war (thus by implication, never really sharing the hardships of the siege). Zhdanov accused Zoshchenko of 'hunkering down in Alma-Ata, far from the frontlines,' and not helping the Soviet people 'in their struggle against the German invaders.' In a note to Zhdanov, Stalin called the report 'superb' and instructed him to run it in the papers immediately and to publish it later as a stand-alone pamphlet. The news reverberated throughout the Soviet Union and, indeed, the entire world.

Writing three decades later, in emigration, Svirsky asked himself why Stalin did not kill Akhmatova and Zoshchenko, whether in the Gulag, like Mandelstam, or through an arranged 'accident,' like Mikhoels. His answer was that had it been only Akhmatova and Zoshchenko, it would have been simple to quietly liquidate them. The problem was that there was an entire generation of poets and writers returning from the War, who were simply too numerous to be wiped out. Instead they had to be frightened into toeing the line. After Zhdanov's report, Akhmatova and Zoshchenko were expelled from the Writers' Union, their ration cards were taken away, and their works could no longer be published. The whole spectacle was an object lesson for anyone thinking of literature and poetry as a profession in the Soviet Union. There was, however, a deeper import to the message that the State was sending.

In July 1946, only a month before the Zhdanov speeches, Konstanin Simonov and Ilya Ehrenburg, along with a supporting cast of characters that included Simonov's wife, the actress Valentina Serova, arrived to Paris with nearly unlimited funds, to wine, dine, and charm Ivan Bunin along with other émigrés, in order to persuade them to repatriate. Earlier in the summer, a law was passed granting the right to receive a Soviet citizenship to citizens of former Russian Empire and to persons who gave up their Soviet citizenship and were now residing abroad. The Soviet delegation painted enticing pictures of Soviet literary life to the impoverished émigré community, but relatively few literary émigrés took the bait. The biggest disappointment was Ivan Bunin's rejection of the invitation to repatriate. As the first Russian recipient of the Nobel Prize for Literature, Bunin was not only the face of Russian literature in exile, but – as he was introduced at the Nobel Prize banquet – the inheritor of the 'glorious traditions of the great Russian literature.'

It seems no coincidence that it was only *after* Bunin made it clear that he wouldn't repatriate that Zhdanov unleashed the attack against Akhmatova and Zoshchenko. Zhdanov's 'unmasking' of nationally respected writers as cowardly, sexually promiscuous, egotistic, vulgar and mendacious sent an unambiguous message that poets and writers, whether Soviet or émigré, were neither moral compasses nor voices of conscience. That role was claimed by the State. In his memoirs, Simonov said that after Zhdanov's attacks, which became instantly known in the émigré community, there was no wooing back the émigré poets and writers.

If during the War the State had done so much to encourage poetry through publishing, broadcasting and promotion, after the war the situation was reversed. Poets were discouraged from writing about the hard truths of the war, journals were shut down as warnings to other journals, poetry readings were restricted, and poets themselves were demoted from truth-speakers into tangential figures in the building of Communism. An article in *Literaturnaia gazeta* in October 1946 called 'Life Moves Forward' attacked the recent work of soldier poets like Alexander Mezhirov, Sergey Orlov and Semyon Gudzenko, describing them a 'ceaseless howl of complaint' and urging poets to follow the lead of their former fellow-soldiers, who are 'toiling and building communism.' Although these young poets were eventually allowed to reply to these charges in print, critics continued to level similar accusations against them and other poets trying to write honestly about what they had experienced in the War.

Something unforeseen happened, however, as the State began to clamp down on poets and their poetry. The silencing of the wartime poets and the shutting down of venues led to an increase in the private circulation of good but unsanctioned poetry, old and new, handwritten and typed, and in private poetry readings. These later became more self-conscious and deliberate, eventually growing into the phenomenon known as Samizdat. Publicly demoted poets and writers also gained in stature outside of the official State structures of recognition, becoming viewed as cultural heroes and their unpublished work regarded as source of wisdom and a moral authority.

After the War

The period between the end of the war and Stalin's death was not a good one for poetry of any kind in the Soviet Union. A chapter entitled 'Post-War Literature; 1946–1953,' in the *History of Soviet Russian Literature* published in 1968 takes issue with the damning assessments of the literature of the period by hostile and unobjective Western critics, citing a number of important and internationally recognized works from this period. It is telling, however, that the only poem cited is Alexander Tvardovsky's long poem, *A House by the Road* (1946). Although it is, without a doubt, one of his finest, a moving meditation on how a war affects a family, Tvardovsky wrote most of it in 1943 and 1945, and published it *before* Zhdanov's attack on Akhmatova and Zoshchenko.

Remarkably little memorable war poetry was written and published in that early post-war period. The first book by Yulia Drunina came out in a small print run in 1948 (*In a Soldier's Overcoat*), followed by *Poems* in 1952. Sergey Orlov published several books of poetry during this period. Nonetheless, the best poems in these poetry collections are those that were written during the war. Semyon Gudzenko also had difficulties. Although Gudzenko 'travelled the country, worked a lot, and had the reputation of being an exemplary optimist,' he once said to Ehrenburg, 'I now know how to write, but I write worse than I used to.' In his notebooks Gudzenko wrote, 'I read my poems... People were listening... [but] I was bored by my own poetry.'

Writing in 1951, Gleb Struve proposed the existence of a 'submerged' Soviet Russian literature.[17] This written-for-the-desk-drawer prose and poetry had indeed existed in Russia for almost as long as the Soviet Union itself; the full scale of this phenomenon, partially overlapping with but not nearly encompassed by Samizdat, only became graspable after the fall of the Soviet Union, with an avalanche of publications that keep coming to this day. Many poets learned to publish their 'publishable' poems while writing other poems for the desk drawer. In 1949 Olga Berggolts, who chose to publish what she could and to keep for the desk drawer what she couldn't, wrote a long poem *Pervorossiisk*, about the first Soviet commune. The poem, not one of her best, was published in 1950 and received the State Stalin Prize in 1951. At the same time, Berggolts was writing her heart-breaking and unpublishable 'Triptych of 1949'. Nikolai Glazkov took a different route when he began putting together small handwritten booklets of his unpublishable poems, calling them 'sam-sebia-izdat' ('publishing-myself-by-myself'), thus heralding the Samizdat era.

Meanwhile, the poets of the first and second wave of emigration wrote whatever they wished about the War, and did so with a vengeance (sometimes, literally). Poems about the War appeared notably in *Grani* (founded in 1946 by second-wave émigrés and published in Frankfurt am Main), *Novyi zhurnal* (founded in 1942 by first-wave émigrés who moved on to New York). The poets of the second wave emigration were especially active; incredibly, they managed to set up a number of publishing presses in the Displaced Persons camps where they led a precarious existence, in danger of being shipped back to the Soviet Union at any moment. The DP presses printed books on a variety of subjects (they even brought out a volume of Nikolai Gumilyov's poems) that could be purchased for cigarettes and coffee. In 1946 Olga Anstei started to publish her poetry in émigré journals in Germany and the USA. In 1947 her poems were included in an anthology of poetry published in the DP camp where she was held. In 1949 she published her first collection of verse, *A Door in the Wall,* including her devastating poem about the massacre of Jews in Baby Yar.

Then, in 1953, the unthinkable happened: Stalin died. During national mourning, the Doctors' Plot quietly folded, anti-cosmopolitanism receded, the feeling of growing terror declined, and there was even something akin to a sense of closure. The poet David Samoilov observed, 'World War Two finished not in May 1945, but in March 1953.' Hopes for real change arose in the wake of the 20th Congress of the CPSU in February 1956, when Nikita Khrushchev delivered his secret speech, denouncing Stalin's dictatorship, criticizing the pre-war purges of the army, blaming him for the terrible Soviet losses in the first year of the War, condemning the deportations of entire nations, and, most importantly, denouncing Stalin's appropriation of the people's victory. Ehrenburg, who knew better than anyone what the situation was like on the ground, and whose novel *The Thaw* (1954) gave the name to this period of relaxation of State controls, wrote that by 1961 (when Stalin's body was finally removed from the mausoleum on the Red Square) Soviet poetry had finally thawed after being 'frozen in the snows.' By then it was possible to reinsert the lines cut out or changed by censorship in the poems of the frontline poets.

The Khrushchev Thaw, and Beyond

It is said that 'the first poet of the Thaw, the first poet of the 'de-Stalinization' of consciousness' was Boris Slutsky. In 1957 Slutsky was accepted into the Writers' Union (an unheard-of case, since he had not yet published a single book). The poet Mikhail Svetlov said to the members of the poetry section of the Union: 'I hope it's clear to all of us, that a poet has come who is better than us all.' A prewar student of the Moscow Law Institute and, simultaneously, of the Maxim Gorky Literary Institute, Slutsky also took part in Ilya Selvinsky's poetry seminars, where he joined a tightly-knit poetic circle that included Mikhail Kulchitsky and Pavel Kogan, neither of whom made it through the War, and Sergei Narovchatov and David Samoilov, who did. Slutsky served as a soldier, a political instructor, a military prosecutor in the tribunal courts and as a scout on reconnaissance missions. The War was the central event of his life, the central theme of his poetry and prose, and he wrote about it, according to Joseph Brodsky (who, incidentally, began to write poetry after reading Slutsky's poem 'Monument') in a tone 'tough, tragic and unemotional... the way the survivor calmly tells, if he wants, about how and in what he survived.'

Slutsky, who only began to publish his poetry in earnest in the late 1950s (with the help, once again, of Ilya Ehrenburg), was astonishingly prolific. He wrote most of his poems, however, for the desk drawer (many were circulated as Samizdat and some published in the West as Tamizdat – the latter of which, Slutsky, who retained an 'us' and 'them' mentality until the end of his poetic career, disapproved). The real scope of Slutsky's poetic legacy became clear only after Perestroika, when his literary executor brought out three volumes of Slutsky's poems (representing only a part of his poetic output). Slutsky's published poems pushed the limits of what was possible during the Thaw; his famous poem 'Hospital', written and rewritten over many years, and published in his debut book of poems, *Memory*, shows how the notion of shared humanity is denied during war. Slutsky's ironic treatment of the 'glorious death' of the Motherland's defenders (he radically suggests that death is death for everyone) was shocking even during the Thaw. On the other hand, his poem 'A Ballad About a Dogmatist', written during the Thaw, couldn't be published until 1989, because it questions what Slutsky himself had been taught, and what he had preached to the soldiers on the frontlines as a political instructor, about Communism, Socialism, and the proletariat.

While Slutsky, Samoilov, Mezhirov, Dudin and Drunina tried to interrogate the War and its meanings, rejecting decorative elements in poetry in favour of common and colloquial speech, the majority of published Soviet poets, writers, and historians, persisted in presenting an edited version of the war as an undiluted national triumph. This perspective was encouraged politically and was soon bolstered by Leonid Brezhnev's ascendancy in 1964. Victory Day became a national holiday again in 1965 and countless memorials to the War sprang up all over the Soviet Union (although veterans were only granted privileges by the State in 1980). Looking back, Lazar Lazarev said that 'those of us who had fought in the war thought, at first, that at last the war was getting the attention in merited... But in fact, that attention was purely an official attempt to turn the war into a show made up of concocted legends.'

This master narrative was fiercely guarded. There were rigid limits on what was allowed to be said about the war. Literature about the War that didn't subscribe to prevalent views, was variously criticized as 'trench truth' (having a narrow view of the war), 'Remarquist' (Pacifist) or 'Naturalist' (needlessly graphic in description of wartime horrors).

The situation was paradoxical. On the one hand, the 1950s and 1960s were a momentous time for Russian poetry in the Soviet Union, when there were several poetic generations and many different groups of poets sharing the same poetic space – older poets associated with the 'Silver Age' of Russian poetry, veteran poets, nonconformist poets and 'stadium' poets, at a time of ever-growing interest in poetry. On the other hand, there were continued and growing State restrictions imposed on both producers and consumers of poetry, and stiff controls on what could be written, published, and read, especially about the war. It is not surprising then, that so much of the Soviet Russian poetry of the time that either countered the official narrative of the War or explored some of the forbidden war-related topics, could not be published and had to be either written for the desk drawer to wait for better times, or else had to find other, unofficial ways of reaching the readers.

Coinciding with this social change and pressure was another poetic phenomenon: the rise of the unofficial poem-song (also called bard song or author song). Poem-songs, whose roots went back to the 1930s, had numerous points of origin (university student songs, geologist songs, tourist songs, etc.). They gained legitimacy as an unofficial poetic genre, however, through the role played by songs during the War, when hundreds of poems were set to music, and many of these became vitally important both on the national and personal level. When Anna Akhmatova saw a singing column of soldiers during the War, she is said to have exclaimed, 'Oh, how happy I would have been, if they were singing a song of mine!' Vladimir Vysotsky once said that his favourite song of all time was Vasily Lebedev-Kumach's 'Sacred War,' played every morning on the State radio during the war: 'This song would send a shiver down your spine, if you actually understood what stands behind it!' What 'stands behind' the song, of course, is the national need for unity in face of critical danger, the national resolve to sacrifice in the name of a common victory, but also the ability of poetry and song to speak for the nation. The popularity of poem-songs in the 1960s was also spurred by the Soviet manufacture and sales of the 'Yauza' tape recorders beginning in the late 1950s, which facilitated a wide distribution of these unsanctioned songs that the State couldn't control, that became known as *Magnitizdat.*

The three best-known masters of the genre – Vysotsky, Bulat Okudzhava and Alexander Galich – wrote many songs about the war. Okudzhava, who enlisted as a soldier at eighteen, wrote about the vulnerability of young soldiers, their fear, naivety, bravery, bewilderment, and their longing for their mothers even as they were going into battle. Galich, who was rejected for military service for health reasons, and who spent the war entertaining the troops and the wounded, wrote songs about how returning soldiers were brutalized by the authorities, about the lack of appreciation for the war dead despite official pieties, and about the way relationships changed after the war. His poem-song 'Waltz Dedicated to the Regulations for Guard Duty' written in the mid-sixties, gained particular resonance as a reflection on the fate of the entire wartime generation. While Vysotsky wrote many poem-songs about his wartime childhood, he also wrote a large number in which he convincingly spoke through a persona of a soldier, a pilot, an officer from a penal battalion etc. He also wrote what is without doubt the most famous poetic text about penal battalions.

Meanwhile, the émigré poets, spared the freeze-thaw cycle of Soviet internal policies, but saddled with the usual literary émigré problems in a new Cold War situation, were free to write what they wanted about the war. Predictably, it was the second-wave émigrés, like Gleb Glinka and Ivan Elagin, who experienced the brutal annihilation war on the Eastern Front, the instability and fear of the DP camps, often combined with the loss of their families—either because the latter were killed during the war, or because they were cut-off by the iron curtain, who kept returning to the topic in their poems,

The third wave of emigration in the 1970s and early 1980s, brought a different group of poets and writers into the mix of Russians abroad. Some of the newcomers were adults during the War and had war memories to spare, like Alexander Galich, who was forced to emigrate in 1974, Naum Korzhavin, in 1973, and Alexander Solzhenitsyn in 1974. Some were younger, like Joseph Brodsky, who was evacuated from Leningrad with his mother during the war, and was thrown out of the Soviet Union in 1972. Notably, many first publications in the West of these third-wave poets and writers were related to the War. The first poem Brodsky published in the very first issue of *Kontinent* (a journal founded in

1974 by third-wave émigré writer Vladimir Maximov) was his ambivalent ode 'On the Death of Zhukov'.

Poetry and the Post-Soviet Period

The watershed moment for Soviet Russian poetry about the War came in the late 1980s, with Gorbachev's Glasnost, and stretched beyond the collapse of the Soviet Union in 1991, when it finally became possible to publish much of the literature that was waiting for better times in desk drawers all across the Soviet Union. Many wartime poets did not live to see this era (Boris Slutsky, for instance, died in 1986, after suffering from a mental illness for the last nine years of his life, during which he wrote nothing), and it was up to their literary heirs and executors to publish these texts, which sometimes didn't happen because of the economic and social crises that gripped post-Soviet society. The poetic legacies of both major and minor poets suffered; Slutsky's poetry has not been published in its entirety to this day. Many poets of the Leningrad siege have yet to be published fully or at all. Anna Alekseeva, who wrote extraordinary poems about the realities of life during the siege, not only about courage, loss, and loneliness, but also about those who thrived while others starved, had some of her poems published only after the fall of the Soviet Union; most still await publication.

When the Soviet Union fell apart, ex-Soviet citizens could finally travel without restrictions to the West, including Germany, which made for inevitable comparisons and irresistibly brought home the difference between the postwar lives of the conquered and the conquerors. That experience and the publications of new historical research, led many to reassess their understanding of what happened during the War, on a global level and as a part of their own personal and family history. In a 1995 interview Bulat Okudzhava declared that the War

> 'was a collision of totalitarian regimes, a showdown. Yes, we won, but we turned out to be the vanquished in the end... The Soviet Union was a fascist, totalitarian state, which dreamed of world domination, and suppressed the individual. The same as Germany. The differences were merely superficial: they had the swastika; we had the hammer and sickle. They had the scumbag Hitler, we had the 'genius' Stalin. But the essence was identical. Two totalitarian systems grappled in a showdown.[18]

This view gained considerable currency in the twenty-first century. But the main difference between the Soviet Union and Nazi

Germany never lay in their systems of government so much as what they preached to their citizens and, consequently, in the belief systems of these citizens as they went to war. On the Nazi side there was antisemitism, racial 'science', anti-intellectualism, and the idea of world domination; on the Soviet side, social, racial and gender equality and the future happiness of all mankind (however compromised this was by the practices of regime itself).

The generation who experienced the War firsthand is now very old. Their personal experience of the War has been passed to their descendants, who have inherited a legacy of pride, but often also that of silences, gaps, bitterness, and anger. Contemporary poets writing in Russian often turn to the subject of the War as a way of working out the legacy of the conflict in their own families, dealing with the inherited memories of the war that have informed their lives, often as a means of engaging with questions of broader national and world history.

Memory and commemoration are, of course, two vastly different things. On a state level, the Russian Federation has made sustained efforts to devise a system for a national commemoration of the war, focussing primarily on the Soviet victory over Nazi Germany and on the national sacrifice behind that victory, including the St. George Ribbon, worn on the days leading up to 9 May; and a Victory Day parade at which families carry the portraits of veterans.[19] The State has affirmed through the State-funded and sponsored organization 'The Immortal Regiment of Russia,' that it intends to be the main shaper and keeper both of the memory and the central narrative of the War. Poems about the War continue to be important in Russia and in the Russian diaspora as a way of commemorating the War and keeping its memory alive. There are yearly programmes around 9 May in theatres, schools, and universities, as well as on national television, featuring classic wartime poems and songs (there are analogous programs commemorating the wars in Afghanistan and Chechnya, but on a much smaller scale). Contemporary poems about the War are in demand mostly around anniversary years, when competitions are announced for the best new poem on the subject or for top new poems numbering as many years as in the anniversary.

All in all, the imprint of the War on Russian poetry remains palpable to this day, not only because the war was responsible for shaping the poetic voices and poetic destinies of so many influential Russian poets, but because the cataclysm of the War forced Russian poets to develop new strategies for writing. The German philosopher Theodor Adorno argued in 1949 that 'after Auschwitz poetry is barbarism'. We now know, however, that poetry was one of the ways that people survived the horror of the concentration camps. Seventy-five years after the Soviet defeat of Nazi Germany, there is every indication that the War will continue to engage Russian poets for many years to come, not only as one of the largest sites of intersection of personal and national history, but also as an endlessly compelling complex narrative – thrilling, horrifying, awe-inspiring, nauseating, chilling, elating, and heartbreaking.

Notes

[1] The number of Soviet dead is contentious. During Stalin's era, the official number of dead in the USSR (both military and civilian) was 7 million. Khrushchev announced that the actual number of dead was 20 million. During Gorbachev's era, the number was raised to 26–27 million, which remains the internationally accepted estimate. In 2017, however, one of the deputies of the State Duma announced that the number of Soviet dead was actually 42 million, based on recently declassified files of the State Planning Committee (GOSPLAN).

[2] For a discussion of the differences in the perception and memory of the First World War among Soviet and émigré communities, see Aaron J Cohen, 'Oh, That! Myth, Memory, and World War I in the Russian Emigration and the Soviet Union,' *Slavic Review,* Vol. 62, No. 1 (Spring, 2003).

[3] Boris Lukin (ed) *War and Peace: The Great Patriotic War (1941–1945) in the Poetry of XX–XXIst Centuries* (Tiumen, 2015–2016) consists of five volumes, each around 700 pages long, and more than a thousand poets. Altogether, 12 volumes are planned.

[4] 'Concerning the Work of War Correspondents at the Front,' from the 'Rules and Regulations,' instated by the Department of Propaganda and Agitation and the Main Political Directorate of the Red Army in 1942.

[5] Gefter and Lazarev are quoted in Nina Tumarkin, *The Living and the Dead: the Rise and Fall of the Cult of World War II* (Basic Books, 1994).

[6] Marietta Chudakova, *The Literature of Soviet Past* (Iazyki russkoi kul'tury, 2001).

[7] Ilya Ehrenburg, *People, Years, Life* (MacGibbon and Kee, 1964).

[8] Irena Verblovskaya, *Loved with a Bitter Love: the St Petersburg of Anna Akhmatova* (Zhurnal Neva, 2003).

[9] Polina Barskova (ed) *Written in the Dark: Five Poets in the Siege of Leingrad* (Ugly Duckling Press, 2016).

[10] Alexander Galich, *Dress Rehearsal: A Story in Four Acts and Five Chapters* (Slavica, 2008).

[11] *Ibid.*

[12] AN Yakovlev (ed) *The State and the Artistic Intelligentsia. Documents of TsK RKP(b) – VKP(b), VChK – OGPU – NKVD about Cultural Policy 1917–1953* (International Fund for Democracy, 1999).

[13] A Gladkov, *Meetings with Pasternak* (Art-Fleks, 2002).

[14] Galina Vishnevskaia, *Galina: The Story of a Life* (Gorizont, 1993).

[15] Evgeny Dobrenko, *Late Stalinism: The Aesthetics of Politics* (Yale, 2020).

[16] Elena Zubkova, 'The Soviet Regime and Soviet Society in the Postwar Years: Innovations and Conservatism, 1945–1953,' *Journal of Modern European History*, (2004, II.1).

[17] *Epokha* (18 May 1995).

[18] The St. George Ribbon is an orange and black strip of ribbon (referencing the 1945 medal 'Victory of Germany') distributed annually in the days before and following 9 May in Russia since 2005. It was an initiative by the State News Agency RIA, and has become the main commemorative symbol in the RF (much like the red poppy in the UK). The origin of the parade with photographs of war veterans goes back to 2012, when several journalists in Tomsk came up with the idea as a way for families to perpetuate the memory of their veterans and to publicly assert their family's connection to the War; they called it 'The Immortal Regiment.' In 2015, one of the organizers of the Moscow parade broke with the original movement, and (with the Kremlin's backing) founded 'The Immortal Regiment-Moscow' (subsequently known as 'The Immortal Regiment Russia'). There are currently two separate movements: the former, still a grass-roots, family-centred effort to perpetuate the memory of the 'generation that went through the war', the latter a State-sponsored 'Russia-wide public civic-patriotic movement'.

Subscribers

Thanks to the following for supporting this book:

Teddi Ahrens
Anoushka Alexander-Rose
Leonie Barron
Elaine Bradshaw
Maurice Casey
Nancy Charley
Cliff Cocker
Nicholas Costello
Robert Dale
Dr Vicky Davis
Martin Edwards
Eduardo Embry
Five Leaves Bookshop
Philippe Frison
Ian Garner
Andrea Gullotta
Bill Herbert
Stuart Hill
David Holmes
Geoffrey Hosking
Andrew Jameson
John Jess
William Kerr
Christine Lindey
Alexis Lykiard
Robbie MacDonald
Edward Mackinnon
Eamonn Meadows
Kevin Morgan
Alan Morrison
John Nelson
Dave Puller
Chris Purnell
Christopher Read
Ann Shukman
Southampton Communist Party Branch
Kathryn Thompson
Jonathan White
Patrick Zuk

Daria Aleeva
John Barber
Polina Barskova
Andy Byford
Robert Chandler
Kate Clark
David Colmer
Holly Daffurn
Lucy Daniels
Rosemary Edney
Julie Egdell
Annie Fisher
Georgie and Nigel Foxcroft
Elena Gapova
Jim Greenhalf
Adrienne Harris and Steven Jug
James Heyworth-Dunne
Ashley Holdsworth Quinn
Irina Holmes
Vika Ivleva
Rien Jansens
The Jess Family
Claire Knight
JS Litherland
Alexander McConnell
Irene and George MacDonald
Nick Matthews
Paul Mills
Ekaterina Morozova
Mike Munford
Sean O'Brien
Mike Quille
Peter Raynard
Elliot Short
Richard Skinner
Ben Thompson
Bryn Waters
James Womack